Season of Conspiracy

Calvin, the French Reformed Churches, and Protestant Plotting in the Reign of Francis II (1559–60)

Season of Conspiracy
Calvin, the French Reformed Churches,
and Protestant Plotting in the Reign
of Francis II (1559–60)

Philip Benedict

American Philosophical Society Press
Philadelphia

> Transactions of the
> American Philosophical Society
> Held at Philadelphia
> For Promoting Useful Knowledge
> Volume 108, Part 5

Copyright © 2020 by the American Philosophical Society for its Transactions series.

All rights reserved.

ISBN: 978-1-60618-085-3
Benedict ebook: 978-1-60618-090-7
US ISSN: 0065-9746

Library of Congress Control Number: 2019953261

Contents

Abbreviations   vii
Preface   ix

1. Introduction   1
2. The Weight of Past Historiography and the State of the Question   7
   First Reports from the Crown and Foreign Ambassadors   10
   Early Protestant Apologias and Denials   17
   The Revelations of Pierre de La Place and Louis Régnier de La Planche   29
   New Discoveries, Limited Impact   44
     Amédée Roget, Émile Doumergue, and Alphonse de Ruble   46
     Lucien Romier and the Question of English Complicity   50
     Henri Naef, Alain Dufour, and the Geneva Connection   63
     Recent Work   73
3. The Testimony of Gilles Triou   83
4. From Amboise to Lyon   107
5. From Lyon to Orléans   131
6. Conspirators from Geneva: Men and Motives   147
7. Conclusion: Rethinking the Nature and Significance of the Plotting of 1560   167

Appendix. The Deposition of Gilles Triou   197
Index   213

Abbreviations

AD	Archives Départementales
ADE	*Archivo documental español: Negociaciones con Francia*, vol. 1 (1559–60), Madrid: Real Academia de la Historia, 1950.
ADHG	Archives Départementales de la Haute-Garonne (Toulouse)
ADPA	Archives Départementales des Pyrénées-Atlantiques (Pau)
AEG	Archives d'État de Genève
AM	Archives Municipales
AS	Archivio di Stato
BnF	Bibliothèque nationale de France (Paris)
BSHPF	*Bulletin de la Société de l'Histoire du Protestantisme Français*
CO	*Joannis Calvini Opera quæ supersunt omnia*, eds. Guillaume Baum, Édouard Cunitz, and Édouard Reuss, 59 vols., Brunswick and Berlin: C. A. Schwetschke and Sons, 1863–1900.
Corr Bèze	*Correspondance de Théodore de Bèze*, eds. Hippolyte Aubert, Alain Dufour, Béatrice Nicollier, et al., Geneva: Droz, 1960–2017.
CSP For	*Calendar of State Papers, Foreign Series, of the reign of Elizabeth, 1558–1563*, ed. Joseph Stevenson, London: His Majesty's Stationery Office, 1863–69.
CSP Ven	*Calendar of State Papers and Manuscripts, relating to English affairs existing in the archives and collections of Venice*, vol. 7, *1558–1580*, eds. Rawden Brown and George Cavendish Bentinck, London: Longman Green, 1890.
FP[1]	*La France protestante*, eds. Eugène Haag and Émile Haag, 10 vols., Paris: Cherbuliez, 1846–59.

*FP*²	*La France protestante*, 2nd ed., eds. Eugène Haag, Émile Haag, and Henri Bordier, 6 vols., Paris: Sandoz et Fischbacher, 1877–88.
HE	[Theodore Beza], *Histoire ecclésiastique des Eglises réformées au royaume de France*, eds. Guillaume Baum and Édouard Cunitz, 3 vols., Paris: Fischbacher, 1883–89.
La Planche	[Louis Régnier de La Planche], *Histoire de l'Estat de France, tant de la Republique que de la Religion: Sous le regne de François II*, n.p., 1576.
LB	*Le livre des bourgeois de l'ancienne république de Genève*, ed. Alfred Coville, Geneva: J. Jullien, 1897.
LH	*Le livre des habitants de Genève*, I: *1549–1560*, ed. Paul-F. Geisendorf, Geneva: Droz, 1957.
MC	*Mémoires de Condé, servant d'éclaircissement et de preuves à l'Histoire de M. de Thou*, 6 vols., London: Claude du Bosc & Guillaume Darrés, 1743.
Naef	Henri Naef, *La conjuration d'Amboise et Genève*, Geneva: A. Jullien, 1922.
Paillard	C. Paillard, "Additions critiques à l'histoire de la conjuration d'Amboise," *Revue Historique* 14 (1880): 61–108, 311–35.
R Consist	Registres du Consistoire.
RCG	*Registres du Consistoire de Genève au temps de Calvin*, vols. 1–12 (1542–58), eds. Thomas A. Lambert, Isabella M. Watt, and Jeffrey R. Watt, Geneva: Droz, 1996–2018.

Preface

My research for the past seventeen years has focused on the critical years of the French Reformation from circa 1552 to 1563. My ultimate goal remains to write an in-depth, narrative history, built from the sources upward, of the sequence of events that led from the first clandestine foundation of Reformed churches "*à la mode de Genève*" by refugee pastors returning from the Swiss borderlands, through the remarkable proliferation of such churches and their knitting together into a synodal network capable of imposing common practices and coordinating collective action in 1559–61, to the ultimate shattering of the great dreams of religious and social renewal aroused by the Reformed movement amid a bloody civil war. This monograph covers just one portion of that story, the sequence of plots developed by an activist faction within the movement during the 513-day reign of king Francis II (July 10, 1559–December 5, 1560). Examined here are not only the well-known conspiracy of Amboise, which resulted in a failed attempt to seize control of the king in March 1560, but also several subsequent ventures that did not impress themselves on the consciousness of subsequent historians to the same extent but are no less significant for understanding the story of Francis II's reign and the political strategies pursued by the Reformed in this period: First, a planned seizure of Lyon in early September canceled at the last minute but nonetheless discovered by the authorities through a chance encounter with some of the arms and men infiltrated into the town; then, wider, ultimately unsuccessful efforts to pressure the first prince of the blood, Antoine of Navarre, to march to court at the head of a massive cavalcade of armed men.

The evidence I have assembled, some of it new, much of it brought to light by previous historians but overlooked or underappreciated by those writing after them, convinces me that the latter episodes deserve more prominence in accounts of this period than they have heretofore received. It also convinces me that all of these conspiracies were more closely linked to both John Calvin and the emerging network of Reformed churches than the current historiography, still under the shadow of an apologetic tradition begun in the immediate aftermath of the events, allows. Here I seek to set out that evidence in detail. As with two previous articles and an edited volume of documents with a long introduction that I prepared together with Nicolas Fornerod,[1] this is thus a prolegomenon to the larger narrative history to come. Where these previous works focused chiefly on the years 1561–63, this monograph looks at the nationally coordinated political action of the Reformed in the period 1559–60, when the synodal network was not yet as well established and actively functioning.

Several colleagues provided essential assistance for this project as it grew from what I initially expected to be an article into this larger work. I owe them all a great debt of gratitude. Jeffrey Watt called my attention to a previously unnoticed entry in Geneva's consistory records for 1560 concerning participants in the conspiracy of Amboise that is perhaps the most important new archival find reported here. He deserves the credit for its discovery. He also generously gave me access to the electronic files of the transcribed consistory registers that he and his collaborators editing these records from Calvin's lifetime have compiled, along with its accompanying biographical data base. This has been a key resource that enabled me to locate information about nearly a dozen otherwise anonymous or little-known participants in the conspiracy who came from or passed through Geneva. Natalie Zemon Davis provided equally essential aid in identifying obscure Lyon residents mentioned in the central document for this study, the deposition of a Lyon cabinetmaker actively involved in both the Amboise conspiracy and the plan to seize

---

[1] Philip Benedict and Nicolas Fornerod, "Les 2150 'églises' réformées de France de 1561–1562," *Revue Historique* 311 (2009): 529–60; Philip Benedict and Nicolas Fornerod, eds., *L'organisation et l'action des églises réformées de France, 1557–1563* (Geneva: Droz, 2012); Philip Benedict and Nicolas Fornerod, "Les députés des Églises réformées à la cour en 1561–1562," *Revue Historique* 315 (2013): 289–332.

that city. During her long years of research on Lyon that culminated in two magisterial articles,[2] Professor Davis built up an immense card file of information about its inhabitants that she hopes soon to make generally accessible. I must thank her for taking the time to dig through her card boxes multiple times to answer my queries. Céline Borello, Robert Descimon, Mack Holt, David Potter, Bernard Roussel, and—at the last minute with a particularly important find—Sylvie Daubresse also responded helpfully to questions and shared information from their own research with me. Margo Todd alerted me to important resources for understanding the affairs in Scotland that were so closely intertwined with those in France in this period. Claire Moutengou Barats checked my transcription of the Triou deposition and helped research its provenance. Pierre-Olivier Léchot and Camille Serchuk generously responded to late calls for help and furnished reproductions of difficult-to-obtain materials. Barbara Diefendorf, Mark Greengrass, and Bernard Roussel read earlier versions of this study and greatly improved it with their suggestions. I also profited from the comments of an anonymous reader for the APS. A visiting appointment in the History Department of the University of Pennsylvania gave me access to its library resources that were so important for completing the project. Pamela Lankas oversaw the production of the book with rare suppleness. To all of these individuals and institutions, I offer my heartfelt thanks.

---

[2] Natalie Zemon Davis, "Strikes and Salvation in Lyon," *Archiv für Reformationsgeschichte* 56 (1965): 48–64, reprinted in Natalie Zemon Davis, *Society and Culture in Early Modern France* (Stanford; Stanford University Press, 1975; Natalie Zemon Davis, "The Sacred and the Body Social in Sixteenth-Century Lyon," *Past & Present* 90 (1981): 40–70.

One

Introduction

When he was first arrested in Lyon on September 7, 1560, he said that his name was Pierre Menard and that he was a fifty-year-old cabinetmaker from Surgères, near La Rochelle. He lived in Geneva and had only come to Lyon to pick up some furniture that he had stored in the house of Jean Constantin, a goldsmith and leading member of Lyon's Reformed church. He had no idea why he had been detained, unless perhaps it had something to do with the recent trouble at that house. Three days previously, after stockpiles of weapons had been observed there by a delivery person, a company of harquebusiers had gone to investigate, only to be greeted by heavy fire from scores of armed men inside. Those inside the house drove the harquebusiers away, assembled hundreds of collaborators hidden elsewhere in town, marched with them in battle order through the streets at midnight, and then slipped out of town before daybreak. The cabinetmaker hid in the cellar during the tumult. Soon thereafter, he and a few other unfortunate collaborators left behind were arrested. The episode has come to be known to historians as the "Maligny affair." It was the fizzled squib of a Protestant conspiracy to seize Lyon cancelled just prior to the chance discovery of the arms in Constantin's house.

The cabinetmaker came clean after the interrogators showed him a list in his handwriting entitled "roll of arms per battalion," confronted him with another arrestee who said he knew him by a different name, and ushered him into the torture chamber. His real name, he confessed, was Gilles Triou. Traveling under the pseudonym of Gilles

Le Gantier, he had been sent from Geneva by close associates of John Calvin as part of a conspiracy that aimed, after securing Lyon, to summon an Estates-General and impeach and remove the brothers Guise from their pre-eminent place at the court of Francis II. He had also played a role in the conspiracy of Amboise six months previously and subsequently carried messages between the conspirators and the prince of Condé. Indeed, the conspiracy of Amboise and the Maligny affair were connected parts of the same larger enterprise, one in which, he said, Geneva's pastors had become deeply involved.[1]

Gilles Triou's deposition is not totally unknown to historians. Several historians of the sixteenth century were aware that a man they identified simply as a glover (*gantier*) had revealed many details about the conspiracies after being arrested.[2] The local historian of Lyon, Gabriel de Saconay, seems to have had access to Triou's deposition or a résumé of it, for he provided many details that agree closely with it in his highly polemical 1569 *Discours des premiers troubles advenus à Lyon*. These details in turn found their way into Jean Le Frère de Laval's 1573 *Vraye et entiere histoire des troubles et guerres civiles, avenues de nostre temps pour le faict de la religion*, only to largely disappear thereafter.[3] Three centuries later, the baron Alphonse de Ruble rediscovered a copy of the deposition in the departmental archives in Pau and drew on it for his richly documented multi-volume account of the lives and political activities of Antoine de Navarre and Jeanne d'Albret.[4] Since then, it has again slipped from the view of those who have written about either the conspiracy of Amboise or the Maligny affair, even as subsequent research has brought to light new details about these plots and about some of the conspirators named in the deposition whom neither Saconay nor de Ruble could identify.

Most striking, de Ruble wrote within a long-established framework of interpretation that minimized the role of Reformed pastors

---

[1] ADPA, E 582 (13). A full transcription of this document is provided in the Appendix.
[2] La Planche, 579-80, 700; Lancelot Voisin de La Popelinière, *L'histoire de France, enrichie des plus notables occurrances survenues ez provinces de l'Europe et pays voisins* ([La Rochelle: Pierre Haultin], 1581), I, 207. Neither of these Protestant historians provided much of his testimony.
[3] Gabriel Saconay, *Discours des premiers troubles advenus à Lyon* (Lyon: Pierre Jove, 1569), 31-33; Jean Le Frère de Laval, *Vraye et entiere histoire des troubles et guerres civiles, avenues de nostre temps pour le faict de la religion* (Paris: Jean Hulpeau, 1573), fos. 109v-110v.
[4] Alphonse de Ruble, *Antoine de Bourbon et Jeanne d'Albret* (4 vols., Paris: A. Labitte, 1881-86), II, 342-43.

and churches in the conspiratorial activity and saw it as a venture of noblemen. Calvin had rebutted accusations of his own involvement in the conspiracy of Amboise in letters that had long been known to historians, who found his rebuttal convincing in light of the other evidence available to them. De Ruble consequently discounted Triou's assertion that Calvin and other ministers in Geneva had sponsored the recruitment of troops for the Maligny affair. Then, in 1963, Alain Dufour demonstrated from other pieces of the reformers' correspondence that, whatever their attitude toward the conspiracy of Amboise, Calvin and Beza helped to direct the second round of plotting that eventuated in the aborted plan to seize Lyon, with Calvin even contributing much of his modest fortune to financing it.[5] But since the Triou deposition had been lost to sight, Dufour could not exploit the information that it has to offer confirming the Genevan church leader's involvement in this plot. And since Dufour's article appeared in a relatively obscure regional history journal, many subsequent historians of the Protestant conspiracies of 1560 and virtually all Calvin scholars have overlooked it in the half-century since its publication. Neither of the best and fullest biographies of Calvin to appear in conjunction with the five-hundredth anniversary of his birth in 2009 gives any hint of his deep involvement in the Maligny affair. Nor does the review of Calvin's political engagement in Geneva and France that opens theologian Matthew J. Tuininga's recent, probing reexamination of the reformer's political thought and its relevance for today.[6] The failure of Calvin specialists to take on board Dufour's findings has in turn led the most prominent contemporary writer who self-identifies as a Calvinist, the author and critic Marilynne Robinson, to write: "Calvin had his supernumeraries, great French lords who were more than ready to take up arms in his cause, which was under severe persecution. He managed to restrain them while he lived, saying that the first drop of blood they shed would become a torrent that

---

[5] Alain Dufour, "L'affaire de Maligny (Lyon, 4–5 septembre 1560) vue à travers la correspondance de Calvin et de Bèze," *Cahiers d'Histoire* 8 (1963): 269–80.
[6] Bruce Gordon, *Calvin* (New Haven: Yale University Press, 2009), passim; Yves Krumenacker, *Calvin. Au delà des légendes* (Montrouge: Bayard, 2009), passim; Matthew J. Tuininga, *Calvin's Political Theology and the Public Engagement of the Church: Christ's Two Kingdoms* (Cambridge: Cambridge University Press, 2017), 87–88.

drowned France."⁷ We will see that matters were a bit more complex than that.

The fate of Triou's deposition is just the most striking illustration of how, over the past century, much has been both learned and forgotten about the conspiracy of Amboise, the Maligny affair, and their interconnection. This study seeks to provide a detailed re-examination of these linked plots. The Triou deposition will receive special attention because of its interest. Contemporary diplomatic and administrative correspondence, the letters of Calvin and Beza, the revelations contained in early histories of this era, documentation in Swiss archives first brought to light by Henri Naef and others, and heretofore unknown evidence from Geneva's consistory records concerning the Amboise conspirators will also be used. The goal is not to produce a sequential narrative of these events, but to explore in detail the new or forgotten evidence that most strongly compels rethinking Protestant political action in the year 1560. Considerable effort has also been devoted to learning as much as possible about the many little-known individuals from different walks of life mentioned in the sources, a task much facilitated now by the Internet.

The structure of this study might be likened to a forensic investigation of a cold case reopened after new evidence is found. Gilles Triou's testimony forms its hinge, for it was the rediscovery and close reading of this document that convinced me that there might be important new things to say about the Huguenot plots of 1560. To grasp the implications of his testimony, however, prior knowledge of the ample stock of documents about these events used by previous historians and the current *status quaestionis* is required. Chapter Two provides this. Reader beware: This chapter is very long. Even though specialists in the history of sixteenth-century France are likely to find information new to them here, and even though the chapter can also be read as a case study in how historical knowledge about an important event in a country's past changes—or does not change as much as might be expected—over time, readers with a firm grasp of the sources and literature about the 1560 conspiracies may wish to skim this chapter and move ahead quickly to Chapter Three. This tells of the adventures of Gilles Triou and draws out the implications of his

---

⁷ Marilynne Robinson, "Fear," *The New York Review of Books*, September 24, 2015, 28.

testimony. Chapters Four through Six then set forth complementary pieces of evidence, either new or previously underexploited, that speak to the plausibility of Triou's testimony. Chapter Seven outlines the revised understanding of the nature and significance of the plotting of 1560 that emerges when all of the evidence is combined.

Conspiracies by their very nature defy complete elucidation, and the sources do not dispel all of the mysteries surrounding Protestant plotting during the reign of Francis II. Nonetheless, combining old and new documentation in this manner alters comprehension of the plotting in at least five important ways. First, as already suggested, and as Alphonse de Ruble and, after him, Lucien Romier already understood a century ago (although many subsequent historians appear to have forgotten it), it highlights that the enterprises of Amboise and Lyon were two phases of a single, larger conspiratorial undertaking that continued even after the Lyon mission was called off at the last minute. Second, in addition to confirming Calvin and Beza's engagement in the Lyon enterprise, it suggests that, if Calvin and the other Genevan pastors did not baldly lie when they sought to distance themselves from the conspiracy of Amboise after its failure, they at the very least engaged in lawyerly evasion. Third, in revealing and enabling us to identify many previously unknown participants in the conspiracies, some of them pastors, deacons, or prominent members of important urban churches, others ordinary *roturier* converts to the Protestant cause, it shows that the plots were more closely connected to the emerging network of the French Reformed assemblies and less a matter of aristocratic adventurism than the most recent literature, following an ancient historiographic tradition, still asserts. Fourth, it suggests that the conspiratorial activity was characterized throughout Francis II's reign by considerable internal tension. Many of those from humbler walks of life recruited as foot-soldiers in the ventures appear not to have been apprised of the full political and military goals defined by the national and regional organizers and ideologues of the movement; they believed that they were simply acting to gain greater freedom to practice their faith. Among those aware of the larger political aims, tension was persistent between more adventuristic captains and organizers, eager to act once they had invested their time and reputation in assembling what they believed to be sufficient support, and the leading grandees and Genevan ministers, who each to their own ends sought to restrain this eagerness and channel the discontent into the course that they judged most legally justifiable and most likely to succeed. In the end, a strike carefully prepared by the adventuristic elements would be called off by some combination of Calvin, Beza, Antoine, and Antoine's brother, the prince of Condé, all of whom were working closely with one another at the time, but among whom ultimate responsibility for this decision cannot be precisely apportioned. Then the course advocated by the first two would be rejected by the last two. The aborted ventures came to the attention of the royal authorities. The result was a harsh wave of repression that, had Francis II not suddenly died as it was gathering strength, might well have cost Condé his life and undone the rapid growth that the French Protestant movement had experienced over the immediately preceding months and years. The fifth manner in which the documentation assembled here alters our understanding of this era is thus that it forces us to reconsider Calvin's political engagement and sagacity. In allowing himself to be convinced for a period that an armed enterprise might succeed and throwing himself into its financing and directing, he may well have helped bring the French Reformed churches to the brink of a catastrophe that was only averted by an unexpected stroke of fate.

Two

The Weight of Past Historiography and the State of the Question

How successive generations wrote about the plots of 1560 from the first signs of trouble around Amboise to the present is a lengthy tale that reveals a good deal about the nature and history of historical scholarship. It shows how enduringly the first accounts of events can shape both their subsequent narration across the centuries and the terms in which later generations debate their interpretation. It shows surprising continuities across what is typically taken to be the great watershed in historical writing that occurred in the nineteenth century, when university-based historians supplanted gentlemen, clerics, and *litterateurs* as the leading authors of histories. It shows the twisting path of progress that scholarship in the would-be cumulative age of academic history actually follows about a specific historical topic. Most important for our purposes, it enables us to grasp the current state of understanding of Huguenot conspiratorial activity under Francis II and the documentation on which it rests. Only with such knowledge can the full interest and importance of Triou's testimony be grasped.

It must first be noted that the historiography about the conspiracy of Amboise is far more extensive than that dedicated to the subsequent Protestant plotting. No history of sixteenth-century France fails to discuss what contemporaries variously called the "enterprise," "conjuration," or "tumult" of Amboise. Widely publicized at the time, this has been seen ever since as an essential link in the chain of events leading up to the French Wars of Religion, if not the first episode of the civil wars themselves. In the twentieth century, it was the subject of a hefty monograph by Henri Naef, important chapters of major books by Robert M. Kingdon and Arlette Jouanna, and several substantial articles.[1] By contrast, the Maligny affair or the larger plots underway at the time that it fizzled out never entered the standard narrative of France's national history. Most Protestant historians either passed over the Maligny affair completely, as Theodore Beza did in the *Histoire ecclésiastique des Eglises réformées au royaume de France*, or said far less about it than the Catholic Jean Le Frère de Laval. This is true even of the one important Protestant historian to reveal important details about it, Louis Régnier de La Planche.[2] Jacques-Auguste de Thou, the great *politique* historian of the turn of the seventeenth century whose work did so much to shape the later national historiography of the Wars of Religion, followed in their footsteps.[3] Certain recent histories of sixteenth-century France do not mention the Maligny affair at all.[4] Those that do accord it far less space than the conspiracy of Amboise.[5] The one important contribution made during the past century to understanding this second phase of plotting is Dufour's important but often overlooked article.

---

[1] Henri Naef, *La conjuration d'Amboise et Genève* (Geneva: A. Jullien, 1922); Robert M. Kingdon, *Geneva and the Coming of the Wars of Religion in France, 1555–1563* (Geneva: Droz, 1956), ch. 7; Arlette Jouanna, *Le devoir de révolte. La noblesse française et la gestation de l'État moderne, 1559–1661* (Paris: Fayard, 1989), ch. 5; N. M. Sutherland, "Queen Elizabeth and the Conspiracy of Amboise March 1560," *English Historical Review* 81 (1960): 474–89; Jacques Poujol, "De la Confession de Foi de 1559 à la conjuration d'Amboise," *BSHPF* 119 (1973): 158–77; Corrado Vivanti, "La congiura d'Amboise" and Elizabeth A. R. Brown, "La Renaudie se venge: l'autre face de la conjuration d'Amboise" in eds. Yves-Marie Bercé and Elena Fasano Guarini, *Complots et conjurations dans l'Europe moderne* (Rome: Ecole Française de Rome, 1996), 439–50, 451–74.
[2] La Planche, 572–80.
[3] De Thou devotes one brief paragraph heavily dependent on Régnier de La Planche to the episode. De Thou, *Histoire universelle* (London, 1734), III, 538–39. On de Thou's enduring influence, see pp. 43–44.
[4] E.g., Mack P. Holt, *The French Wars of Religion, 1562–1629* (Cambridge: Cambridge University Press,1995), passim; Olivia Carpi, *Les guerres de Religion (1559–1598)* (Paris: Ellipses, 2012), passim.
[5] This disproportion is clearly visible in Lucien Romier's standard account of the reign of Francis II, *La Conjuration d'Amboise. L'aurore sanglante de la liberté de conscience. Le règne et la mort de François II* (Paris: Perrin, 1923). The entire first half of the book is devoted to the Amboise conspiracy. A single twenty-page chapter recounts "le nouveau complot." Similarly, in briefer compass, Robert J. Knecht, *The French Civil Wars, 1562–1598* (Harlow: Longman, 2000) devotes five pages to the conspiracy of Amboise and a half page to the second phase of the plotting. Arlette Jouanna et al., *Histoire et dictionnaire des guerres de Religion* (Paris: R. Laffont, 1998) devotes sixteen pages to the former and four to the latter.

From the start, unraveling the nature and goals of these conspiracies has been complicated by the loss of the records of nearly all the interrogations carried out in their aftermath. They were almost certainly destroyed amid the reshuffling of power that followed King Francis II's sudden death in December 1560 and the constitution of a regency government that, while headed by Catherine de Medici, also accorded a significant role to Antoine de Bourbon as the first prince of the blood. When the king fell ill, Antoine's younger brother Louis, Prince of Condé, was in prison facing likely execution for what a specially appointed team of judges had learned about his role in the plots of the preceding year. The new power dynamics of a regency period in which it was commonly accepted that Antoine deserved an important seat at the table enabled him to gain his brother's release, insist on the rehabilitation of his good name, and make the documents disappear in return for ceding precedence to the queen mother. The interest of the Triou deposition is that it is the fullest record of an interrogation to have survived.[6] The extant version, a clean copy, appears to have been sent to Antoine in the fall of 1560 to let him know the evidence the crown had about his brother's involvement in the plots. Its preservation in the archives of the family of Foix–Albret–Navarre enabled it to escape destruction.

In the absence of more interrogation transcripts of arrested conspirators, and with Triou's deposition tucked away in Pau, historians from the seventeenth century onward relied primarily on three other kinds of sources to unravel the details of the conspiracies. The first category is composed of the ample, often contradictory or speculative reports about the conspirators and their aims written by crown officials and foreign ambassadors amidst the initial alarms and arrests around

---

[6] A transcript of the September 22, 1560 interrogation of one of Condé's servants, Robert de La Haye, also survives among the manuscripts of the Bibliothèque nationale de France and was published in Louis Paris, ed., *Négociations, lettres et pièces diverses relatives au règne de François II* (Paris: Imprimerie Royale, 1841), 568–75. De La Haye denied any knowledge of plotting and revealed no details of importance. The *arrêt du Conseil* of June 13, 1561, proclaiming Condé's rehabilitation offers an indication of how many records were destroyed. It alludes to "interrogatoires et responses de Jaques de La Sague, et Gilles Triou, dit Le Gantier, . . . deffunct Messire François de Vendosme, Chevalier de l'Ordre dudit Seigneur Roy, Vidasme de Chartres: Depositions, Mémoires ou advertissemens de Jacques De la Bigne, Jean Landier, Florent Boulanger, Jean Du Point, Jean De la Borde, un nommé Calandrin, Jean Coderc prisonnier au Chasteau de Nismes, et du Seigneur Bellines." This arrêt has been published numerous times since it was first appended to the 1561 pamphlet *Sommaire récit de la calomnieuse accusation de monsieur le prince de Condé*, most accessibly in *MC*, II, 391–95, quotation here at 391–92.

Amboise. While struggling to understand just what was happening, these observers quickly perceived that those involved were driven by a range of motives. From the start, their dispatches foregrounded the question of whether (to use the categories of the contemporary chronicler Pierre Bruslart) "malcontentedness" or "Huguenoterie" lay at the heart of the matter.[7] The second major group of sources consists of the private letters and printed histories written by Protestant pastors and publicists after the failure of the Amboise conspiracy. The authors of these documents were interested in putting as much distance between that disastrous misadventure and the Reformed churches and their ministers in either Geneva or France as they could. At the same time, they offered such circumstantial accounts of the background and unfolding of the conspiracies and were so rich in previously secret details, so careful to include ample direct quotations from otherwise lost documents, and so forthright in identifying hitherto unknown participants that they enduringly molded understanding of these events in a way that put aristocratic discontent at the heart of the story and minimized ministerial involvement. Finally, in the past century, Swiss archives have yielded up a number of interrogations of participants in the Amboise conspiracy that confirm some of the details offered by the early Protestant histories, add new information about the recruitment of participants, and permit the identification of still more of them. It is this information that constitutes the third category of sources. It is also this information that, together with the Triou deposition, forces reconsideration of the role of Huguenoterie in general and Calvin in particular in the plotting of 1560.

First Reports from the Crown and Foreign Ambassadors

The Amboise plotters intended to assemble near Blois and launch their venture during the first half of March, with different sources specifying March 6, 10, and 15 as the planned date. Advance warning

---

[7] Pierre Bruslart, "Journal des choses les plus remarquables arrivés en France despuis la mort d'Henry second" in *MC*, I, 8: "Au mois de Mars [1560], advinrent grands troubles et mutations en Court, à raison de quelques gens qui s'éleverent contre le Roy et son Conseil, soubs pretexte de Religion; combien que le bruict fust qu'il y avoit plus de malcontentment que de Huguenoterie."

that something was afoot reached the crown by February 19.[8] Foreign ambassadors became aware that the king and his advisors feared a major threat after the castle of Amboise, where the royal entourage was staying, was locked down each evening between March 6 and 8 and the royal family guarded throughout the night by the greatest lords of the order of Saint Michael. At this point, diplomatic dispatches began to bristle with contradictory reports. The Mantuan ambassador wrote on March 8 of a newly discovered conspiracy directed by unidentified *"grandi"* against the king, the queen mother, the cardinal of Lorraine, and the duke of Guise that everybody believed was *"per conto della religione."* The English ambassador, who probably had prior contacts with the plotters, reported that Lorraine and Guise had learned that the conspiracy was directed solely against them but "bruited" (to make the matter more odious) that it was "ment only against the king." The Venetian ambassador said that those of Geneva and the chief cantons of Switzerland were also involved. The goal may have been to kill the king, although this was not yet confirmed. The Guises were unquestionably targeted for death. Ferrara's envoy alluded to rumors that Germans, as well as Swiss and Genevans, were involved.[9] Four days later, after several arrests had been made and alarm had died down enough for members of the court to begin to go out hunting once again, the two Guise brothers wrote to their sister Mary, regent in Scotland, that the conspirators had intended to kill the two of them, take the king, and give him new masters who would instruct him in Protestantism.[10]

Over the days that followed, the king's men continued to come across and arrest suspicious groups in the woods and hamlets around Amboise. Some were armed, others not. The papal nuncio Lenzi asserted on the 15th that those taken fell into three categories: lowborn

---

[8] Paillard, 85; Daniel Cuisiat, ed., *Lettres du cardinal Charles de Lorraine (1525–1574)* (Geneva: Droz, 1998), 384.
[9] AS Mantova, Archivio Gonzaga 652, Herculo Strozzi to duke, Blois, March 8, 1560; Patrick Forbes, ed., *A Full View of the Public Transactions in the Reign of Q. Elizabeth* (London: J. Bettenham, 1740–41), I, 353, Throckmorton to Cecil, Amboise, March 7, 1560; Paillard, 86, Chantonnay to Margaret of Parma, March 8, 1560; *CSP Ven*, VII, 154, Giovanni Michiel to doge and Senate, Amboise, March 6, 1560; AS Modena, Ambasciatore Francia, busta 36 (I), fos. 39, 42, Giulio Alvarotti to duke, Amboise, March 7 and 12, 1560.
[10] Cuisiat, ed., *Lettres du cardinal de Lorraine*, 388.

people moved only by religion, soldiers and malcontents whose pay and pensions had been discontinued, and grandees recruited on the promise of a change in government.[11] A letter of the Venetian ambassador dated March 16 reported that a courier arriving the previous night had brought word of a plan, hatched in the towns of the Southwest and other regions where the Protestants were strongest, to establish municipal cavalry units of two hundred horse apiece, supported through the revenue of Catholic religious houses, as protection against all who might harm them on account of their faith; the towns would retain their allegiance to the king. A source told him that ciphered documents addressed to the conspirators had been seized telling them to come punish the two miscreants, a phrase the duke of Guise and cardinal of Lorraine took as referring to them. Initial interrogations, he also reported, revealed that a number of conspirators felt themselves ill used by the crown for their previous services, having been dismissed without back pay, and consequently joined the other insurgents concerned about religion.[12]

By the 16th the crown was confident enough that the worst threat had been averted to issue a decree that pardoned those who had come simply to present their confession of faith if they would return home immediately in groups of no larger than three. Interrogations in the king's presence, the royal letters patent explained, had revealed that many of those arrested were simple, ignorant people who had been lured into coming on such a mission by "seditious spirits" whose real goal was to "sack all the rich cities and households of our kingdom." These latter and all who persisted in the enterprise rather than turning back, were to be seized and hanged on the spot.[13] An accompanying letter, known to have been sent to the municipal authorities of Agen, Châlons-en-Champagne, and Lyon, then subsequently printed in Lyon, expounded at greater length on how the

---

[11] Jean Lestocquoy, ed., *Correspondance des nonces en France: Lenzi et Gualterio, légation du cardinal Trivultio (1557–1561)* (Rome, Presses de l'Université Grégorienne, 1977), 224, Lenzi to Borromeo, Amboise, March 15, 1560.
[12] *CSP Ven*, VII, 157–59, Giovanni Michiel to doge and Senate, Amboise, March 16, 1560.
[13] "Le pardon et abolition à tous ceux qui s'estans trouvez en armes es environs de la ville d'Amboise et acheminez pour y aller se seront retirez suyvant le commandement dudit seigneur, avec permission aux dessusdits de deputer et envoyer vers le Roy leurs requestes et remonstrances," Antoine Fontanon, ed., *Les édicts et ordonnances des rois de France* (4 vols., Paris, 1611), IV, 262–63; slightly varying copies in BnF, MS Nouvelles Acquisitions Françaises 7176, fos. 167–68; *MC*, I, 11–14.

crown wished the conspiracy to be understood by the public. It was a "detestable conjuration by certain unfortunates... secretly made against our person, the princes, our chief ministers, our state and our loyal subjects. Abusing the name of religion under the pretext of the same," the ringleaders had incited foreign rulers to raise troops to enter the kingdom and recruited participants from "secret assemblies in several cities" in order to spark a "great sedition in various places in our kingdom... that at the very least would have created such trouble and confusion that they were able to pillage the richest churches and sack the best houses of our towns."[14]

Then new alarms sounded. On the same day that the royal pardon was issued, a score of noble conspirators led by the former *écuyer* of Henry II's stables, the baron Charles de Castelnau-Tursan, had been found in a nearby chateau, led to the king, interrogated, and imprisoned. The next morning at dawn, a raiding party of five hundred men approached Amboise expecting to find the Porte des Bonshommes opened for them. From there they planned to fight their way into the chateau with the aid of collaborators already infiltrated into the lower city. They were spotted as they approached. The watchmen's cries alerted the lords lodging with the king in the castle. The king's men poured forth to defend the town, foiled the attempt, and killed

---

[14] "Il a pleu à Dieu, par sa grace te bonté, faire venir à nostre cognoissance et metre en lumiere la detestable conjuration que aucuns malhureux habandonnez de Dieu avoyent secretement faicte contre nostre personne, celles des princes et de noz principaulx ministres, nostre estat et loyaulx soubgectz, lesquels conjurés, pour parvenir à l'effect de leurs dampnés entreprinses, auroient inventé tous les moyens que peuvent penser les malings speritz pour atraire et persuader les hommes, entre autres, abusans du nom de religion soubz le pretexte d'icelle, auroient solicité aucuns princes estrangiers de favoriser leur conspiration, de lever gens de guerre pour entrer dedans nostre royaulme, leur donnant assurance de venir sans difficulté à chef de leurs desseings, et à cest fin suposoyent faulcement que aucuns sieurs et gentilshommes avec grand nombre de noz autres subgectz habitans des villes et plat pais estoyent complices et adherans à ladite conspiration, prendroient les armes et se esleveroyent à jour certain et determiné entre eulx. D'autre part, afin de plus facilement seduire nosdits soubgectz, ont praticqué de faire secretes assemblees en plusieurs villes et autres lieux de nostredit royaulme, desoubz le pretexte de religion ont tenté les voluntés de ceulx qui se sont trouvez esdits assemblees et efforcez par tout moyen de crainte, peynes et esperance de bien les aliener de la fidelité et affection qu'ilz nous doyvent et les tirer à ladite conspiration, ... et tendoyent iceulx conjurez à ce but d'esmouvoir en mesme temps sa grande sedicion en plusieurs endroictz de nostre royaulme, qu'il seroict aprez impossible d'estaindre le feu qu'ilz auroient alumé, qui pour le moingz n'eussent mys toutes chozes en tel troble et confusion qu'ilz auroyent le moyen de piller les plus riches eglises et sacager les melheurs maisons de noz villes." *Archives Historiques de la Gironde* 29 (1891): 8–10; Georges Hérelle, ed., *La Réforme et la Ligue en Champagne. Documents* (2 vols., Paris: Champion, 1888-92), I, 30–32; *ADE*, I, 201–03. On the same day the cardinal of Lorraine wrote to the French agent in Solothurn that the conspirators sought nothing less than a change in the state. Cuisiat, ed., *Lettres du cardinal de Lorraine*, 388.

or captured many of those involved.[15] Two days later, the man by now identified as the leader of the conspiracy, Jean Du Barry, seigneur de La Renaudie, was discovered by a patrol in a nearby wood and killed in an exchange of gunfire. The scion of a well-off noble family from the Périgord, familiar with the milieu of the court, La Renaudie had lived abroad for a dozen years, chiefly in Lausanne, following his 1546 condemnation for using falsified documents in a dispute over an ecclesiastical benefice, but had recently been allowed to return to France. His dead body was hung from a gibbet with a placard around his neck reading *"chef des rebelles."*

As arrests, interrogations under torture, and executions multiplied, ambassadors at court were able to dispatch more information that they had learned from their contacts. The Spanish ambassador Chantonnay reported on March 18 that Lorraine told him three days previously that ciphered documents found on certain prisoners showed that the conspirators recognized the authority of the king over their persons but not their souls and were seeking freedom of worship. Their mobilization was aimed against the Guises. They hoped to finance the troops they had raised from the royal coffers and church wealth.[16] In another dispatch of March 19, Chantonnay claimed to have learned, largely from Habsburg intelligence in the Low Countries, that the plan was for four to five hundred men to take over the chateau of Amboise, seize the king and his brothers, and convoke the Estates-General. If the king could be brought over to their sect, he would be allowed to continue to rule; if not, another would be chosen in his place. If the Guises would not go along with this, they would be proscribed, as the ministers of Strasbourg, Augsburg, and other cities had urged. Geneva's ministers, for their part, approved killing them.[17] The Mantuan ambassador Herculo Strozzi said he had been told that the confessions of the plot leaders

---

[15] The "Récit inédit du tumulte d'Amboise" published by Naef, 257–60, and the account provided by Agrippa d'Aubigné, *Histoire universelle*, ed. André Thierry (Geneva: Droz, 1981–2000), I, 278, appear to be the most reliable sources for these events. Hugues Daussy, *Le parti huguenot. Chronique d'une désillusion (1557–1572)* (Geneva: Droz, 2014) places the arrest of Castelnau and his associates on the 15th, but the letter of Claude de L'Aubespine to the constable Montmorency, Amboise, March 19, 1560, published in the pièces justificatives of de Ruble, *Antoine et Jeanne*, II, 458, clearly suggests it occurred on the evening of the 16th.

[16] Paillard, 104, Chantonnay to Margaret of Parma, Amboise, March 18, 1560.

[17] *ADE*, I, 208, Chantonnay to Philip II, Amboise, March 19, 1560; Paillard, 84–85.

revealed that, once the conspirators had entered the chateau at Amboise, one group under Castelnau planned to take Francis II away and make him live as a Protestant, a second group under Mazères meant to kill the Guises, and a third group under Maligny was charged with killing the queen and queen mother.[18] Both the Venetian ambassador and Chantonnay reported that sixty or more men living in Geneva for religion came to aid the plot. The former also mentioned that Germans, Swiss, Savoyards, Englishmen, and Scots were among the insurgents. And he passed along information that suggested that nonreligious concerns motivated some of the conspirators. The baron of Castelnau and his men had previously been dismissed from the crown's service without being paid back wages due them, he wrote; aggrieved against the Guises and finding themselves without means, they joined the other insurgents who were acting for religion's sake.[19] The Florentine ambassador Alfonso Tornabuoni, who believed that the conspirators came "to kill the king and his council, being resolved to establish an independent republic," reported that while nine tenths of those involved were heretics, not all were.[20] Two weeks later the Mantuan ambassador wrote that the better part of the leaders came from the "house and adherents of the king of Navarre and the prince of Condé," while most of the men arrested were from Poitou, Touraine, and Gascony. He had earlier reported that among the dozens executed in the aftermath of the plot were three ministers.[21] The Ferrarese ambassador, who previously had spoken of German involvement, wrote on March 23 that the cardinal of Lorraine now told him that the plot was based solely in France, but that it had been fomented by England.[22]

So many different accounts of just who the plotters were and what they aimed to do would confront later historians with a perplexingly difficult problem of determining which were accurate once these reports were exhumed from the archives, but few of the precise details

---

[18] AS Mantova, Archivio Gonzaga 652, H. Strozzi to duke, Amboise, March 29, 1560.
[19] *CSP Ven*, VII, 156, 161, Michiel to doge and Senate, Amboise, March 15 and 17, 1560; Paillard, 108, Chantonnay to Margaret of Parma, Amboise, March 18, 1560.
[20] Abel Desjardins, ed., *Négociations diplomatiques de la France avec la Toscane* (Paris: Imprimerie Impériale, 1865), III, 409, Alfonso Tornabuoni to Cosimo I, Amboise, March 23, 1560.
[21] AS Mantova, Archivio Gonzaga 652, H. Strozzi to duke, Tours, April 6, 1560 and Amboise, March 29, 1560.
[22] AS Modena, Ambasciatore Francia, 36 (I), fo. 66v, Alvarotti to duke, Amboise, March 23, 1560.

that they provide about the aims of the plotters found their way into the most important statement that the crown issued about the event in its aftermath. This was a royal letter to the Parlement of Paris explaining the conspiracy that was subsequently sent to regional courts throughout the kingdom and gained wide currency when published in pamphlet form.[23] It simply spoke of "an abominable treason aimed at the complete subversion of our State (*Estat*)" that could have led either to the extermination of the royal family and principal ministers or to subjects dictating the law to their rulers. According to it, the conjuration originated with "certain of our subjects brought to justice for various crimes and banished from this kingdom." They subsequently recruited the assistance of "certain preachers of new doctrine scattered throughout our kingdom," who in turn induced many of their auditors to approach the king with a petition to worship according to the rules of their sect and told them that they would only gain access to the king if they bore arms. Soldiers given to pillaging, men who had exhausted their resources and wanted to live off those of others, and other factious and turbulent people of ill will also were drawn in. They were led to believe that some princes would step forward to lead the scheme, but the document declared that this was not true.[24]

---

[23] The letter was received by the Paris Parlement on April 18. BnF, MS Français 16517, fo. 93v. A printed version is *Lettres du roy, Contenans le succinct du fait de la conspiration entreprinse contre sa majesté* (Lyon: Pierre Merant, 1560).

[24] "Nous avons descouvert et veriffié tant par déclarations que les complices mesmes de la conjuration nous ont faict, comme par lettres des conjurez, informations envoyées de divers lieulx, confession de ceulx qui ont esté apprehendez, et toute autre sorte de preuve, comme depuis quelque temps encza aucuns de noz subgectz qui avoitent esté prevenuz en justice de plusieurs crimes, condamnez et bannyz de ce royaume ... ont à la fin osé machiner une abominable trahison qui tendoit à l'entiere subversion de nostre Estat, ce qui ne povoit estre sans que Nous, nostre tres-honorée Dame et Mere, nostre tres-chère et tres-aimée compaigne la Royne, noz Freres et autres Princes ayans le principal manyement de noz affaires, ne feussent du tout estainctz, ou bien que à tout le moins Nous ne feussions reduictz à tel party que l'auctorité du Roy fust rabaissée à la mercy du subject qui donnast la Loy à celluy duquel il la doibt prendre. Or comme il leur semblast que telle oeuvre ne se peust bonnement exploicter sans assistance de grand nombre de personnes et sans venir aux armes, ce qu'ilz desesperoient de pouvoir impétrer envers noz subjectz pour la naturelle obéissance et dévotion qu'ilz portent à leur Roy, ... ils s'adviserent de s'aider d'aucuns prédicans de nouvelle doctrine, dispersez en nostre Royaulme, lesquelz apres avoir dogmatisé en assemblées secrettes et conventiculles reprouvez par toutes loyx, voyans beaucoup de gens estre imbuz de leur doctrine et désirer mutation touchant la religion, feirent tant à la longue par leurs persuasions qu'ilz induirent ceulx qui les escoutoient à s'eslever de divers endroictz de nostre obéissance, en intention de venir en gros nombre Nous présenter une requeste, tendant à ce que sans les rechercher sur les doctrines qu'ilz tenoient, ilz peussent seurement vivre selon la nouvelle institution de leur secte, encores qu'elle feust contraire à l'ancienne observance de Saincte Eglise; laquelle exhortation voyans estre receue, ilz obtindrent après que ceulx qui viendroient devers Nous seroient armez, leur ayant faict entendre que sans les armes il n'y avoit seur accès envers Nous.... Ainsi, la chose ayant esté

The March 31 account was extremely important for shaping the subsequent understanding of the conspiracy of Amboise. When juxtaposed against the range of ambassadors' reports, its identification of men banished for unspecified crimes as the initiators of the plot, and of unemployed soldiers and factious people as participants can be seen to place it closer to the malcontent pole of interpretation than to that of Huguenoterie. Nevertheless, its prominent mention of the role of preachers and assemblies of the new sect in a subversive enterprise threatened potentially fatal damage to the clandestine Reformed churches then multiplying in France. Catholic controversialists had long charged that heresy and sedition went hand in hand, a charge that Calvin went to great pains to deny. If it now came to be believed that the Reformed churches and pastors had indeed abetted an armed attack on the king, the link would seem confirmed, as many subsequent Catholic authors who wrote about the event indeed took it to be. In response, Huguenot publicists rushed to promote another narrative.

Early Protestant Apologias and Denials

To counter the March 31 account, four anonymous Huguenot tracts set out what they claimed to be the true nature of what two of them called the "assembly held before Amboise." It was, they insisted, a legitimate act of service to the crown, in no way seditious. It was also a political, rather than a religious, enterprise, directed against Guise

---

deliberée soubz la masque de Relligion, et par la persuasion de ceulx que les simples avoient en estime et comme ministres de la Parolle de Dieu, et soubz asseurance qu'on leur avoit faulcement imprimée que aucuns Princes embrasseroient leur desseing et se constitueroient chefz et conducteurs de leur menée, combien que la preuve du contraire les ait exemptez de toute soupson, les aulteurs de la trahison... s'étans renforcez d'aucuns autres nos subjectz, personnaiges factieux, dont les uns ayans suivy les guerres et vescu comme la licence du temps et l'impugnité leur avoit tolleré, voyans les moyens de piller durant la paix leur estre du tout ostez, les autres après avoir malheureusement consumé leurs biens voulloient vivre de ceulx d'aultruy, aucuns turbulentz de leur nature desiroient toujours changement de temps, et tous ensemble seduictz, les ungs de mauvais conseil, les autres de mauvaise volunté, actenterent si avant en ce qu'ilz avoient désigné, que sans la bonté de Dieu lequel comme par miracle feist descouvrir peu auparavant la conspiration et sur l'instant de l'execution livra entre noz mains les principaulx aucteurs et conducteurs de l'entreprinse, les plus malheureux d'entre eulx eussent... procéder à si damnable exécution dont ne se pouvoit ensuyvre que désolation et subversion de l'Estat institué de Dieu." *MC* I, 348–50.

misrule, not the king.[25] The longest and most often reprinted of these four tracts, the *Histoire du tumulte d'Amboise*, quite possibly written by François Hotman, also provided considerable narrative detail about the events around the town and chateau.[26] It sought to cast in the best possible light the actions of the participants, especially two of their leaders whose notoriety was established by their very public deaths, La Renaudie and Castelnau.

According to these tracts, well-established precedent dictated that when a minor inherited the throne, the task of constituting the regency council fell to the Estates. The princes of the blood were to occupy a leading place within it, whereas foreigners should be excluded. The Guises, a foreign house from Lorraine, had nonetheless seized power on Francis II's accession. They embroiled France in foreign adventures, drove up taxes, left soldiers unpaid, enriched themselves, and undercut the autonomy of the Parlement of Paris. The tumult at Amboise came about because several gentlemen could no longer bear this tyranny. They banded together to remove the Guises on behalf of the Estates, vowing at the same time not to do anything contrary to the king's interests. They chose as their leader La Renaudie, "a man of great spirit and almost incredible energy," and sur-

---

[25] *Brieve remonstrance des Estats de France, Au Roy leur souverain seigneur, sur l'ambition, tyrannie et oppression du tout intolerable des de Guyse*; *Briefve exposition des Lettres du Cardinal de Lorraine envoyees au nom du Roy aux Cours des Parlemens de France*; *Response chretienne et defensive sur aucuns points calomnieux contenus en certaines lettres envoyées aux baillis, senechaux et lieutenants du Roy*; *L'Histoire du tumulte d'Amboise*. The text of all four of these pamphlets can be found in *MC*, I, 320–30, 352–97, 405–10. Much of the first of these tracts may have been drafted even before the Amboise attack, as portions correspond to the contents of the ciphered document reported by the Spanish ambassador to have been found on arrested conspirators, and a printed version entitled *Les estats de France opprimez par la tirannye de Guise, au Roy leur souveain seigneur* was already circulating by April 15, when a copy was placarded on the church of St Hilaire in Paris and another sent by Geneva's authorities to Bern. The *Brieve remonstrance* nonetheless clearly was completed after the plot's failure. It opens by noting that the king found "this new assembly" (the gathering of the conspirators as they approached Amboise) strange, before then justifying it. On these tracts and their circulation, see Jehan de La Fosse, *Les "mémoires" d'un curé de Paris (1557–1590) au temps des guerres de Religion*, ed. Marc Venard (Geneva: Droz, 2004), 36; Romier, *Conjuration*, 131; Naef, 173–74; Daussy, *Parti huguenot*, 152–53.

[26] François Baudouin, Hotman's bitterest academic rival and political opponent at the time, first identified him as the author of this work, an attribution that the editor and translator of Hotman's *Francogallia* find convincing. Hotman, *Francogallia*, ed. Ralph E. Giesey, trans. J. H. M. Salmon (Cambridge: Cambridge University Press, 1972), 20. Donald Kelley, Hotman's biographer, does not venture a guess as to which of the pamphlets justifying the Amboise conspiracy he wrote but considers him a key progenitor of the legal argument undergirding them all. Donald Kelley, *François Hotman: A Revolutionary's Ordeal* (Princeton, NJ: Princeton University Press, 1973), 115.

rounded him with a council of thirty experienced military men. As they approached Amboise to present their grievances, however, the Guises deluded the king into thinking that he was threatened by "Lutherans" seeking revenge for their recent harsh persecution. When Castelnau and his men were discovered as they gathered at the chateau of Noizay, the duke of Nemours induced them to lay down their arms on the promise that they would be led to the king and allowed to tell him their concerns without being harmed. That promise was broken. They were imprisoned, tortured, and executed for *lèse majesté*.[27] La Renaudie crossed paths with one of the king's men scouting the surrounding area and was fatally run through with a sword in the ensuing firefight. Five hundred horsemen were able to make it to Amboise, but they were given away by traitors suborned by the Guises.

The tracts rebutted in different manners the charge that the conspirators were drawn from the ranks of the Reformed and sought to establish a new religion. The *Briefve exposition des Lettres du Cardinal de Lorraine envoyees au nom du Roy aux Cours des Parlemens de France* flatly denied any intention to present a request concerning religion. So, too, did the *Response chretienne et defensive sur aucuns points calomnieux contenus en certaines lettres envoyées aux baillis, senechaux et lieutenants du Roy*, which also denied all involvement in the enterprise of those labeled in the king's letter "preachers of new doctrine." On the other hand, the *Histoire du tumulte d'Amboise*, like the *Brieve remonstrance*, admitted that some participants embraced Reformed doctrine. It even asserted that some had dared hope that an assembly of the Estates would give them the opportunity to present their confession of faith to the king. The *Brieve remonstrance des Estats de France* said that it was true that some of those who gathered in the name of the three estates sought to live "according to the reformation of the Gospel."

---

[27] It should be noted that this portion of the apologetic history receives confirmation in the Protestant diplomatic correspondence of the era. The English ambassador reported to Elizabeth that Castelnau was originally sentenced to three years of galley service. However, on the urging of the Guises, the death sentence was substituted at a special meeting of the knights of the Order of Saint Michael and his captor, Nemours, absolved at the same time of any taint on his honor for breach of promise. The beheading took place on March 29. *CSP For*, II, 505, Throckmorton to Elizabeth, Amboise, April 6, 1560. AS Mantova, Archivio Gonzaga 652, H. Strozzi to duke, Amboise, March 29, 1560, confirms Castelnau's execution on that date but adds none of the other details furnished by Throckmorton.

"Nonetheless, this cause alone would never have led them to take up arms if there had not also been a civil and political cause, that of [the Guises'] oppression of Your Majesty."[28]

In sum, these four apologias cast the enterprise as one launched by noblemen committed to upholding the kingdom's fundamental constitution. The legal rationale they foregrounded, which corresponded with what was stated in the documents found on the conspirators and reported in Chantonnay's letters, was intended to remove all taint of sedition from the venture. Nothing was admitted about other elements that the Spanish ambassador and other informed contemporaries believed were also part of the enterprise, such as killing the Guises if they resisted or removing the king from power if he could not be brought over to Protestantism. All sought to minimize or deny that the tumult had a religious component, even if two admitted that some participants were Reformed converts and one said that these men wanted to present the movement's confession of faith to the king. None said anything about any foreign involvement.

Calvin and Beza in Geneva also did their utmost after the conspiracy's failure to squelch rumors that they had supported the venture, to downplay their prior knowledge of it, and to minimize the participation of Geneva's larger exiled French community. They could not, however, distance themselves and Geneva entirely from the conspiracy. Among those captured around Amboise, as the ambassadors had reported, were scores of men who had come from the city. Among those executed for their role in the plot was Adrien de Beauvais de Briquemault, seigneur de Villemongis, an immediate neighbor of Calvin's in Geneva with ties of loyalty to the Admiral Coligny.[29] Who knew what else his interrogation and that of other Genevans arrested might have revealed about the contacts between the plotters in France and the ministers in Geneva that had in fact been going on since the latter half of the preceding year?

These prior contacts are known to us chiefly from two sources: the letters of Calvin and his collaborators published in two main installments in the nineteenth century, and a trial in Geneva brought

---

[28] *MC*, I, 410.
[29] Villemongis will reappear several times in this study. For his life course and networks, see Naef, 102–05, pp. 161–62 here.

to light by Henri Naef in 1922.[30] The Calvin correspondence shows that already in the first months after Henry II's death, leading ministers of the Paris church aided by jurists in their milieu and in Strasbourg elaborated the legal argument set forth in the post-Amboise treatises about the role that the Estates and princes of the blood should play under the fifteen-year-old Francis II and lobbied Antoine de Bourbon to assert the rights they claimed he had. At the same time, they apprised Geneva's pastors of their actions and convinced the legally educated Calvin of the soundness of their juridical argument in support of a role for the first prince of the blood—this even though Jean Du Tillet would soon marshal substantial evidence indicating that French law set the age of majority for rulers on their fourteenth birthday.[31] The trial brought to light by Naef shows that over the course of the fall and winter of 1559, the minister Antoine de La Roche Chandieu (whose brother Bertrand led the cavalry contingent that sought to enter Amboise) and La Renaudie both made trips to Geneva during which they met with Calvin and sought his approval for their plan of an enterprise in the name of the Estates that did not involve Antoine.[32]

The most important direct evidence about what Calvin knew and thought about these initiatives before the fact is a letter he wrote just after the venture was launched but before he learned its outcome to the Strasbourg schoolmaster Jean Sturm, a key agent in efforts to build support for francophone Protestants among Germany's Lutheran rulers and hence a man aware that plotting was going on. When first approached by those who conceived the enterprise, Calvin told Sturm, he informed them that he did not like either the general idea or the details of their scheme. Now that they had foolishly launched their stupid venture he was disgusted that they were moving so slowly and hadn't yet done what they had planned to do a week earlier. Meanwhile, several groups in Provence had already shown

---

[30] Calvin's French letters were published by Jules Bonnet in 1854. His complete correspondence and related letters were published between 1871 and 1879 in volumes 10 to 20 of the *CO*. Naef's book and his discoveries are discussed at length further along in this chapter, pp. 63–68.

[31] *CO*, XVII, cols. 597, 609, Morel to Calvin, Paris, Aug 15 and 22 1559; Naef, ch. 4; Romier, *Conjuration*, 57–62; Vittorio de Caprariis, *Propaganda e pensiero politico in Francia durante le guerre di religione I (1559–1572)* (Naples: Edizione Scientifiche Italiano, 1959), 29–54; Jouanna, *Devoir de révolte*, 129–32; Jean Du Tillet, *Pour l'entiere majorité du Roy treschrestien, contre le legitime conseil malicieusement inventé par les rebelles* (Paris: Guillaume Morel, 1560).

[32] Naef, 69–91, 113–50.

themselves in public even though he had told them to lay low until the purge of court was completed.[33] This letter, which previous historians have not always read attentively, shows that although Calvin was contemptuous of the conspirators and their plan, he was also aware of many details of it and advised believers elsewhere in France how to coordinate their actions with it.

Beza was in an even more delicate situation. Although he had written to Bullinger in September 1559 that Geneva's ministers were often asked by those in France whether they could resist and replied in the negative, by the end of that year he had become sufficiently convinced of the legitimacy and potential interest of some sort of coordinated action to pass along to Paris a treatise written in Strasbourg, almost certainly with the input of Hotman, his old law school classmate and colleague at the Lausanne Academy, making the legal case for action in the name of the Estates. After La Renaudie's visit to Geneva, Beza also gave him a going-away present of his recent translation of psalm 94, which begins, "O Lord, thou God of vengeance, thou God of vengeance, shine forth! Rise up, O judge of the earth; render to the proud their deserts!"[34]

Because it was impossible after the conspiracy's failure for Calvin and Beza to deny all prior connection to the conspirators, they instead protested to allies how strenuously they had opposed La Renaudie's plan once they learned of it. They also minimized the extent of Genevan participation and claimed that those residents of the city who had gone off to Amboise left without their knowledge or against their advice. They even went so far as to initiate legal action against a man reported to have suggested that they had supported the venture.

Calvin's longest self-justification, and the letter most often cited by subsequent historians as evidence of his attitude toward the conspir-

---

[33] *CO*, XVIII, col. 39, Calvin to Sturm, Geneva, March 23, 1560: "Quum me principio consulerent qui primi ad hoc negotium agitandum aliis fuerunt autores, libere respondi, mihi non placere totam agendi rationem, rem vero ipsam multo minus probari. Quod stulte cogitaverant pueriliter deinde aggressi sunt. Nunc me ignaviae eorum piget, quia quod ante idus Martias exsequi statuerant, scio nondum tentatum fuisse quinque post diebus. Nunc in singula momenta exspectamus quorsum magnifici eorum conatus eruperint. . . . Interea in oppidis quibusdam Provinciae plus ausi sunt boni viri quam vellem. Suaseram ne ante aulicam lustrationem in publicum prodirent: nunc festinatio eorum maiores gignet motus." Also Naef, 155.

[34] *CO*, XVII, col. 638; Naef, 80, 163–72. The psalm is quoted in the Revised Standard Version, which offers the closest English equivalent to Beza's translation: "Eternel, Dieu des vengeances, O Dieu punisseur des offenses, Fay toy cognoistre clairement. Toy gouverneur de l'univers, Hausse-toy pour rendre aux pervers, De leur orgueil le payement."

acy, came in an undated letter to Coligny whose final paragraphs make it clear that it was written after the Maligny affair as well, hence in late 1560 or early 1561.[35] The reformer's fullest but also most complaisant biographer, Emile Doumergue, called this *"grande lettre"* "a masterpiece."[36] Many subsequent historians have cited it as evidence of his attitude toward the conspiracy. As its most recent editors observe, however, it is best understood not as a full and forthright statement of his involvement with and attitude toward the plots of 1560, but as an *"excuse"* or apologia meant to provide Coligny with as much evidence as possible that could be used to defend Calvin's and Geneva's innocence at the French court without incriminating anybody else.[37] For months prior to the Amboise affair, Calvin declared, he told those who had sought his advice about the conditions under which resistance was justified that religious persecution alone could never be opposed by force; the only situation in which they could think of taking up arms legitimately was to aid the princes of the blood if they collectively demanded that their rights be respected. When La Renaudie came to Geneva seeking approval for another plan of action, Calvin opposed it, so he said, and saw immediately that its ringleader was vain and arrogant. He recurrently tried to dissuade an unnamed mutual acquaintance of theirs, almost certainly Villemongis, from joining the adventure. If he did not speak out openly against the plot or alert the Genevan or French authorities, this was because he "scorned it as a childish endeavor," "didn't think it was a big affair (*grand mestier*)," and feared innocent participants would suffer if he did. Furthermore, "nobody left here except secretly in small numbers, so much so that we had no idea what was brewing underground." In the same letter, Calvin also denied or minimized any connection to subsequent tumultuous episodes. Regarding the iconoclastic raiding in Provence led by Paulon de Richieu, seigneur

---

[35] *CO*, XVIII, no. 3374. Its first editor, Jules Bonnet, dated it to April 16, 1561. The editors of the *Opera Calvini* profess their ignorance of why that date was chosen but also place it amid the letters of April 1561.

[36] Émile Doumergue, *Jean Calvin. Les hommes et les choses de son temps* (7 vols., Lausanne: Georges Bridel, 1899–1927), VII, 242.

[37] Jean Calvin, *Oeuvres*, eds. Francis Higman and Bernard Roussel (Paris: Gallimard, 2009), 1205–07. If Bonnet's dating of the letter to mid-April is correct, it would have been sent soon after Coligny joined the Privy Council. J. Shimizu, *Conflict of Loyalties: Politics and Religion in the Career of Gaspard de Coligny Admiral of France, 1519–1572* (Geneva: Droz, 1970), 56.

de Mauvans he wrote, "Excesses occurred in Provence; some took up arms; several people were killed; but I never had any communication with those responsible." As for the Maligny affair, "We have heard talk of a certain tumult in Lyon, but whatever might have occurred the source came from elsewhere ... and I never saw the person who is considered responsible."[38] Readers will be better able to appreciate the artfulness of this last denial once all of the evidence about the enterprise of Lyon has been reviewed.

Many elements found in this self-justification also appeared in earlier letters to ministerial colleagues in Zurich and Winterthur written in response to reports from them that Geneva and its pastors were being widely blamed for the conspiracy. On May 11, 1560, Calvin wrote to Heinrich Bullinger, "You can certainly deny the accusation against us concerning the Amboise tumult. When these projects started to be debated eight months ago, I used all my authority to oppose them." As in his later letter to Coligny, the reformer felt obliged to explain why he did not make his opposition publicly known or denounce those involved to the authorities in either Geneva or France. This was because he feared all of the faithful would be butchered if word reached "the enemy." "I thought I had calmed the intemperate zeal of these imprudent souls."[39] But, as he wrote at greater length that same day to Bullinger's Zurich colleague Peter Martyr Vermigli:

> I soon learned—too late to stop it—that they had misunderstood my advice and followed up on their original plan. Despite my remonstrations, about sixty left here as if under a spell. They claimed that they did not act lightly, as they had the authorization of a leading man who by the ancient custom and written law of the kingdom is able to claim primacy in council with his brother absent.... I had told them that should a single drop of blood be spilled, rivers would inevitably follow that would inundate France. Additionally, the ill-planned affair was carried out even

---

[38] *CO*, XVIII, cols. 429, 430, 431.
[39] *CO*, XVIII, col. 84: "Quum ante octo menses agitari consilia haec inciperant, meam autoritatem interposui ne longius progredi tentarent. Occulte id quidem et placide, quia verebar ne, si rei fama ad hostes manaret, ad carnificinam pios omnes traherem. Putabam tamen mea opera repressos atque sedatos impetus.

less well. The imbecile who boldly pushed himself forward sent all to ruin in his worthless vanity.[40]

Late that month, after the former reformer of Constance then pastoring in Winterthur, Ambrose Blaurer, passed along the rumor that upward of a thousand people had left Geneva to participate in the enterprise, Calvin assured him that this was wildly exaggerated. "No more than seventy set out, half of them artisans of the lowest sort." Furthermore, those who went did so "either without my knowledge or openly against my strong urging."[41] For his part, Beza offered verbal assurances to foreign students in Geneva that the city's ministers had not supported the conspiracy.[42]

The most striking evidence of the lengths Calvin and Beza went to kill reports of their complicity is the trial record found by Naef.[43] On April 9, the two pastors informed Geneva's Small Council that a minor nobleman then in town had defamed their reputation by telling an acquaintance that they, especially Beza, had approved of what they called "the recent enterprise of certain shallow and reckless men undertaken without the consent of their Lordships or the ministers" and had even written to churches in France urging them to fund it. The object of their complaint was Jean Morély, who would later gain notoriety for proposing a system of church government that anticipates modern congregationalism. Imprisoned and interrogated posthaste, Morély explained that he did not think that Geneva's pastors, unlike some in France, could be held responsible for the enterprise, because the conspirators did not follow their advice.[44] He had

---

[40] *CO*, XVIII, cols. 81–82: "Paulo post cognovi (sero tamen quia iam non erat remedio locus) repudiato meo consilio sequi quod iam animis praesumpserant. Hinc etiam profecti sunt me reclamante circiter sexaginta, ut clare diceres esse fascinatos. Excusant quidem, se non temere sumpsisse arma quia permiserat unus ex proceribus, qui secundum veterem regni morem et scriptas leges summi consilii fratre absente gradum primum sibi iure vendicat. . . . Dicebam enim fieri non posse quin ex gutta una mox profluerent fluvii qui Galliam obruerent. Caeterum res non satis prudenter suscepta deterius tractata fuit. Ac certe nebulo unus, qui se audacter ingesserat, omnes pessumdedit sua futilitate."
[41] *CO*, XVIII, col. 95, Calvin to Blaurer, Geneva, May 28, 1560: "Quin etiam ex hac urbe quidam me vel inscio, vel palam et fortiter reclamante, profecti sunt. Quanquam rumor ille, quem dicis apud vos fuisse sparsum, de aliquot milllibus, vanissimus fuit. Non enim plures septuaginta egressi sunt, et quidem ex dimidia parte infimae sortis opifices."
[42] *CO*, XVIII, col. 80, Hermann Folkertzheimer to Vermigli, Geneva, May 9, 1560.
[43] AEG, Procès criminels, 2e série, 1215. This document and Naef's long synopsis and explication of it (113–50, 163–70) form the basis for this entire paragraph.
[44] "Il scait bien qu'on n'a pas suivi le desir des ministres de ceste cité mais qu'il a esté mal executée combien que les ministres de par dela ont esté prins aux affaires." AEG, Procès criminels, 2e série, 1215, fo. 4v.

simply said the following things: that La Roche Chandieu had visited Geneva, consulted with the city's ministers, and subsequently put it about that they approved the enterprise; that Beza had received from Strasbourg a short "*Discours sur l'affaire Themistyque*" setting out arguments against the tyranny of the Guise and sent it along to Paris; that Beza gave La Renaudie a copy of his translation of psalm 94 "thoroughly a propos for such an affair"; and that Morély himself had received advice from Beza about what course to adopt before a recent trip to France. All this led him to believe that Beza consented to the general scheme of the enterprise, if not the precise way in which it was carried out.[45]

After his deposition was shown to the Company of Pastors so that it could reply, the city's ministers came as a body to the prison to confront Morély in the presence of the syndics and councilors. Calvin, speaking on their behalf, denied Morély's assertion that Chandieu had come to speak to the group and said he testified falsely. But after Morély modified his testimony to specify that La Roche Chandieu spoke not to the ministers generally, but to Calvin individually, Calvin admitted that this was true. It would appear that the city's pastors felt so threatened by any suggestion of their complicity in the conspiracy that they initially used the lawyerly strategy of seizing on an erroneous detail in an accusation to justify a denial of the general charge. Calvin then explained that although he had, indeed, been contacted by certain conspirators, he sought to prevent the plan as it was presented to him unless the first prince of the blood supported it. Beza now confirmed the truth of Morély's statements concerning him. His defense was that he was not the author of the manuscript in question and (quite implausibly) that the psalm could not be read as offering support for the endeavor. Calvin and Beza acted shrewdly in appealing to the Council, for it was well inclined to them and deeply concerned for the city's safety if it came to be believed that Geneva had become a base for sedition against the French crown. It declared it untrue that the pastors had consented to "an armed enterprise to prevent the persecutions in France" or "advised using force or taking up arms for religion's sake." Morély was ordered to ask

---

[45] AEG, Procès criminels, 2e série, 1215, fo. 4v; Naef, 123.

pardon for having spoken in a manner that suggested otherwise—not, it should be noted, for having spoken falsely—and told never again to say anything that could be similarly construed.[46]

The initial ambassadors' reports devoted much attention to rumors that the conjuration was led by *grandi* and mentioned that many of those involved appeared to be clients of Antoine of Navarre and his brother. Calvin's letter to Vermigli indicated that the conspirators claimed to have Condé's support for their venture. The published Protestant responses, on the other hand, said nothing about the possible role in the conspiracy of either Condé or Antoine. The royal letter of March 31 generously asserted that good evidence showed the Bourbon brothers not to have been involved.

In point of fact, when the conspirators approached Amboise, Antoine was at Nérac, but Condé had just recently come to court. At just the moment when Castelnau and his companions were arrested, the standard-bearer of his ordinance company and a man who had been raised alongside him at the abbey of Saint Denis, Edme de Ferrières-Maligny, the younger of the two brothers both often simply identified as "Maligny" in the documents of the time, fled precipitously from Amboise on one of the best horses in Condé's stable. Arrested conspirators rapidly implicated the younger Maligny as a plot leader.[47] Suspicion fell on Condé as well. Even the royal declaration of March 31 could not stanch such talk. By the first week of April rumors that arrested conspirators had implicated the prince ran so rife at court that Condé felt compelled to deny hotly any connection with the tumult in the king's presence and dare any courtier who believed otherwise to say so to his face. According to the Spanish ambassador, the cardinal of Lorraine kept his eyes glued to the floor and said nothing throughout the scene. The duke of Guise graciously replied

---

[46] AEG, Procès criminels, 2e série, 1215, fos. 11v–12; Naef, 145–46.

[47] *CSP Ven*, VII, 182–83, Michiel to doge and Senate, Amboise, April 4, 1560, reports the flight of "Maligni" at the time and makes it clear from the additional information provided about him that the individual in question is the younger brother Edme. The episode and its importance in stimulating suspicion of Condé is also reported in Pierre de La Place, *Commentaires de l'Estat de la Religion et Republique soubs les rois Henry et Francois seconde et Charles Neufieme* ([Orléans: E. Gibier], 1565), fo. 53v; and La Planche, 232, who both clearly identify the man involved as "le puisné de Maligny" or "le jeune Maligni." For Edme de Ferrières' upbringing alongside Condé and early career in his service, see Jean-Denis Léon de Bastard d'Estang, *Vie de Jean de Ferrières, vidame de Chartres, seigneur de Maligny* (Auxerre: Perriquet et Rouille, 1858), 35–39.

that he was happy to hear this, and that he was sure that the king had never doubted Condé's loyalty.[48]

For his part, Antoine expressed dismay on receiving news of the attack on the chateau and offered to come to court to defend the king. He was told to stay put and to seize any Protestant preachers active in the region, especially two known to have preached under his protection "whom prisoners confessed to be two of the chief seducers who incited this lovely enterprise," François Boisnormand and Pierre David. The same letter informed him that some had said that his brother was part of the affair, but the king did not believe it.[49]

Not long after Condé so vigorously defended his innocence in the king's presence, he slipped away from court. In June, he went to join his brother in Nérac, where none other than Boisnormand, who had not been arrested, preached at the first church service they attended together. All of this would heighten the suspicion of both men's possible involvement in the plotting, even before seized letters brought new evidence to light in late August linking Condé to ongoing conspiratorial activity and leading ultimately to his arrest and trial. He would be saved by Francis II's sudden death in December and would deny involvement in the conspiracies for the rest of his life, but belief to the contrary always hung heavily around him. As for Antoine, his relationship to conspiratorial activity throughout the reign of Francis II seems clear enough in retrospect, but again was uncertain at the time. As the first prince of the blood, he was the man the conspirators always tried to get to lead their endeavors. Prior to 1559, he had shown himself sufficiently well inclined to Protestantism

---

[48] Paillard, 348–49, Chantonnay to Margaret of Parma, Amboise, April 6, 1560; *ADE*, I, 246, Chantonnay to Philip II, Amboise, April 10, 1560. AS Modena, Ambasciatore Francia, 36 (II), fo. 2, Giulio Alvarotti to duke of Ferrara, Amboise, April 8, 1560, reports the scene differently; according to him, the Cardinal was not present and Guise's response was that he personally had always known Condé to be the king's virtuous servant.

[49] *MC*, I, 398–401, Francis II to Antoine, Marmoutier, April 9, 1560. This letter incorrectly names the second preacher "Martin David." On Pierre David's salaried preaching to the king and queen of Navarre in 1557–58, see *HE*, I, 123–24; *CO*, XVII, col. 70, Calvin to Antoine, Geneva, n.d., probably c. Feb 1558; col. 134, Macar to Calvin, Paris, April 12, 1558; Kingdon, *Geneva and the Coming*, 60–61, 72–73. The accuracy of the denunciation of him as a conspirator may be questioned. Calvin and the ministers inside the kingdom who were then establishing the boundaries of French Reformed orthodoxy viewed David with suspicion as one who "swam between two waters" and worked to discredit him in the eyes of his patrons, with Boisnormand leading the attack inside the Bourbon–Albret household. As Kingdon remarked, it would be surprising if, after their long quarrel, David and Boisnormand "co-operated on anything, even a plot."

to protect Reformed preachers and correspond with Calvin, giving cause to hope that he might openly champion the movement. When pressed to stake a claim to a greater share of authority, however, he always vacillated and ultimately decided not to provoke a showdown that might prove disastrous for him and the country.

The Revelations of Pierre de La Place and Louis Régnier de La Planche

Although the initial public Protestant response was to cast the Amboise conspiracy as an enterprise of lesser noblemen unconnected to Condé, Navarre, Calvin, Beza, or the French Reformed churches, and although the first Protestant tracts presented those actions that could not be denied in the most innocent light possible, Huguenot histories written over the next decades chose to reveal a great deal more about the secret organization of the plot. After Condé's death in 1569, they did not hesitate to say that he had been involved. Since these histories were written later, they also revealed details of the second phase of conspiratorial activity in the latter half of Francis II's brief reign. While still maintaining silence about any connections to either Calvin or Beza and casting the conspiracies as driven above all by resentment of the Guises, they appear to have been operating on the insight that the more they revealed that fit with the story line of a chiefly aristocratic and primarily political venture, the better their chances of shaping the narrative that they hoped would prevail.

The first Huguenot historian to disclose important new details of the Protestant plotting was Pierre de La Place, a high legal official and superintendent of Condé's household affairs. His 1565 *Commentaries on the State of Religion and the Commonwealth under Kings Henry II, Francis II and Charles IX*—the title echoes that of Johann Sleidan's history of the politics of the Reformation in the Empire under Charles V and shows that he was working in the same tradition—made it known that the conspirators worked out their plan of attack at an assembly in Nantes summoned by La Renaudie.[50] There, the formerly banished nobleman was chosen to act as the lieutenant of an unnamed

---

[50] Pierre de La Place, *Commentaires de l'Estat de la Religion et Republique soubs les rois Henry et Francois seconde et Charles Neufieme*. Fos. 50v–54 examine the conspiracy of Amboise.

"*prince muet*," who was the real leader. A six-person council and approximately thirty captains were named to aid him. La Place did not reveal exactly what plan of action was adopted at Nantes, other than that, after the court moved from Blois to Amboise, the conspirators were supposed to assemble at the house of La Fredonnière three leagues from the town and recognize one another by carrying black-and-white court tennis balls (*esteufs*). He presented the goals of the enterprise as being to evict the Guises from power without attempting anything else against the king or his state, and to "ensure the observation of France's ancient custom through a legitimate assembly of the Estates," adding that "some adherents of the so-called new doctrine who are called *huguenauds*" also associated themselves with this "civil and political cause" in order to present their confession of faith to the king and obtain a moderation of the persecution.[51]

La Place recounted what befell the conspirators around Amboise in the same manner as the *Histoire du tumulte d'Amboise*, adding a few additional details such as the flight of the younger Maligny. A few pages further along, he introduced through a striking vignette both a topos that would long endure in the historiography of French Protestantism and an explanation of La Renaudie's motives in terms of vengeance and rivalry. According to this tale, Catherine de Medici, eager to learn the real story behind the tumult at Amboise, summoned to court a protégé of the constable Montmorency whose political sagacity she respected, Louis Régnier de La Planche. La Planche, "a political rather than a religious man" in his nephew's words, seized the occasion to denounce the pretentions of the Guises and explain to the queen mother that "insofar as those who troubled the kingdom are called *huguenauds*, there are two kinds of them: *huguenauds de religion* and *huguenauds d'estat*." The former had been convinced by La Renaudie to take up arms so that they could present a request for the moderation of their persecution and could be easily satisfied by means of concessions and dialogue on the religious front. The latter were harder to appease without a significant restructuring of power at court since they had personal motives. Among them, La Renaudie was exhibit A, for he burned to avenge the secret execution of his

---

[51] La Place, *Commentaires*, fo. 51v.

brother-in-law, Gaspard de Heu, which he blamed on the house of Lorraine.[52]

Those knowledgeable about the life and fate of Gaspard de Heu might not have found this a very good illustration of the importance of personal rather than religious motives for many Amboise conspirators. De Heu was a member of one of the patrician families that dominated the government of Metz during the two centuries in which the town enjoyed the status of a free imperial city of the Holy Roman Empire. He was also the leader of the Protestant group that in 1542–43 encouraged Guillaume Farel to come preach in the city and that succeeded, with the backing of nearby Protestant territories, in obtaining a grant of toleration for evangelical worship from an imperial mediating committee, only to be prevented from enjoying that grant when armed troops directed by members of the house of Lorraine crossed the border, broke up the Reformed assemblies, and forced Farel and de Heu to flee.[53] Fifteen years later, after Henry II had taken Metz under French protection, de Heu got involved in efforts to end the French tutelage over the city, restore its independence, and at last establish Protestant worship. These efforts may have involved seeking armed support from Protestant princes in Germany. They certainly included contacting Antoine of Navarre; both de Heu, then using his title of "seigneur de Buy," and La Renaudie can be determined to have carried messages to him in the spring of 1558. This cost de Heu his life after he was recognized in Paris in May of that

---

[52] La Place, *Commentaires*, fos. 62v–64. The qualification of La Planche as an "homme politique plustost que religieux" comes from the history written by his nephew of the same name, La Planche, 404. This latter history also recounts the story told by La Place, although it paraphrases the elder Régnier de La Planche as distinguishing between Huguenots concerned with their consciences and those concerned with the *bien public* and also expresses skepticism about the explanation of La Renaudie's motives suggested by the story. It seems highly likely that the original source for this tale told by both historians was a now-lost pamphlet describing the interview written by the elder Régnier de La Planche. See Charles Delizy, "Louis Régnier de La Planche, historien du règne de François II" (thèse de bachelier, Faculté Libre de Théologie Protestante Paris, 1938), 30–32.

[53] Key documents and the fullest account of the events in Metz in these years are in Guillaume Farel, *Traités messins*, eds. Reinhard Bodenmann, Françoise Briegel, and Olivier Labarthe (2 vols., Geneva: Droz, 2009–18). I would like to thank Olivier Labarthe for giving me access to the invaluable introduction to Volume 2 prior to publication. See also *Guillaume Farel 1489–1565. Biographie nouvelle écrite d'après les documents originaux par un groupe d'historiens, professeurs et pasteurs de Suisse, de France et d'Italie* (Neuchâtel: Delachaux et Niestlé, 1930), 486–503; Henri Tribout de Morembert, *La Réforme à Metz* (2 vols., Nancy: Memoires des Annales de l'Est, 1969–71), I, 127–203; Thomas A. Brady, Jr., *Protestant Politics: Jacob Sturm (1489–1553) and the German Reformation* (Atlantic Highlands, NJ: Humanities Press, 1995), 81–86.

year, arrested, interrogated under torture, and executed on September 1 inside the chateau of Vincennes on orders of the king. Since the cardinal of Lorraine exercised administrative oversight over the bishopric of Metz and watched events in the larger region closely, many Protestants considered him responsible for de Heu's fate. Hotman, also involved in building this larger Protestant alliance, specifically mentioned de Heu's secret execution in his most acrimonious anti-Guise philippic, *Le Tigre de France*.[54] All this might suggest that La Renaudie was involved in clandestine Protestant activity even before de Heu's death, and that whatever hatred he felt toward the Guises for what he believed to be their role in the killing of his brother-in-law was not a mere family vendetta, but was also related to the house of Lorraine's engagement in suppressing Protestantism in Metz in both 1543 and 1558. Few later historians of France were aware of these details of Metz's history in its last years as a free imperial city, however. The idea that there were two kinds of Huguenots, political and religious, would have a long afterlife in French historiography, as would the idea that personal motives animated La Renaudie's engagement in the conspiracy of Amboise.

The pages of La Place's *Commentaries on the State of Religion and the Commonwealth* devoted to the remainder of Francis II's reign say nothing about the Maligny affair, other local disorders of the summer of 1560, or plots that the author connects to the Protestant cause. The lion's share of the discussion of these six months is devoted to the Assembly of Notables held at Fontainebleau in August. But La Place does mention a rumor that circulated in September 1560 of a scheme involving a coalition of aristocratic opponents of the Guises that, as we will see, could be pertinent for understanding Protestant plotting in the summer and fall. According to this rumor:

> The king of Navarre with the prince of Condé, accompanied by large forces from Guyenne, were supposed to pass through Poitiers, Tours and Orléans, towns devoted to him, on the pretext that they were going to see the king. Damville, the constable [Montmorency]'s second son,

---

[54] *CO*, XVII, cols. 81–82, 108, 115, 162, 183, 249, 349, 355, all cited in Naef, 46–47; "Mort de Gaspard de Heu, seigneur de Buy, le 1 septembre 1558," *BSHPF* 25 (1876): 164–68; Roger Mazauric, "La tragique destin d'un patricien messin: Gaspard de Heu, sieur de Buy," *Mémoires de l'Académie nationale de Metz* 159 (1978): 118–42, esp. 140–42; *Farel biographie nouvelle*, 505; Kelley, *Hotman*, 105–07.

was supposed to go to meet them at Poitiers with five to six hundred soldiers. The constable held Paris in his hand and could turn it as he wished when needed. The duke of Etampes would take care of Brittany, the count of Tende Provence and Senarpont and Bouchavannes Picardy. Having thus arranged things, if the king, prince and lords could not immediately master those of the Guises, they would hold their gathering and assembly at Orléans, the navel of the kingdom, and continue it until the Guises had been tried.[55]

Eleven years later, in 1576, a host of additional revelations about the conspiracies of 1560 would appear in a history of the reign of Francis II with a title very similar to La Place's, the *History of the State of France, both of the Commonwealth and of Religion, in the Reign of Francis II* (*Histoire de l'Estat de France, tant de la Republique que de la Religion: sous le Regne de François II*). Perhaps no other work would shape so profoundly the subsequent historiography of the topic. Its author was another Louis Régnier de La Planche, not the advisor to the constable Montmorency interviewed by Catherine de Medici, but his nephew of the same name. In light of the importance of this history, it is unfortunate that little is known about this Régnier de La Planche other than that he came from Poitou and that, although his grandfather was lieutenant-general of the sénéchaussée of Poitiers and his father a regent of law at the university, he pursued a military career as a captain of a gendarme company rather than studying jurisprudence like the previous generations. His date of birth is unknown, but as his parents only married in 1545, he could have been no more than fourteen when Francis II came to the throne, which suggests that he learned the previously untold stories about the reign that he recounted in his book from older informants, among whom his uncle was probably one. His text reveals that he shared his uncle's deep hostility to and suspicion of the house of Lorraine while developing a stronger Reformed faith.[56]

---

[55] La Place, *Commentaires*, fo. 105v.
[56] The two Louis Régniers de La Planche were long conflated, as in *Dictionnaire de biographie française* (Paris, 1933–ongoing) XIX, cols. 881–82, s.v. "La Planche [Louis Régnier, sieur de]." But see Paul Raveau and Joseph Salvini, *Le Château de la Planche de Vivonne* (Poitiers: Imprimerie Moderne, 1935), 16–17, 20–31, 60; Delizy, "Régnier de La Planche," 63–74; Myriam Yardeni, "La pensée politique de la première historiographie huguenote: Pierre de La Place et Louis Régnier de La Planche," in *Cité des hommes, cité de Dieu. Travaux sur la littérature de la Renaissance en l'honneur de Daniel Ménager* (Geneva: Droz, 2003), 101–10; Guilhem de Corbier, "Les ouvrages historiques des guerres de Religion de Lancelot Voisin de La Popelinière: élaboration et postérité" (thèse de doctorat, Université de Poitiers, 2015), 426–29.

La Planche's account of the reign of Francis II opens by focusing the reader's attention immediately on noble rivalries and attributing whatever sway the Guises exercised over other great lords to corruption. At Henry II's death, it declares, the Guises came to the fore, the nobility split between those they could bribe to join their faction and the "*connestablistes*." The third estate was "beaten down (*matté*)" and grew passive.[57] Unlike previous Protestant accounts, however, this history divulges connections between Reformed ministers and the politics of the reign. The author reveals what Calvin's correspondence would later confirm for the pastors of Paris, namely, that after Henry II's death ministers from the capital, Orléans, Tours, and other cities approached Antoine and urged him to come out as a Protestant. The Amboise conspiracy, on the other hand, is said to have originated in aristocratic resentment of governmental abuses. The monopolization of offices and appointments by the Guises, their corruption of judges, their skimming off of revenues, "in brief, their violent and . . . illegitimate government sparked marvelous hatred against them and led several lords to awaken as if from a deep sleep." These lords banded together and sought "some just defense to restore the kingdom's ancient and legitimate government." For this, they consulted with leading jurists and theologians in France and Germany, who declared that opposition to the Guise usurpation of power would be legitimate so long as one or more of the princes of the blood—not necessarily the first one—undertook the venture, and so long as it was done at the request of the "better (*plus saine*) part" of the Estates.[58] With Condé now safe in his tomb, La Planche did not hesitate to identify him as the prince muet. According to his account, Condé was approached by the initiators of the plan, heard them out, opened an investigation of the Guises' government, determined that grounds existed to have the brothers tried by the Estates, and agreed to lead the enterprise. La Renaudie was placed in charge of organizing the Nantes assembly, which took place on February 1. It decided that on March 10 five hundred nobles would attempt to seize Guise and Lorraine at Blois. At the same time, others would secure the kingdom's main cities to ensure that nobody went to their rescue. Captains were

---

[57] La Planche, 5–6.
[58] La Planche, 125–26.

appointed for different provinces. La Planche provided a name for nine of them and indicated that a tenth, whom he only identified as "N.," was the captain for Champagne, Brie, and the Ile-de-France. A generation later, Agrippa d'Aubigné would augment La Planche's list with seven more names, among them his own father's, and put a name on "N." That name was Maligny. Unfortunately, he did not specify whether the Maligny in question was Edme de Ferrières, the *guidon* in Condé's ordinance company, or his older brother Jean, a still more experienced military man who in 1560 was the lieutenant of the ordinance company of their cousin through the maternal line, François de Vendôme, Vidame de Chartres.[59]

In addition to providing many important revelations about the Amboise conspiracy, Régnier de La Planche, unlike La Place, did not hide that a second round of Protestant plotting soon got underway. Indeed, he set out quite a few details about the events leading up to the discovery of armed men in Lyon on September 4, albeit in convoluted prose that does not always make it easy to follow the story. It is a sign of how little attention has been paid to the Maligny affair that nobody seems to have remarked that the modern historians who have written about it have disagreed about which of the two Maligny brothers directed it. Virtually all historians from the elder Maligny's mid-nineteenth century aristocratic biographer, Jean-Denis Léon de Bastard d'Estang, through such recent scholars as Alain Dufour and Hugues Daussy assign the leading role to the younger Edme. On the other hand, the two historians to draw most heavily on the Triou deposition, Alphonse de Ruble and Lucien Romier, place Jean in charge—correctly, as we shall see.[60] The confusion and uncertainty probably must be traced back to La Planche's account, which distinguishes between the two brothers and makes the elder's involvement clear yet appears to indicate that Edme led the enterprise.

According to La Planche, the elder Maligny had not been involved in the Amboise conspiracy but was nonetheless summoned to court to answer for a role that was improperly attributed to him.

---

[59] La Planche, 127–35; Agrippa d'Aubigné, *Histoire universelle*, ed. André Thierry (11 vols., Geneva, 1981–99), I, 270–71.
[60] Bastard d'Estang, *Jean de Ferrières*, 55; Dufour, "Affaire de Maligny," 280; Jouanna et al., *Histoire de dictionnaire*, 74; Daussy, *Parti huguenot*, 174. Cf. de Ruble, *Antoine et Jeanne*, II, 345; Romier, *Conjuration*, 228.

Was Régnier covering up for him here, as he may also have been when he chose to identify the captain of the conspiracy for Champagne and the Ile-de-France only by the letter "N"? Since at the moment when he wrote, Maligny was still alive and was seeking to return to France after having been banished following the Saint Bartholomew's Massacre for his role in the early civil wars, whereas most of the captains of the conspiracy whom Régnier identified by name were now dead, this is a real possibility. On the other hand, no evidence of which I am aware unequivocally ties Jean de Ferrières to the Amboise conspiracy. Whatever the accuracy of La Planche's claim about the elder Maligny's prior innocence, it was his summons to court, La Planche explains, that led the Burgundian nobleman to realize that he needed to protect himself. To do so, he launched a second round of organizing. He gathered some nobles willing to back him, sent several to Condé to assure him of their support, and dispatched the rest to warn the churches throughout the kingdom of the need to work together against continued Guise tyranny.[61] For his part, Condé, after leaving court, went to join Antoine at Nérac, where the two brothers received several groups that urged them to act on behalf of the Estates. A new enterprise was hatched to seize Lyon "in order to give the princes courage and convoke there all who wished to see the proper order of the kingdom restored." This was "arranged (*dressée*)" by the younger Maligny, who went to Provence and so dexterously handled the matter that everything was in place for a successful mission. (This is the passage that led most later historians to give Edme the leading role in organizing the affair.) Then, at the last minute, a letter arrived from Antoine calling the mission off and instructing "Maligny" (no further specification) to take his men to Limoges instead. Very soon thereafter, the infiltrated men and their weapons were spotted in Lyon and had to fight their way out of town.[62] Even after the Lyon mission was cancelled, efforts to push Antoine to undertake some forceful action did not cease. Over the subsequent months further groups of people, including Beza, pressed him in this direction.[63]

---

[61] La Planche, 391.
[62] La Planche, 570–72.
[63] La Planche, 600–10. Pages 107–09 and 134–35 return in greater detail to the information provided about these later efforts to spur Antoine to act.

Together, the *Histoire du tumulte d'Amboise*, La Place's *Commentaires*, and La Planche's *Histoire de l'Estat de France* built the essential structure of interpretation and provided most of the specific details that would be repeated in subsequent histories, Catholic as well as Protestant, for generations to come. Their influence in shaping the Huguenot memory of the conspiracies was particularly direct since, in this era when directly copying large chunks of a prior historical work into a new one was common practice, large extracts were reproduced verbatim in several other Protestant histories of the time. The book that shaped later Huguenot memory like no other, Jean Crespin's *Histoire des martyrs*, directly lifted its accounts of the Amboise enterprise from the *Histoire du tumulte d'Amboise* for the 1564 edition and from La Place's *Commentaires* for editions from 1570 onward. Casting the Protestants as eternal victims as demanded by the martyrological genre, it also added the novel claim that subsequent talk of a second enterprise to displace the Guises in favor of the princes of the blood was a false rumor circulated by the Lorrainers so that they could renew the persecution of the faithful under the guise of combating sedition. Crespin's telling of the event in turn served as the source for the pictorial representations of the events around Amboise created by Jacques Tortorel and Jean Perrissin for the series of forty graphic images of *The Wars, Massacres and Troubles of Our Time* published in Geneva in 1569–70 (Figures 2.1 [pp. 40–41], 6.1 [p. 162]).[64] A decade later, Theodore Beza copied La Planche's account of the preparations for Amboise into the 1580 *Histoire ecclésiastique des Eglises réformées au royaume de France*.[65] Lancelot Voisin de La Popelinière's 1581 *Histoire de France* reproduced what Régnier wrote not only about the preliminary planning of that enterprise, but also the pages about the second round of the plotting that Beza had significantly omitted.[66] La

---

[64] Jean Crespin, *Actes des martyrs deduits en sept livres* (Geneva: Crespin, 1564), 991–95; Crespin, *Histoire des vrays tesmoins de la verité de l'Evangile* (Geneva: Crespin, 1570), 557–58; Crespin, *Histoire des martyrs persecutez et mis à mort pour la vérité de l'Evangile, depuis le temps des apostres jusques à présent (1619)*, eds. Daniel Benoit and Matthieu Lelièvre (3 vols., Toulouse: Société des Livres Religieux, 1885–89), III, 64–70; Philip Benedict, *Graphic History: The 'Wars, Massacres and Troubles' of Tortorel and Perrissin* (Geneva: Droz, 2007), 130–34, 244.
[65] *HE*, I, 285–90, 303–04.
[66] La Popelinière, *Histoire de France*, eds. Jean-Claude Laborie, Benoist Pierre, Pierre-Jean Souriac, and Denise Turrel (Geneva: Droz, 2009–ongoing), II, 247–80, 421–25 and passim. This critical edition reveals the full extent of La Popelinière's borrowing from La Planche and his inclusion of some details from La Place as well.

Planche's influence may also be discerned behind the far more condensed account of the reign of Francis II provided in the last major account of the period written by a Protestant who lived through it, Theodore Agrippa d'Aubigné's 1616–18 *Histoire universelle*.

This last work also added some startling details not found in any of the previous histories. As has already been mentioned, d'Aubigné enlarged the list of captains of the Amboise enterprise provided by La Planche with seven additional names. He also placed the future chancellor Michel de L'Hospital and Coligny's brother d'Andelot among the conspirators, "as I will maintain despite all that has been written about this, since the original [document] of the enterprise was given for safekeeping to my father and [L'Hospital's] seal was there between those of d'Andelot and a Spifame." Finally, he asserted that even before the Nantes assembly met "to fix the plan of attack (*pour reigler l'execution*)," a first gathering of La Renaudie and unnamed collaborators took place in Aubonne, near Geneva, "to fix the guiding principle (*pour résoudre la these generale*)."[67] D'Aubigné's work, written in his old age, is considerably less reliable about dates and details of the early Wars of Religion than the other contemporary histories.[68] Because other sources also point to a meeting in the vicinity of Geneva in December 1559, d'Aubigné's indication of an initial conclave in Aubonne has nevertheless been accepted by twentieth- and twenty-first-century historians.[69] The claim that L'Hospital and d'Andelot were involved has not, even though the involvement of d'Aubigné's father in the conspiracy might be thought to have given him access to reliable information about it.[70]

Initial speculation about the Amboise conspiracy had focused attention on the relative importance of malcontentedness and Huguenoterie. The royal letter of March 31 came down somewhere in the middle by identifying exiled laymen as the core plotters and

---

[67] D'Aubigné, *Histoire universelle*, I, 269–78, 286–87.
[68] My own fact checking confirms the judgment of Henri Hauser, *Les sources de l'histoire de France. XVIe siècle (1494–1610)* (4 vols., Paris: Picard, 1906–15), III, 75–76.
[69] Naef, 42, 51; Daussy, *Parti huguenot*, 141.
[70] Seong-Hak Kim, *Michel de l'Hôpital. The Vision of a Reformist Chancellor during the French Religious Wars* (Kirksville, MO: Sixteenth Century Journal Publishers, 1997), 50, provides strong reasons for rejecting the assertion concerning the chancellor.

unemployed fighting men or impoverished nobles as important participants, yet also emphasizing the role of ministers of the new sect in inducing members of their assemblies to join these malcontents under the guise of religion. In contrast, the post-Amboise Protestant apologias and histories consistently insisted that the plotting was born of a political, not a religious, cause. Calvin and Beza denied having supported the Amboise affair, got Geneva's authorities to silence anybody in the city who suggested otherwise, and said as little as possible about Maligny's venture. La Place's and La Planche's ample revelations about the clandestine preparation of the Amboise conspiracy mentioned consultation with ministers and legists about the legitimacy of opposing Guise tyranny in defense of the ancient constitution, but the venture itself was presented as having been launched by noblemen and backed by a prince muet identified as Condé once he was safely dead, with the few additional participants also mentioned by name likewise coming from the ranks of the aristocracy. Most of the accounts of the events around Amboise mentioned the attack on the Bonshommes gate, but more attention was given to Castelnau's voluntary surrender to Nemours on the promise of being led safely to the king to present a remonstrance, then the subsequent breaking of that promise. D'Aubigné would reiterate several times that the Reformed churches did not have anything to answer for in the Amboise conspiracy as it was a political act. The overall effect was to distance the Amboise conspiracy from Geneva and the French Reformed ministers and churches while associating it with noblemen and their discontents. The second round of plotting was largely, if not entirely, shrouded in silence.

One very different Protestant presentation of the Amboise venture must be noted. When Beza reviewed the history of the Reformed churches across the period of the civil wars in a long memorandum for the 1594 national synod of Montauban, he put the question of religion at the heart of the affair, asserting that the intention of those involved was never to do anything but present the confession of faith to the king to get him to show some compassion. The petitioners had to go armed because those around the young king had left him a king in name alone, much to the discontent of "all good and true

Figure 2.1. *(this and facing page)* Jacques Tortorel, *The Enterprise of Amboise Discovered on March 13, 14 and 15 1560*, woodcut, [1569–1570], 32 x 50 cm, collection of the author. This synoptic view, which compresses discrete events that occurred over several days into a single scene, depicts the events around Amboise as they came to be narrated in the earliest Protestant histories. Foregrounded in the left half of the image immediately above is the firefight in which La Renaudie was killed. In the right middle ground *(facing page)*, the baron of Castelnau and his companions in the chateau of Noizay negotiate with the duke of Nemours, shown on horseback in front of the building. According to the caption that accompanied this print, Nemours pledged on his honor as a prince during this negotiation to escort those in the chateau safely to the king. In the valley in the middle ground, Castelnau and his men (to quote the legend), "having put down their arms, are being led to Amboise, where subsequently they

were executed." In the far upper left (*facing page*) a company of horsemen said to have ridden through the night is thwarted as it attempts to enter Amboise. At the top of the image on this page, a band of cavalrymen ride out from the city toward a nearby wood where they encounter and capture an unsuspecting group of foot soldiers. The caption explains that many of these men would also be hanged or drowned. The narration thus focuses on the betrayal and harsh fate of many of those who had come to Amboise to speak to the king, while not entirely omitting to show that some tried to fight their way into the city. Because specific turns of phrase in the legend exactly match the wording of Crespin's 1564 recounting of these episodes, that edition of his martyrology may be presumed to have been the source used by the artists as they imagined these scenes a decade after the event.

Frenchmen."[71] This was a manuscript for internal church use. It had none of the enduring influence of the published histories.

Meanwhile, arch-Catholic historians from Saconay and Le Frère de Laval through the author of the 1579 *Grandes annales et histoire generale de France*, François de Belleforest, to the important seventeenth-century historian Scipion Dupleix (1569–1661) offered a very different picture of the conspiracies, their key actors, and their motives. In this telling, both the Amboise and the Lyon conspiracies were primarily inspired by ministers from Geneva who detested monarchy in both the secular and the ecclesiastical realms. Those who took part, far from seeking to defend the king and the true principles of the French monarchy, were prepared to harm Francis II or even change the existing form of government. Both Belleforest and Dupleix adduced evidence about Amboise in support of their assertions that they claimed to have learned from oral informants. The former wrote that a servant of La Renaudie's told him that the conspirators wanted to have no king. The latter, who hailed from Aquitaine, claimed to know a man who had gone with Castelnau to Amboise, only to learn at the last minute that hands might be laid on the sovereign. He turned back at once, renounced Calvinism forever, and fought on the Catholic and royal side in the subsequent civil wars.[72] The depiction of the conspiracies offered by these works would persist in certain Catholic circles through the seventeenth century and beyond. Strikingly, however, it ultimately exercised surprisingly little influence over the most prominent historians during the last centuries of the Ancien Régime, even though these historians shared the Roman faith. Even while casting the conspirators' aims in sinister hues and depicting their noble captains as dancing to a tune played by the ministers, the arch-Catholic historians copied most of the specific details they provided about the Amboise conspiracy from their Protestant predecessors. Their tone was more obviously partisan, virulently so in the

---

[71] "Mémoire de Théodore de Bèze sur les guerres de religion," *BSHPF* 21 (1872): 30–31, quoted in Naef, 171.

[72] François de Belleforest, *Les grandes annales et histoire générale de France* (2 vols., Paris: Gabriel Buon, 1579), II, 1608–13; Scipion Dupleix, *Histoire générale de France* (3 vols., Paris: Claude Sonnius, 1634–44), III, 575–78. The story told by Belleforest is repeated by Brantôme. Pierre de Bourdeille, seigneur de Brantôme, in *Oeuvres complètes*, ed. Ludovic Lalanne (11 vols., Paris: Veuve Jules Renouard, 1864–82), IV, 290–91.

case of Saconay, who offered the most circumstantial account of events in Lyon. None provided other than hearsay evidence that the conspirators meant to alter or abolish the monarchy. For these reasons, later generations of historians looking for reliable evidence generally discounted them. In this instance, as in many others related to the Wars of Religion, the history that came to prevail in the following centuries was that first written by the losers, not the winners. The richer documentation, more ample details, and more measured tone enabled the early Protestant histories to carry the day.

Political considerations around the turn of the century also contributed to the victory of the Protestant narrative. As the civil wars drew to a close, a growing fraction of the political class recognized that if France wished to live in peace, it had no choice but to tolerate its Huguenot minority. An account of the recent civil wars that cast them as arising from aristocratic rivalries and opposition to the evil house of Guise offered more hope for confessional reconciliation than one that suggested that Protestantism was intrinsically seditious. Furthermore, the leading role of the next generation of the house of Guise in the Catholic League's futile attempt to bar Henry of Navarre's accession seemed to accredit La Planche's picture of the previous generation as no less malevolent and power-mad. The more general failure of the League after a long and supremely destructive civil war discredited the larger tradition of Catholic ultras like Saconay. When Henry IV's *politique* Catholic advisor and supporter de Thou sat down to write the history of these years, he relied primarily on earlier Protestant historians, especially La Planche, at virtually every step in his account of the conspiracies of the reign of Francis II. In his telling, as in the works of the early Protestant historians, the conspiracies were driven more by discontent with the Guises than by religion. La Renaudie and other noble captains, not any pastors, were the organizers and actors of the plots, with Condé operating behind the scenes. The conspirators' early consultation with leading Protestant theologians did not go unmentioned, but no links were made with Calvin or Geneva, nor were the French Reformed ministers or churches given any role in recruiting participants.[73] Nothing from

---

[73] De Thou, *Histoire Universelle* (6 vols., The Hague: H. Scheurleer, 1740), II, 753–73.

Saconay was added to La Planche's terse mention of the plot against Lyon canceled at the last minute.[74]

For as long as Latin remained the chief language of learning, de Thou's weighty and eloquent *Historia sui temporis* remained the fundamental work about the period. As French came to replace Latin, full translations appeared in Paris, The Hague, and Basel between 1734 and 1742. The most important enrichment of the source base for understanding the period from 1559 to 1572 to appear during the Ancien Régime, the six volumes of documents published in 1743 under the title *Mémoires de Condé*, may offer the best testimony to the work's enduring influence; it bears the subtitle "*servant d'éclaircissement et de preuves à l'Histoire de M. de Thou*."[75] The general picture of the conspiracies given by de Thou continued to structure understanding of them from the time of François Eudes de Mézeray, the most authoritative historian of the age of Louis XIV, to that of François Guizot, the preeminent historian of the early nineteenth century.[76] Through de Thou's influence and because the Protestant sources were simply the fullest ones available, the distancing of the conspiracies from the Reformed churches initiated by Huguenot pamphleteers and historians would have remarkable staying power within the subsequent historiography, as would Calvin's denial of personal involvement.

New Discoveries, Limited Impact

Already in 1743, the *Mémoires de Condé* made widely available many of the pamphlets and royal declarations of the year 1560 and substantial

---

[74] De Thou, *Histoire Universelle*, II, 806.
[75] The complex publishing history of de Thou's work is told by Samuel Kinser, *The Works of Jacques-Auguste de Thou* (The Hague: Nijhoff, 1966). The work's influence on subsequent French historical writing about the Wars of Religion is sketched in Philip Benedict, "Shaping the Memory of the French Wars of Religion: The First Centuries," in *Memory before Modernity. Practices of Memory in Early Modern Europe*, eds. Erika Kuijpers, Judith Pollmann, Johannes Müller, and Jasper van der Steen (Leiden: Brill, 2013), 119–122; and Benedict, "Were the French Wars of Religion Really Wars of Religion?" in *The European Wars of Religion: Interdisciplinary Reassessment of Sources, Myths, and Interpretations*, eds. Wolfgang Palaver, Dietmar Regensburger, and Harriet Rudolph (Farnham, UK: Ashgate, 2016), 73–74.
[76] Mézeray, *Histoire de France* (3 vols., Paris: Thierry, 1685), III, 14–23; Guizot, *L'histoire de France depuis les temps le plus reculés jusqu'en 1789, racontée à mes petits-enfants* (5 vols., Paris: Hachette, 1877), III, 264–70.

extracts from the Habsburg diplomatic correspondence of the time. The pace of discovery and publication of new documents then accelerated in the second half of the nineteenth century. Britain's state papers were calendared. The ambassadorial correspondence in Venetian, Florentine, and Belgian repositories came to light. Between 1854 and 1876, the judge and legal historian Rodolphe Dareste published or summarized letters from and to Francois Hotman that revealed his enthusiasm about the conspiracies and his role in promoting efforts to gain support for it from the Protestant princes of Germany. One particularly important letter from Jean Sturm, the rector of the academy of Strasbourg where Hotman taught law, charged Hotman with being so intoxicated at one point with confidence in the Amboise conspiracy's strength that he indiscreetly revealed the plan to all and sundry, boasting that all of the males of the Guise family would soon be slain.[77]

A particularly important event was the publication in the 1870s of Calvin's complete correspondence. This made available not only his and Beza's letters about the conspiracy of Amboise, themselves not without ambiguity when read closely, but also letters from later the same year that pointed to their becoming ever more directly involved in efforts to induce Antoine to stake his claim to authority within the royal council. Volume 18 of the correspondence, published in 1878, contained the great bulk of letters from the second half of 1560. These revealed three major points of note. First, in response to a request from the king of Navarre, Calvin dispatched Beza in July to join Antoine at Nérac, "partly to correct his sloth, partly to counter the turbulent advice of the multitude."[78] Second, both Calvin and Beza had made contact with an unnamed "fervid one of ours," hesitantly identified by the editors in a note as the younger Maligny, at some point before September 10, when Calvin wrote to Beza to say that he had tried to urge him to be patient even before this latest change

---

[77] Rodolphe Dareste ed., "François Hotman et la conjuration d'Amboise: deux lettres inédites de Jean Sturm," *Bibliothèque de l'École des Chartes* 15 (1854): 360–75, esp. 370; "François Hotman d'après sa correspondance inédite," *Revue Historique* 2 (1876): 1–59, 367–435.

[78] *CO*, XVIII, col. 208, Calvin to Bullinger, Geneva, Sept 30, 1560: "De Beza nostro sic habe: non fuisse illuc sponte profectum, sed evocatum Regis literis, quibus et humaniter et magna contentione me rogabat ut hoc sibi beneficium concederem. Non putavi id negandum, partim ut corrigerret pigritiem, partim ut turbulentis multorum consiliis occurreret."

of plans.[79] Third, after Maligny's mission was canceled, Calvin felt that action by "our leaders" was even more urgent. He remained confident for several months that if the first prince of the blood acted promptly and firmly, he would be able to assume his rightful place within the council without bloodshed by following the plan prepared for him, only to splutter with rage and disappointment when "the tortoise" ignored his and Beza's counsel, rejected the offers of aid from numerous noblemen, and proved too cowardly to do what was right.[80] Volume 20 of the Calvin correspondence, published in 1879, made available two other pertinent letters. The first dated from 1560 but was not published alongside the others of that year because the editors of the correspondence only found it later. It showed that Beza wrote to Calvin from "Racney," an anagram easily decoded as Nérac, telling him to put the brakes immediately on "the production being prepared in your direction," to wait until he gave word to proceed, and to send as much remaining money as possible to Nérac.[81] The second, dating from June 1563, contained an appeal from Calvin to Jeanne d'Albret, by then Antoine de Bourbon's widow and a committed Protestant, asking her to repay the ten thousand francs he had sent Maligny in Lyon at her late husband's request. Calvin wrote that he personally had contributed "even the coins I use to buy my daily provisions," but this was not his chief concern. Above all, he wanted to reimburse the friends from whom he had borrowed most of the money.[82]

Amédée Roget, Émile Doumergue, and Alphonse de Ruble

One of the nineteenth century's leading historians of Geneva, the independent-minded Liberal Conservative politician Amédée Roget, quickly saw the import of the letters in volume 18, even if he did not

---

[79] *CO*, XVIII, col. 177, Calvin to Beza, Geneva, Sept 10, 1560. This important letter had already been published in Johann Wilhelm Baum, *Theodor Beza nach handschriftlichen und anderen gleichzeitigen Quellen* (2 vols., Leipzig: Weidmann, 1851), II, Appendix, 15–17; and in English translation in *Letters of John Calvin*, ed. Jules Bonnet, trans. Marcus Robert Gilchrist (4 vols., Philadelphia: Presbyterian Board of Publication, 1855–58), IV, 126–30. Both editors had likewise suggested that Maligny was the "fervent one."
[80] *CO*, XVIII, nos. 3207, 3215, 3242, 3246, 3248, 3253, 3254, 3260, 3269, 3285, 3291.
[81] *CO*, XX, col. 473.
[82] *CO*, XX, col. 36, Calvin to Jeanne d'Albret, Geneva, June 1, 1563.

notice those hidden two volumes further along. In 1881, as he reached the year 1560 in his monumental *Histoire du peuple de Genève depuis la Réforme jusqu'à l'Escalade*, Roget turned briefly to Calvin's role in events in his natal kingdom and their implications for Geneva's security. In the pages that he devoted to this topic, he provided extensive quotations from the newly published letters and deduced from them a number of points that could have served to inject the plotting of the summer and fall of 1560 into the mainstream of the narrative of Francis II's reign, had historians of France been motivated to read with care a seven-volume history of Geneva. He admitted to having some difficulty in seizing the reformer's precise stance toward the tumult in France. "At times he condemns the impetuosity of the Protestants, at others their irresoluteness and delays," he wrote. Nonetheless, he suggested that Calvin probably approved the project of a *pronunciamento* of nobles in favor of Antoine's right to a leading role in the government but sought to ensure that the explosion did not come too soon. Maligny's goals in seizing Lyon, he asserted, were to provide a rallying point for the militant Protestants of Dauphiné and Provence and to encourage Navarre to act. Calvin was aware of Maligny's plan and "worked in concertation with [him], even while criticizing the haste with which he proceeded." After the cancellation of this venture, the reformer believed that it was even more urgent that Antoine and Condé make a show of force.[83] Roget deserves credit as the first modern historian to call attention to Calvin and Beza's active support in the summer and fall of 1560 for a demonstration of strength led by Antoine and to note their concertation with Maligny. But few historians of France had occasion to open his book. What he wrote on the subject was rarely cited.

One French historian who did engage with Roget a generation later was Emile Doumergue, the professor of church history at the Protestant Theology Faculty of Montauban who was at once Calvin's most thorough biographer and his greatest defender. His *Jean Calvin. Les hommes et les choses de son temps* appeared in seven massive folio volumes between 1899 and 1927. The final volume examined what

---

[83] Roget, *Histoire du peuple de Genève depuis la Réforme jusqu'à l'Escalade*, (7 vols., Geneva: Jullien, 1870–83), VI, 18–29, 39–58, quotations at 50n, 57. Roget died before he could take his history beyond 1567, but to this day his work remains the best study of the politics of the Genevan Reformation during Calvin's lifetime.

Doumergue considered to be the triumphant culmination of Calvin's life work, the dramatic expansion of his movement in France in the years 1555–62. The Montauban professor did not appreciate Roget's depiction of his hero as inconsistent and criticized him for failing to see that Calvin always opposed disorder or resistance except when led by lesser magistrates with constitutional authority to exercise a share of power; hence, he condemned the impetuosity of Protestants who seized churches, engaged in unsanctioned acts of iconoclasm, or took part in plots led by anybody other than the first prince of the blood, but encouraged Antoine to act when he had a legitimate claim to authority. Nor would Doumergue grant Calvin's involvement in the Maligny affair. A letter from Calvin to Bullinger a month after the fact saying that he had tried to cut short Maligny's enterprise but failed was proof for him that there was no concertation between the reformer and the adventurer. His own close examination of the evidence did, however, lead him to grant that Roget had correctly seen that Calvin pressed for a demonstration of strength on Navarre's part. "Insofar as one can grasp [his idea], Calvin wanted the king of Navarre to issue an appeal to all friends of the Gospel and enemies of the Guises, loudly assert his place in the royal Council, and go take it at the head of a large demonstration. In this plan, the surprise capture of Lyon could even play a role if the king of Navarre wished it done."[84] Like Roget's book, Doumergue's might have drawn the attention of French historians to Calvin's support for assertive action by Antoine in the summer and fall of 1560, if not to his contacts with Maligny, had it been widely read. But it, too, was not. By 1927 most leading figures in France's determinedly *laïc* university system had come to dismiss Doumergue as little more than a hagiographer. They were as unlikely to read his latest volume from cover to cover as they were Roget's history of Geneva.

Meanwhile, in the same years between 1870 and 1882 when the Strasbourg team was editing Calvin's letters and Roget was writing his history of the Genevan people, the baron Alphonse de Ruble was scouring French and Spanish repositories in search of evidence about the lives of Antoine de Navarre and Jeanne d'Albret. A lawyer and

---

[84] Doumergue, *Jean Calvin. Les hommes et les choses de son temps. Tome VII, Le triomphe* (Neuilly-sur-Seine: Editions de "La Cause," 1927), 241–48, quotation at 247.

monarchist who withdrew to private life after the fall of the Second Empire, de Ruble earned enough prominence among his contemporaries as a historian to be chosen as president of the Société de l'Histoire de France and gain election to the Académie des Inscriptions et Belles-Lettres. The extraordinary pains that he took to accumulate original documentation for the six volumes that he devoted to his biographies of Henry IV's mother and father led him to a number of previously unexploited pieces of evidence about the conspiracies of 1560, most notable the Triou deposition.[85] Triou's testimony in turn enabled him, when he published the second volume of *Antoine de Bourbon et Jeanne d'Albret* in 1882, to detect the involvement of the Lyon church in the Amboise conspiracy and to narrate in detail the preparation of Maligny's plot to seize the city. He could not, however, identify the individuals close to Calvin mentioned in Triou's testimony, because the detailed investigation of Geneva's archives that has subsequently brought to light so much information about those around the reformer, an enterprise to which Doumergue contributed heavily, had not yet begun. Although de Ruble does not appear to have used the just-published Calvin correspondence, other sources showed him that the Protestants continued to lobby Antoine to act even after the fiasco at Amboise and that Hotman and Beza went to Nérac on such a mission. Separating himself from the Protestant historiographic tradition, he followed Chantonnay's reports in suggesting that the Amboise conspiracy aimed to pressure the king to convert and cede some power on pain of deposition, as well as to force into exile or even kill the Guises. But like so many royalist historians before him, he saw elite politics as chiefly driven by aristocratic rivalries and personalities, with religion a mere pretext.[86] Antoine himself, he grew convinced, was as much a driver of the conspiracies of Francis II's reign as his younger brother Condé. He provided the great bulk of the funding for the Amboise conspiracy, then over the following summer developed an ambitious scheme to raise the entire

---

[85] De Ruble's work on Antoine and Jeanne appeared under three titles: *Le mariage de Jeanne d'Albret* (Paris: A. Labitte, 1877); *Antoine de Bourbon et Jeanne d'Albret* (4 vols., Paris: A. Labitte, 1881–86); and *Jeanne d'Albret et la guerre civile* (Paris: Paul et Guillemin, 1897). Triou's deposition is cited and utilized in *Antoine et Jeanne*, II, 143, 343–48. Note that de Ruble refers to the cabinetmaker as "Pierre Menard," the first name Triou supplied when interrogated.

[86] *Antoine et Jeanne*, II, 350: "Les mêmes aspirations politiques, sous prétexte de religion, avaient animé les conjurés [in both the conspiracy of Amboise and the Maligny affair]."

Midi in revolt, bring in English support by sea, and march northward to impose his will on the court.[87] These last assertions, it must be said, rested more on supposition and the elimination of alternative explanations than positive evidence. Few subsequent historians would repeat them. For those who read the four volumes of *Antoine de Bourbon et Jeanne d'Albret*, however, a fuller account of the Maligny affair than ever before, as well as evidence about the involvement of a group of Lyonnais in the preparations for the Amboise conspiracy, was now available. But the book would not be read for long, because the nature and chief locus of historical scholarship soon changed and de Ruble's interpretations of the conspiracies of 1560 came under sharp criticism.

Lucien Romier and the Question of English Complicity

A generation after the appearance of Roget's and de Ruble's pages on the conspiracies of 1560, a talented young historian destined for a remarkable career that would end with his becoming one of Pétain's most trusted advisors and cabinet members, Lucien Romier, devoted more than a decade of research and six volumes to the years leading up to the outbreak of the Wars of Religion. A product of the Ecole des Chartes, France's elite school for archivists, Romier wrote a thesis on a prominent figure at the court of Henry II that earned him the scholarship to the Ecole Française de Rome given each year to the outstanding graduating student. In Italy he was able to immerse himself in the archives of the smaller Italian states rich in previously unexploited diplomatic letters.[88] These proved crucial for his subsequent work on the origins of the Wars of Religion, for they reported in detail on the tensions between different factions at court. His first work in the sequence of volumes on the period leading up to the Wars of Religion, the prize-winning, two-volume *Les origines politiques*

---

[87] De Ruble, *Antoine et Jeanne*, II, 226–27, 335–36.
[88] Christine Roussel, *Lucien Romier (1885–1944)—historien, économiste, journaliste, homme politique* (Paris: Editions France-Empire, 1980) offers a biography. For the political and economic views of the mature Romier that made him "one of the pillars of liberal bourgeois opinion" in the interwar years, as well as for his increasingly marginalized role in successive Vichy cabinets, see also Julian Jackson, *France: The Dark Years, 1940–1944* (Oxford: Oxford University Press, 2001), 50, 57, 153, 213, 227, 232.

des guerres de religion, was devoted to the reign of Henry II and appeared in 1913. It located the origins of the civil wars precisely in the aristocratic faction fights of that king's reign, a thesis that Henri Hauser judged in the pages of the *Revue historique* "a bit simple" and too indebted to Michelet and the sixteenth-century Protestant authors, even while praising the excellence of the book's research in Italian archives.[89] Romier then did research in French archives and libraries on the spread of Protestantism in the years 1555–62 after his return from Italy. Poor health prevented him from seeing combat during the First World War. Instead, he was assigned to join a commission headed by Hauser charged with investigating the state of France's wartime economy. This would soon launch him on a new career as an economic journalist that would take him to prominence in the opinion columns of leading conservative newspapers, but not before he finished and published four more tomes on the run-up to the civil wars. The two volumes of *Le royaume de Catherine de Médicis: la France à la veille des guerres de religion* (1922), anticipated many of the concerns of later social history with their analytic survey of the workings of the government, the situation of the various orders of society, and the rapidly changing religious situation on the eve of the civil wars. These were quickly followed by two narrative works that skillfully drew together a wide range of primary sources into concise, lively accounts. The first, bearing the awkward three-part title, *La Conjuration d'Amboise. L'aurore sanglante de la liberté de conscience. Le règne et la mort de François II* (1923), covered the reign of Francis II. The second, *Catholiques et huguenots à la cour de Charles IX* (1924), went from December 1560 to April 1562. These six volumes immediately became the obligatory starting point for any serious student of the years 1547–62.

Romier cited de Ruble in several of his books, especially the volume on the reign of Francis II. Here he also narrated scenes that the baron was the first to reconstruct, notably the meetings of the local organizers in Lyon for the Amboise conspiracy in which Triou took part. For all of Romier's extensive research, however, he did not personally examine the Triou deposition. And while he depended on de Ruble for details derived from that document, he found little

---

[89] Quoted in Roussel, *Romier*, 85.

confirmation for most of the baron's distinctive interpretations. One footnote dismissed his presentation of Maligny's venture with a blunt "de Ruble didn't understand the purpose of the ... affair." Other topics on which the two historians parted company were the depth of Antoine's involvement in the two conspiracies, the financing of the Amboise enterprise, and Antoine's subsequent road map to establishing his right to a leading role in government.[90] Even more than Romier's disparaging comments about de Ruble, however, it was the greater literary merit, tighter organization, and sharper analyses of his histories that consigned *Antoine de Bourbon et Jeanne d'Albret* forever after to the category of books that are occasionally consulted for details and references but never read all the way through. Once this happened, the Triou deposition slipped from the view of historians, except those few who mined de Ruble's footnotes and made the effort required to travel to Pau or to obtain a reproduction.[91]

What Hauser observed about *Les origines politiques des guerres de religion* remained true of *La conjuration d'Amboise*: Romier never entirely escaped the influence of the sixteenth-century Protestant historians, even though evidence that ran counter to their depiction of the conspiracies of 1560 had accumulated by his lifetime, and even though he integrated much of that evidence into his retelling of these events. He brought out more clearly than any previous historian the role of the Paris minister La Roche Chandieu in developing the legal justification for the plot and moving it along in its early stages. He noted that the nobles whom he judged central to the plotting got ideological support from Geneva and Strasbourg and men and money from Reformed churches within the kingdom such as Lyon's. As per Calvin and Chantonnay, he stated that sixty or seventy men went out from Geneva. The echoes in the diplomatic correspondence of what had been learned from those arrested and interrogated around Amboise made clear to him that many of these Protestant participants set out without knowing exactly where and why they were going. He

---

[90] Romier, *Conjuration*, passim, esp. 69–73, 227–29, quotation at 228n.
[91] De Ruble's footnotes were what led me to the Triou deposition, as they also did Natalie Zemon Davis, who, however, never cited it in any publication or analyzed it in detail. The document was also examined by Emile Clouard, who drew upon it and cited it—inaccurately and misleadingly—in "Le protestantisme en Bretagne au XVIe siècle. Étude historique et critique," *Mémoires de la Société d'Histoire et d'Archéologie de Bretagne* 17 (1936): 75, 86.

consequently spoke of the "*caractère confus*" of the Amboise enterprise. Yet for all this, he remained convinced that there was more malcontentedness than Huguenoterie in the venture. The highly original analysis that he offered of the background and family connections of the aristocratic captains of the enterprise identified three networks among what he considered the core component of the conspiracy: relatively obscure relatives of the Bourbon family such as François de Vendôme, Vidame de Chartres, and his cousin and successor to that title Maligny; aristocratic friends and clients of Condé's brother-in-law La Rochefoucauld; and a motley collection of discontented gentlemen recruited by La Renaudie. Implicit in such a network analysis was that factional affiliation or personal dislike of the Guises was as or more important than religious conviction. The larger contingents that converged on Amboise, he believed, included many soldiers in quest of a new adventure and payday, some Frenchmen who had been dismissed at the end of the Habsburg-Valois wars with unpaid wages, others the German, Swiss, Savoyard, English, and Scots mercenaries mentioned by the Venetian ambassador.[92] "The conspiracy was not a Protestant enterprise; the facts prove this, and the king and Guises themselves recognized as much." Not only did Calvin consistently oppose it; "no recognized Reformed minister was directly involved in the plot itself."[93]

That a man of the right and a practicing Catholic like Romier would feel moved to assert so strongly the conspiracy's lack of connection to the Reformed churches is less surprising than it might first appear. Romier was a social Catholic by upbringing and education whose political outlook throughout the inter-war and Vichy years aligned with the center right, a milieu in which anti-Protestantism was relatively weak. Furthermore, members of France's small Protestant minority bulked large in the educational institutions of the turn-of-the-century Third Republic that shaped him. Romier's thesis advisor at the Ecole des Chartes was of Huguenot origin, as was the examiner of the thesis who subsequently became his most influential patron, Gabriel Monod.[94] For all their stated commitment to impartial, archi-

---

[92] Romier, *Conjuration*, 55.
[93] Romier, *Conjuration*, 56.
[94] Roussel, *Romier*, 35–58.

vally based scholarship, historians such as these were still inclined to see their ancestors as being on the side of progress and to defend them against the suggestion that they started the Wars of Religion.[95] The authoritative history of the civil wars that Romier would have read as a student, Jean-Hippolyte Mariéjol's contribution to the Lavisse *Histoire de France*, cast the Amboise conspiracy as part of a larger change that occurred when the "truly evangelical," nonresisting Protestant movement of the earlier years was transformed into a political party by an influx of combatative, half-converted noblemen who initiated a descent into violence and rebellion despite Calvin's warnings against all spilling of blood.[96] The weight of this academic formation in leading Romier to emphasize the role of the nobility in the Amboise enterprise and its disconnect from the Reformed churches would have been further reinforced by the focus on factional rivalries at court found within the diplomatic sources on which he so heavily relied.

The chapter that Romier devoted to the subsequent "new plot" of the summer and fall of 1560 cast this as built of the same stuff as the Amboise enterprise, even if Calvin and Beza were drawn in. Maligny's venture was "simply a reprise on a larger scale of La Renaudie's plot, with the same procedures, the same elements and the same end." It was initiated by Condé, his agents, and "those colonies of unfortunate refugees banished from their country who hoped to return home via a revolution." In need of men and money, they turned to the churches for support and pleaded with Calvin and the Company of Pastors to let Beza go to Nérac. Calvin agreed, hoping that this time Antoine would actively assert his rights and support the convocation of the Estates. For a while, he even allowed himself to believe this could happen.[97] Having read Calvin's correspondence with care, Romier

---

[95] Charles-Olivier Carbonell, *Histoire et historiens: une mutation idéologique des historiens français 1865–1885* (Toulouse: Privat, 1976), esp. 414–47; Nathanaël Weiss, "A quoi sert l'histoire du protestantisme," *BSHPF* 51 (1902): 340; André Encrevé, "Réforme et guerres de religion en France selon Jules Bonnet et Nathanaël Weiss, rédacteurs du *Bulletin de la SHPF* de 1866 à 1923," in *L'identité huguenote. Faire mémoire et écrire l'histoire (XVIe–XXIe siècle)*, eds. Philip Benedict, Hugues Daussy, and Pierre-Olivier Léchot (Geneva: Droz, 2014), 501–22.

[96] Jean-H. Mariéjol, *Histoire de France depuis les origines jusqu'à la Révolution*, Vol. 6/1 *La Réforme et la Ligue—L'Édit de Nantes (1559–1598)* (Paris: Hachette, 1904), 12–13. Romier, too, depicted control of the Protestant movement passing from ministers to noblemen in 1560–61 with similar consequences. *Le royaume de Catherine de Médicis. La France à la veille des guerres de religion* (2 vols., Paris: Perrin, 1922), II, 266–68.

[97] Romier, *Conjuration*, 215–31, quotations at 217, 218.

glimpsed what Roget had seen before him: the reformer's active encouragement of concerted action led by Antoine. Still he averred that the Maligny affair was a direct continuation of the conspiracy of Amboise, which was not a Protestant enterprise. In one way, however, he aligned himself here with the early Catholic historians who saw Protestantism as subversive and proto-republican. He declared it "certain" that the Maligny brothers "worked together with Montbrun in Dauphiné and Mauvans in Provence to make Lyon the head of a vast 'canton' that would become the neighbor and ally of Geneva."[98] I am unaware of any subsequent historian who has accepted this claim.

Romier accorded particular weight to an aspect of the conspiracy that so far has only been alluded to but that now deserves further examination: the question of English support for or involvement in the conspiracies. The cardinal of Lorraine was convinced in the immediate aftermath of the troubles around Amboise that the English had fomented them.[99] At the turn of the twentieth century, an article by J. Dureng deemed this highly probable on the basis of the published diplomatic correspondence and Calvin's letters.[100] Romier went a step further. Finding no evidence for de Ruble's claim that the men who assembled around Amboise were financed from the treasury of Navarre and convinced that the Reformed churches could not have raised the funds necessary to pay thousands of mercenaries, he suggested that the English actively financed the venture.[101]

That suspicion of English involvement should have arisen among both contemporaries and later historians was almost inevitable in light of the interconnection of English, French, and Scottish affairs around 1560. In January 1558, the French took Calais, the last vestige of England's once extensive continental possessions. Naturally, the English were eager to regain what they believed to be legally theirs. Three months later, the "auld alliance" between England's northern and southern neighbors was reinforced when Mary, Queen of Scots wed the future Francis II under a marriage contract that gave the

---

[98] Romier, *Conjuration*, 228.
[99] See p. 15. Habsburg correspondence echoes Lorraine's suspicions. *ADE*, I, 221, Chantonnay to Philip II, Amboise, March 20, 1560.
[100] J. Dureng, "La complicité de l'Angleterre dans le complot d'Amboise," *Revue d'Histoire Moderne et Contemporaine* 6 (1904–05): 249–56.
[101] Romier, *Conjuration*, 72–76.

French dauphin a shared role in kingship in Scotland once he became king in France. This came to pass sooner than anybody expected when the hale and hearty Henry II fell jousting in July 1559. Within nine months of her accession, England's new Protestant queen, Elizabeth, thus found her realm sandwiched between the two halves of a dynastic union of its bitterest hereditary enemies. Furthermore, if one accepted the premise that the illegality of divorce under canon law made Elizabeth an illegitimate child, then she did not deserve to sit on the English throne at all. Her half-sister Mary did. English statesmen's fear of the Franco-Scottish threat grew when they learned that Mary and Francis adopted a seal containing the arms of England as well as Scotland and France. But the situation in Scotland offered the English a way to counter this threat. Although the northern kingdom had been ruled for most of the prior decade by its regent queen mother, Mary of Guise—none other than the sister of the French duke and cardinal who assumed so much authority under Francis I—Scotland, too, like France, saw an outlawed Protestant movement burst into public view as the 1550s drew to a close. A number of lords banded together in December 1557 to advance the faith. John Knox returned to the country from Geneva in May 1559. A wave of iconoclasm and the forced closure of monasteries rocked the central portion of the kingdom, culminating in the seizure of Edinburgh and its churches by the so-called Lords of the Congregation. Mary of Guise desperately sought military reinforcements from France even as she was forced to negotiate with the lords to obtain their peaceful departure from Edinburgh in return for a promise of amnesty and liberty of conscience.[102] In this situation, Elizabeth's more strongly Protestant councilors, led by William Cecil, realized that backing the Scottish insurgents might not only advance the faith, but also offer a lever for removing Mary of Guise from power and thus weaken the new dynastic union. They also imagined that connections useful for this project could be made with co-religionists on the continent, both in France, where the new English ambassador, Nicholas Throckmorton, was the hottest Protestant of all of Elizabeth's councilors, and in Germany,

---

[102] An especially good narrative of the events in Scotland at this time is found in Pamela E. Ritchie, *Mary of Guise in Scotland, 1548–1560: A Political Career* (East Linton: Tuckwell Press, 2002), 205–44.

where Strasbourg was a hub of diplomatic efforts to build an alliance of Protestant cities and princes prepared to act in concert to advance the worship rights of co-religionists living under Catholic rulers.[103]

English diplomatic sources show that soon after Francis II's accession Throckmorton arranged a one-on-one meeting with Antoine of Navarre and assured him that his mistress was eager to build a solid alliance with him on the basis of religion.[104] Hotman wrote Calvin in September 1559 that Elizabeth was so committed to the project of an international Protestant diplomatic initiative that she promised two hundred crowns to fund a trip by Villemongis to a high-placed French nobleman identified only by the code name "Eubulus" to urge him to join it.[105] A few months earlier, Throckmorton helped to arrange the escape from France via Geneva of the young James Hamilton, third Earl of Arran, the eldest son of the Scottish first prince of the blood who had been raised at the French court as a diplomatic hostage to the French alliance. Arran was a confirmed Protestant who corresponded with Calvin and had recently established a Reformed congregation in his father's duchy of Châtellerault. On his return to Scotland in September, he and his father were named leaders of the Lords of the Congregation.[106] And not only were the same English diplomats who were working to assist Scotland's Protestants in touch with Antoine and Hotman, a clear ideological affinity can be seen between the political position staked out by the Lords of the Congregation in 1559 and the ideas expressed in the pamphlets justifying the conspiracy of Amboise. Encouraged by Cecil, the Congregation declared itself the born councilors of the kingdom and asserted that it had the authority to name a new regent and depose

---

[103] Conyers Read, *Mr. Secretary Cecil and Queen Elizabeth* (New York: Knopf, 1955), 117–238; Jane E. A. Dawson, "William Cecil and the British Dimension of Early Elizabethan Foreign Policy," *History* 74 (1989): 196–216; Stephen Alford, *Burghley: William Cecil at the Court of Elizabeth I* (New Haven: Yale University Press, 2008), 104–12.

[104] *CSP For*, I, 491-492, "Throckmorton's Address to the King of Navarre"; Forbes ed., *Full View*, I, 211–16, Throckmorton to Elizabeth, Paris, Aug 25, 1559; de Ruble, *Jeanne et Antoine*, II, 48.

[105] *CO*, XVII, col. 645, Hotman to Calvin, Strasbourg, Sept 19, 1559.

[106] *CO*, XVII, no. 2929, Calvin to Arran, Geneva, Aug 1, 1558; XVIII, no. 3251 [Arran] to Calvin, Lislebourg, Sept 23, 1560, signed "vostre bon ami et frere en Jesus Christ"; Jacques Poujol, "Un épisode international à la veille des guerres de religion: la fuite du comte d'Arran," *Revue d'Histoire Moderne et Contemporaine* 8 (1961): 199–210; Rosalind K. Marshall, "Hamilton, James, third earl of Arran (1537/8?–1609), *Oxford Dictionary of National Biography*, https://doi.org/10.1093/ref:odnb/12083 (consulted May 8, 2018).

Mary.¹⁰⁷ This is little different from what the post-Amboise Huguenot pamphlets would argue.

Late in December 1559, Cecil convinced Elizabeth that the potential rewards of sending military aid to the Congregation outweighed the risks that renewed conflict with France might bring. An English fleet sailed into the Firth of Forth in January. A secret treaty of alliance with the Congregation was negotiated at the end of February. Troops were readied, and on March 6—just before the conspiracy of Amboise was supposed to be sprung—Elizabeth issued an ultimatum to the French to abandon Scotland. When she made a more ample proclamation justifying military intervention there two weeks later, it not only emphasized the threat of French invasion from Scotland stemming from Mary, Queen of Scots's claim to the English crown, but cast opposition to Guise domination as a common cause in Scotland and France. The threat of a French invasion from the north, it declared, "arose from nowhere else than the ambitious appetites of the leading members of the house of Guise." Exhibit A for their ambition was their seizure of the authority in France that rightfully belonged, when the king was underage, to the "princes of the blood royal and other Estates of France."¹⁰⁸ The strategic advantage that the English could gain for their intervention in Scotland, and perhaps even for their hopes of recovering Calais, if internal troubles prevented the French crown from sending more troops to Mary's aid or removed the Guises from their positions of authority, was obvious.¹⁰⁹ This was the context that led the cardinal of Lorraine to assert immediately after the troubles at Amboise that he believed that the English had fomented the conspiracy. It is also what convinced Dureng of English complicity on the basis of the calendared English state papers, Calvin's correspondence, the sources collected in the *Mémoires de Condé*, and de Thou. Romier's additional assertion that Elizabeth financed the

---

¹⁰⁷ Ritchie, *Mary of Guise*, 231–33.
¹⁰⁸ *MC*, I, 529; *CSP Ven*, VII, 167–69; *ADE*, I, 248–52. In the aftermath of the trouble at Amboise, the French court sent a copy to Antoine, who in turn wrote to Throckmorton repudiating the claims made on his behalf in the proclamation and telling him to inform the queen that he did not wish to be mentioned in any future declarations. *CSP For*, III, 24, Antoine to Throckmorton, Pau, May 6, 1560; de Ruble, *Antoine et Jeanne*, II, 222–24.
¹⁰⁹ French statesmen feared as much, as is shown by "Les points qui ont esté cottez sur la response de la Royne d'Angleterre," Paris, ed., *Négociations*, 320.

operation rested essentially on inference from the contacts revealed by the state papers.

In 1966, Nicola Sutherland looked closely at the documentation that Romier and Dureng had provided for English involvement. She argued that the project that chiefly engaged Hotman and other Protestant diplomatic activists in Germany in September 1559 was not the conspiracy of Amboise but instead the action on behalf of the Protestants of Metz. Throckmorton and other English diplomatic agents certainly had contacts with the Protestants in France, tried to learn their plans, and reported what they learned to Elizabeth in the hope that it might encourage her to provide some sort of aid, but Sutherland could find nothing to suggest that either Elizabeth or any of her agents actually offered concrete assistance in paying for the mobilization of men around Amboise. "None of the evidence so far produced for the complicity of Queen Elizabeth and her ministers in the conspiracy of Amboise will stand examination," she concluded.[110] Subsequent historians have judged her review of the evidence as authoritative.[111]

It was not, however. Five years before Sutherland's article appeared, Jacques Poujol published a short study in the *Revue d'Histoire Moderne et Contemporaine* about the place of the earl of Arran in the international intrigue of 1559–60 that called attention to other, more striking clues in the British state papers suggesting possible English involvement than those reviewed by Sutherland.[112] Poujol pointed out that while Arran was commanding the troops of the Lords of the Congregation in Scotland after his return from France, he received advance word of the enterprise of Amboise that he in turn passed on in three letters of January 19 and 20 to Cecil, the English captains in Berwick-upon-Tweed, and William Maitland of Lethington, a key negotiator with the English on behalf of the Congregation. His letter in cipher to Cecil is worth quoting at length for what it shows not only about the circulation of advance knowledge of the plot among

---

[110] N.M. Sutherland, "Queen Elizabeth and the Conspiracy of Amboise, March 1560," *English Historical Review* 81 (1966): 474–89, quotation at 488.
[111] E.g., Daussy, *Parti huguenot*, 148n.
[112] Poujol, "Un épisode international à la veille des guerres de religion: la fuite du comte d'Arran," *Revue d'Histoire Moderne et Contemporaine* 8 (1961): 199–210.

France, Scotland, and England, but also about the sources of his information and the goal as he understood it of the planned conspiracy:

> I send to the queen's majeste two lettres that I received from France by ane brother of the larde of Rethes [identified as Walter Melwin in another letter of the same date] who was sent expressly to me with the credit thereof, which I desire you show to her highness, as after followes. The sum . . . is that the faythfull people, seeing the crualte and tyrannye of the rulers of the French king, killing and murthering daily the saints of god, have deliberated and determined to put themselves to liberty, and to this end have chosen to their chieftain and conductor one of the gretest princes of the realm, protestant, who is not suspect; and of this the ministers assured me, as they are faythfulle men. The beginning of this soon shall be as I am informed within three wekes.[113]

Poujol also spotted in the *Calendar of State Papers, Spanish* a report filed two weeks later by Philip II's ambassador to England saying that a certain Tremayne, an agent of Throckmorton's who regularly traveled back and forth across the Channel with messages to the French "heretics," had just left England to go to Brittany. "I am assured that Tremaine is going about a certain treaty of great importance, although he declares he is going on other matters to the house of [Renée de Rieux] the Marchioness de Nesle." Since this letter is dated February 3 and the Nantes assembly prior to the conspiracy of Amboise took place on or around February 1, Poujol conjectured that Tremayne may have been sent there. The presence of an English agent at Nantes prepared to sign an accord with the conspirators would indeed be strong proof of English support for the venture—if we could be sure that this was his destination. As Poujol admitted, his suggestion was unverifiable, no matter how plausible it might seem.[114] What the documents that he examined establish with certainty

---

[113] National Archives of the UK, SP 52/2, Arran to Cecil, Dysart, Jan 20, 1560, accessed via *State Papers Online*, transcription mine with Scots spelling occasionally anglicized and modernized for readability; several words read as per *CSP For*, II, 298–99. Arran's other two letters are calendared in *CSP For*, II, 290–91, 299–300, Arran and Lord James Hamilton to Ralph Sadler and James Croftes, Dysart, Jan 19, 1560; Arran to William Maitland of Lethington, Dysart, Jan 20, 1560, also in *Calendar of the State Papers Relating to Scotland and Mary, Queen of Scots 1547–1603, Volume 1, 1547–1563*, ed. Joseph Bain (Edinburgh: His Majesty's General Register House, 1898), 285–86. This last volume, on p. 220, shows the earl of Rothes, to have been one of the Lords of the Congregation.

[114] A subsequent letter of Throckmorton's (*CSP For*, II, 507, Throckmorton to Queen Elizabeth, Amboise, April 6, 1560) reports that he sent a man to Brittany to "learn the estates of Messieurs de St Maure and du Pont." As Louis de Saint-Maur was the marquis of Nesle, Tremayne's stated reason for his voyage might not have been misinformation.

is that French pastors with knowledge of the Amboise conspiracy sent advance notice of it to Arran in Scotland. He in turn informed Cecil of what was afoot.

Nor is this the only evidence that English state papers provide of French ministers communicating with Arran. In May, according to Throckmorton, "a Gascoigne preacher, the curé of Shery" was "depeched out of Fraunce" to warn the earl of a plan to capture or poison him. The reference could only be to Pierre Desprez, seigneur de La Cour de Chiré, "*surnommé le Curé de Chiré*" according to the *Histoire ecclésiastique*, a military nobleman who is known to have begun preaching Protestant ideas in Poitou some time before the Amboise conspiracy, served as captain of the enterprise for the region of Châtellerault, and would be recognized by the regional synod at some point prior to early 1562 as the legitimate Reformed pastor of the village of which he was also the seigneur.[115] Other documents in the English state archives overlooked by Sutherland hint at further possible cross-Channel connections. As early as October 5, 1559, Christopher Mundt, the English agent in Strasbourg, passed along to Queen Elizabeth intelligence, perhaps funneled to him by Hotman, according to which many in France think that the Guise "usurpation" will be "broken up with some great tumult, for which a head is wanting but not members." Antoine "has been invited to lead but has closed his ears."[116] In an undated Latin letter in a German hand that could have been sent at any point over the subsequent months, a man who signed himself only "N. N." alluded to correspondence among several other people whose identity is similarly concealed before reporting to his unnamed correspondent that it is hoped that Navarre will soon send his response. Meanwhile, "the whole of Aquitaine and Normandy is in good heart and could easily be moved to action if they perceive any movement elsewhere."[117] On December 2 Cecil dated and entered into his letter book another undated missive to an unknown recipient

---

[115] Forbes, ed., *Full View*, I, 466, Throckmorton to Elizabeth, Amboise, May 22, 1560; *HE*, I, 846; *CO*, XIX, 309–12, Desprez to Calvin, Chiré, March 1 1562; "Lettres adressées à Jean et Guy de Daillon, comte du Lude," 99, Charles IX to Lude, Saint-Germain-en-Laye, June 29 1561. La Planche identifies the captain of the conspiracy for the region of Châtellerault simply as "De Chiray," whereas d'Aubigné calls him "le ministre de Chiré."

[116] National Archives of United Kingdom, SP 70/8, fo. 22 (accessed online); *CSP For*, II, 13–14, Mundt to Queen Elizabeth, Strasbourg, Oct 5, 1559.

[117] National Archives of United Kingdom, SP 70/9, fo. 144 (accessed online); *CSP For*, II, 259, "N. N." to unknown. The editor of the *CSP* places this document in December 1559.

signed by "*La Roche au nom de tous*," the standard formula used by La Roche Chandieu and other ministers or elders of French Reformed churches when they were writing on behalf of the collectivity. The letter expressed assurance that the person to whom it was addressed still felt pity for "our afflictions that you occasionally shared" in France and asked him to accord full credence to the message that the bearer would communicate orally.[118] The letter conveys no hint of what the message might have been. It clearly demonstrates, however, that the Paris church was in direct communication with somebody in England about a matter it dared not commit to paper. In light of all this, it appears that the Spanish ambassador in London, de La Quadra, had good intelligence when he wrote in both January and February 1560 of the "close understanding" that Throckmorton had brought about between the "French heretics" and sympathetic Englishmen.[119]

Amboise conspirators thus communicated their plans to their Scottish counterparts. The English, too, were "certainly in the confidence" of the plotters, as Wallace MacCaffrey has written[120]; Throckmorton and his agents had good contacts with them and may even have sent a man to the Nantes assembly. Furthermore, the English had good reason to encourage a coup d'état in France just when they committed themselves to intervention in Scotland. But did Elizabeth or Cecil actively approve aiding the French conspirators and furnish funds? This is where clear, positive evidence has never been found. The most recent synthesis of Elizabethan foreign policy in this period comes down against the thesis of English involvement in the conspiracy of Amboise.[121] The issue of how the conspiracy was financed remains as unresolved as it was before de Ruble proposed that Antoine was its chief paymaster and Romier assigned this role to Queen Elizabeth.[122]

---

[118] National Archives of United Kingdom, SP 70/9, fo. 19 (accessed online); *CSP For*, II, 159, La Roche to unknown.

[119] *CSP Spain*, I, 121, 124, de La Quadra to duchess of Parma, London, Jan 21, 1560, same to Philip II, London, Feb 3, 1560.

[120] Wallace T. MacCaffrey, "The Newhaven Expedition, 1562-1563," *The Historical Journal* 40 (1997): 5.

[121] David Potter, "Mid-Tudor Foreign Policy and Diplomacy: 1547–63," in *Tudor England and its Neighbours*, eds. Susan Doran and Glenn Richardson (Basingstoke: Palgrave Macmillan, 2005), 117, 119.

[122] As noted by Daussy, *Parti huguenot*, 151.

With regard to the question of English complicity, as with so many other aspects of the conspiracies of 1560, historians have focused their attention on the Amboise enterprise, but de Ruble also thought that Antoine's plan later in 1560 was to bring in English aid via Bordeaux before heading north to assert his claims to power. Neither Sutherland nor any subsequent historian has scrutinized this assertion, but it would appear that if Navarre ever developed a clear plan of action, or if others did on his behalf, whoever did so could have been led into thinking that English assistance was possible. Throckmorton was able to learn in May that renewed plotting was underway and sent a messenger to Elizabeth in June suggesting that she take advantage of France's internal divisions to invade Brittany and Normandy. He might also have told his French contacts that he was taking these steps and given them reason to hope for English aid. But if he did, he led them down a blind alley. In this instance, the English state papers make it clear that no aid was ultimately forthcoming. By July, when Cecil had had time to receive and assess Throckmorton's proposal, Mary of Guise was dead. A successful end to the English intervention in Scotland had been negotiated. The French had agreed to remove all their troops from Scotland. With the mission to the north accomplished, Cecil rejected talk of opening a new front of war against France as foolhardy.[123]

Henri Naef, Alain Dufour, and the Geneva Connection

If the cardinal of Lorraine and several Catholic diplomats suspected the hand of the English behind the Huguenot plots of 1560, assertions of Genevan involvement were even more numerous in the first reports about the plots—and with good reason in light of the arrest near Amboise of scores of people from Geneva. In 1922, a year before the publication of Romier's *Conjuration d'Amboise*—thus too late for Romier to rethink his overall picture of the event, but not too late for him to integrate a few findings into his text and notes—discoveries by Henri Naef in Swiss archives cast a great deal of additional light

---

[123] Forbes ed., *Full View*, Throckmorton to Elizabeth, Amboise, May 22, 1560; *CSP For*, II, 104–06; Throckmorton to Cecil, Blois, June 7, 1560; Read, *Mr. Secretary Cecil*, 240.

on this topic. Although virtually all records of judicial interrogations of the Amboise conspirators had been made to disappear in France, the research of this Geneva-born librarian, museum curator, and historian showed that the same had not happened across the border. Not only did he find the interrogation of Jean Morély by Geneva's authorities that revealed La Roche Chandieu's visit to Calvin, La Renaudie's contact with Beza, and the steps taken by Geneva's pastors to silence talk of their complicity in the Amboise enterprise (discussed on pp. 25–27), in Bern's municipal archives, he discovered an April 8 letter written by the bailiff of Gex (a Bernese territory located just outside Geneva) reporting to their Excellencies what the bailiff, Beät-Ludwig von Mülinen, had learned about the conspiracy on a recent visit to Geneva. In sharp contrast to the estimate that Calvin would subsequently furnish Blaurer, von Mülinen reported that, according to common report, four hundred men left the city to go to Amboise or Orléans. Few were expected to return safely. Von Mülinen spoke directly with one participant in the venture who had made it back with his life. This shaken survivor told him that the plot had been an organizational nightmare. Three to four thousand people from all parts of France and beyond had arrived in the vicinity of Amboise, but when they got there they found no captains to lead them and did not know what to do. Royal troops seized and killed many. As the survivor fled back to Geneva, he saw corpses, often still with boots and spurs, hanging in bunches from the walls of towns he passed.[124]

Naef also discovered a highly revealing investigation initiated by Geneva's magistrates in December 1560 after they received information that a ten-year resident who had recently returned from Languedoc, Ardoin de Porcelet, seigneur de Maillane, had recruited men and collected money for the conspiracy in the lower Rhône valley, his region of origin, while claiming to act "in the name of the church of this city."[125] Judging that this "redounds to the dishonor of Mes-

---

[124] Beät-Ludwig von Mülinen, bailiff of Gex, to Avoyer and Council of Bern, AE Bern, Unnütze Papiere 54, no. 44, published by Naef, appendix V, 316–17.

[125] The document in question is AE Genève, Procès criminels, 1st ser., no. 943. Naef published the document in appendix XI, 371–80, and discussed the trial on 217–37. All of the rest of this and the following paragraph draw upon these pages. Naef identified Ardoin along with his brothers Jean and Robert as "natifs de la cité d'Arles" on the basis of the entry concerning Jean in the LH, I, 13. "On ne sait à quel moment Ardoin ... arriva dans la cité," he wrote (p. 218); "la première fois que nous avons pu constater sa présence à Genève, c'est en septembre 1553." But he overlooked LH, I, 22, which records the reception as an inhabitant of Geneva on December 31, 1551, of "noble

sieurs and could give rise to our being blamed for something," the magistrates arrested Maillane and interrogated him for several days to determine just what he had said and done. Testimony was also taken from people who had crossed paths with him in Geneva or France. The resulting dossier, which Naef published in an appendix, showed the same concern of the Small Council to shield the reputation of Geneva and its pastors from suspicion of involvement in the conspiracies that the body had demonstrated after Beza and Calvin complained about Morély's alleged slanders concerning their participation.

The Geneva magistrates pressed Maillane and the other witnesses particularly hard on the question of whether he had asserted that the enterprise had been backed by Calvin or other of the city's ministers. Despite the testimony of one witness to the contrary, Maillane persistently denied that he had ever claimed that Calvin supported the venture. He admitted, however, that when seeking to recruit participants he might have claimed that some other Genevan pastors backed it. Specifically, he pointed the finger at François de Morel, seigneur de Collonges, a pastor shifted back and forth between Geneva and Paris in 1558–59. While in Paris between December 1558 and September 1559, Morel was Calvin's principal source for information about its church and the activities of its ministers, writing him no less than a dozen letters that have survived. From these, we know him to have been abreast of the overtures made to Antoine after Francis II's death and to have communicated to Geneva the legal arguments developed in the capital in favor of Navarre's claim to power within a regency situation.[126] Maillane also testified that La Renaudie had shown him

---

Ardoin de Percellet, seigneur de Maillane" and complicates the question of the family's place of origin by calling him "originaire de la ville de Beauquerre en Languedoc." The village of Maillane is located in Provence 14 kilometers east of Beaucaire and 23 kilometers northeast of Arles. Less than a year after Jean and Ardoin arrived in Geneva their father disinherited them for their apostasy in a will of May 14, 1552. He subsequently repented and converted; a revised will of 1564 used Reformed formulae and did not exclude the four children who by then had all become Protestant. Céline Borello, *Les protestants de Provence au XVIIe siècle* (Paris: Champion, 2004), 36.

[126] Morel's letters to Calvin are CO, XVII, nos. 2996, 3045, 3055, 3065, 3067, 3080, 3084, 3092, 3093, 3105, 3107, 3117. A native of the Angoumois, Morel studied at Lausanne and acted as a chaplain to Renée de France, the heterodox duchess of Ferrara, and as a minister of the church of Sainte-Marie-aux-Mines in the Vosges, before being appointed to a pastorate in Geneva in July 1557. In September 1558 he was granted leave to serve the church of Paris. While there he presided over the first national synod of the French Reformed churches. After returning to Geneva in October 1559, he left for a second time in April 1561 to serve as minister in Renée's household at Montargis, where he remained until 1564 or 1565. He seems then to have served Paris a second time. He died

the psalm given him by Beza and told him that it demonstrated Beza's backing for the enterprise. He confessed that he had shown disrespect to Geneva's leading ministers by retorting that they were not the only pastors governed by the Holy Spirit after a minister in Nîmes who had just arrived from Geneva, Arnaud Banc, put a roadblock in the way of his efforts to convince the leaders of the Languedoc church to adhere to the conspiracy by telling them that Calvin and his colleagues were hostile to the enterprise. The Small Council judged that the simple fact that this long-time legal resident of the city acted as a recruiter for the conspiracy was enough to arouse legitimate suspicion of Genevan involvement and hence endanger the city's security. Maillane was ordered to express his remorse and told not to leave the city for a year without the Council's permission.

Although of no particular concern to the Geneva authorities, what Maillane's testimony revealed about the plotting's links to the network of Reformed churches in France had particularly weighty implications for understanding this important aspect of the Amboise conspiracy. Maillane said that he had been enlisted by La Renaudie and other nobles "who came from France *on behalf of the churches*" (italics mine). The task he was given was to "solicit the *churches of Languedoc and Provence* (italics mine) to provide money and furnish men to go to Amboise," as well as "to induce gentlemen to go to Nantes for the *journée* that was to take place there to determine the mission of the faction."[127] After taking on the task, he first tried to convince three other natives of Provence then in Geneva to accompany him. Unnamed others in the city dissuaded them. He then set forth to visit a series of localities in the lower Rhône valley, including Nîmes, Aix, and Mérindol. In each of these towns, he sought out and spoke to the minister or other members of the consistory. The goal

---

circa 1569. *FP*[1], VII, 500; Philippe Denis, *Les églises d'étrangers en pays rhénans (1538–1564)* (Paris: Les Belles Lettres, 1984), 274, 276–78, 441–43, 451; Kingdon, *Geneva and the Coming*, 25, 61, 64; *Registres de la Compagnie des Pasteurs de Genève au temps de Calvin*, eds. Jean-François Bergier, Robert M. Kingdon et al. (14 vols., Geneva: Droz, 1962–2011), II, 82; Naef, 135; Elsie Anne McKee, *The Pastoral Ministry and Worship in Calvin's Geneva* (Geneva: Droz, 2016), 148–49, 151–52, 786, 794–95; Emmanuel Rodocanachi, *Une protectrice de la Réforme en Italie et en France: Renée de France, duchesse de Ferrare* (Paris: Ollendorff, 1896), 336–37, 346, 367, 369, 379, 385, 391, 394–95, 424; *Corr Bèze*, VIII, 222–23, 227, IX, 158–61; "Testament d'Antoinette d'Aubeterre, dame de Soubise, du Parc et de Mouchamps, 1570," *BSHPF* 13 (1864): 309. I thank Bernard Roussel for furnishing the references to Morel's activity in the latter part of his life.

[127] Naef, 371.

of the enterprise, he told a minister and deacon of Nîmes, was to seize Lorraine and put him on trial before the princes of the blood or have him killed if this proved impossible. "The French *church* (italics mine) had resolved that it would no longer be tyrannized as it was, seeing that there was no legitimate magistrate in France."[128] The response of the Mérindol congregation to Maillane's recruiting efforts is not known. In Aix he was able to convince the church to support the enterprise, send representatives to the "diet" in Nantes, and urge other nearby churches to do the same. In Nîmes his efforts to get the church as a body to raise money and men ultimately failed after Banc's argument that Geneva's ministers opposed it proved dissuasive. According to Maillane, the city's more senior minister Guillaume Mauget had initially been receptive to the plan. Mauget, who was in Geneva at the time, denied this. He also testified that Maillane never appeared at the secret congregation's assemblies and "more readily approached the *libertins* than those who belonged the assembly, except for [one] deacon." Despite this, Mauget admitted that he "had a very hard time preventing the faithful from joining the ... enterprise."[129]

Beyond finding the three major documents already discussed, Naef unearthed from Geneva's archives a considerable amount of biographical information about the individuals named in these documents who could be linked to the plotting, many of whom had not heretofore been identified as conspirators. He supplemented his digging in Swiss archives with extensive research in rare book rooms that enabled him to identify the "little book from Strasbourg" that Morély's testimony forced Beza to acknowledge sending to Paris, the *Discours sur l'affaire Themistyque*, as most likely the work of Hotman. Ultimately, *La conjuration d'Amboise et Genève* constituted probably the most important single contribution by a historian to understanding the conspiracy of Amboise made since Régnier de La Planche completed his *Histoire de l'Estat de France ... sous le règne de François II*. But if this was so, it was more for its archival discoveries than for its stated conclusions. The focus of the book was on the extent of Genevan involvement in the conspiracy. The revisions that Naef proposed

---

[128] Naef, 371.
[129] Naef, 374.

about this were modest. He cautiously upped the number of Geneva residents who participated in the conspiracy to somewhere between seventy (the number mentioned in Calvin's letter to Blaurer) and four hundred (the figure provided by the bailiff von Mülinen). His discovery of Beza's communications with La Renaudie and Paris suggested to him that the man who would ultimately succeed Calvin as the head of the Company of Pastors had initially been excited by the idea of an armed action, but he speculated that his ardor for the venture then cooled under Calvin's influence. As the senior reformer's testimony before the Small Council concerning the Amboise enterprise aligned with his already-known letter to Coligny stating his opposition to it, Naef reiterated the previous consensus about Calvin's noninvolvement in this venture. More striking, although he had read Roget's work since he, too, was a historian of Geneva, he rejected both Roget's identification of Maligny as "the fervid one of ours" mentioned in Calvin's letter to Beza of September 10 and his larger claim that Calvin had aided Maligny. Saconay's assertion of Genevan culpability was dismissed as a calumny. "Torture drew [from those arrested in Lyon] a few questionable (*peu véridiques*) revelations concerning Geneva, but no positive proof of its complicity, and for good reason."[130] His Conclusion made no mention of the revisionist implications of Maillane's testimony for understanding the relationship between the conspiracy and the Reformed churches within France, for that was not his subject.

Subsequent historians of France would realize the importance of the evidence found by Naef and take it on board alongside that highlighted by Romier showing the role of the minister Chandieu in developing the legal justification for the conspiracy. Although Nicola Sutherland argued in 1980 that the plan that Chandieu presented to Calvin was not necessarily one that the Paris minister actually supported, and although she persisted in assigning responsibility for all that happened to "embarrasing recruits whose motives and interests had little in common with those of the evangelical movement,"[131] most of the historians who looked most deeply into the event after

---

[130] Naef, 110–11, 169–70, 196–97, quotation at 197.
[131] N. M. Sutherland, *The Huguenot Struggle for Recognition* (New Haven: Yale University Press, 1980), 62–100, quotation at 63.

Naef and Romier accepted the involvement of a handful of ministers in the conspiracy. Most agreed that the Protestant desire to gain leverage for the faith via political means that could be legitimized as nonseditious was the core impulse behind it, although they rarely ventured to speculate about what precise religious and political changes the conspirators hoped to make if successful. But even the most painstaking of later historians cognizant of Naef's findings still had a hard time escaping the shadow of the Protestant apologetic tradition, which minimized the role of the Reformed churches. In the chapter in *Geneva and the Coming of the Wars of Religion in France* that Robert M. Kingdon devoted to the conspiracy of Amboise, a chapter for which Naef's study was the clear point of departure, Kingdon asserted that Geneva had been a staging point for the conspiracy despite Calvin's coolness toward it, mentioned Maillane's recruiting trip, and noted the involvement of the ministers Chandieu, Morel, Beza, and Boisnormand. He even speculated, incorrectly as he later recognized, that this last minister might have been sent ahead to Nantes to help prepare the way for the assembly of conspirators held there in early 1560.[132] But he also wrote, "aside from a few Provençal churches and elements in the Paris church, practically none of the Calvinist congregations acceded to the pleas of the conspirators"—this even though, outside of what the Maillane investigation revealed about the churches of Aix, Nîmes, and Mérindol, he had no evidence whatsoever about how any local congregation approached by recruiters for the conspiracy responded, whether positively or negatively.[133] Similarly, Arlette Jouanna's excellent chapter on Amboise in *Le devoir de révolte* drew imaginatively on the details that Naef had accumulated to evoke the milieu of the nobles in and around Geneva who took part in the Amboise conspiracy.[134] For the relevant chapter of her authoritative *Histoire et dictionnaire des guerres de religion*, she noted the engagement

---

[132] Kingdon, *Geneva and the Coming*, 68–78, esp. 72. This last supposition rested on an entry in the registers of the Company of Pastors assigning "monsieur Du Gué" (a pseudonym used by Boisnormand) to Nantes in August 1559. But the plan to assemble in Nantes was unlikely to have been made as early as August, and the good evidence we have about the early history of the Nantes church offers no indication of a pastor named Boisnormand or Du Gué serving it in early 1560. Kingdon subsequently retracted this suggestion in his edition of the relevant volume of the *Registres de la Compagnie des Pasteurs de Genève au temps de Calvin*, II, 89, note 1.
[133] Kingdon, *Geneva and the Coming*, 73.
[134] Jouanna, *Devoir de révolte*, esp. 134–36.

in the enterprise of the ministers named by Kingdon and alluded to evidence from unspecified sources showing that aid came from Lyon, Valence, Orléans, and Tours. Yet in the same work, she reverted to tradition by estimating the number of Genevan participants at sixty and stated, again without positive evidence, that "the Reformed who participated only did so on their own account and without the backing of the churches or their pastors."[135]

Forty years after Naef, in 1963, another historian from Geneva, Alain Dufour, linked Calvin and Beza still more closely to the plotting in France by making connections between the two men's letters in volumes 18 and 20 of the Calvin correspondence that previous historians had failed to spot. At the time, Dufour was in the early stages of his monumental life's work editing Beza's correspondence, a project that he would pursue to completion for sixty years alongside a career as a publisher. He realized that Beza's elliptical August 25 letter to Calvin from "Racnay" that the editors of Calvin's correspondence only tardily discovered and published among the Supplementa, could be clarified if read alongside Calvin's letters of 1560 and 1563 to Jeanne d'Albret. Roget and Romier had already seen that Calvin and Beza had probably been in communication with Maligny before his planned surprise attack on Lyon. Dufour would show that they were in far deeper than that.[136]

Beza's letter stated that things were going swimmingly and soon would allow them to initiate their unspecified "action" in a manner closer to their original wishes than the most recent plan had allowed. For the moment, however, it was necessary to put the brakes on "the production being prepared in your direction" and to wait for new instructions before launching anything. As for the funds they had raised, if some money had to be paid the "witnesses" who had already set out on that production to get them to turn back, Calvin should not hesitate to pay it. He should, however, try to disburse as little as possible and send as much as he could to Nérac.[137]

---

[135] Jouanna et al., *Histoire et dictionnaire*, 63, 64.
[136] Dufour, "L'affaire de Maligny (Lyon, 4–5 septembre 1560) vue à travers la correspondance de Calvin et de Bèze," *Cahiers d'Histoire* 8 (1963): 269–80.
[137] *CO*, XX, cols. 472–73 and *Corr Bèze*, III, 63, Beza to Calvin, Nérac, Aug 25, 1560. The key passages from this letter are also reproduced in Dufour, "Affaire de Maligny," 271–72n.

Calvin did not reply until September 10, by which time Maligny and his men had been flushed from Lyon. The reformer's long, somewhat panicked letter explained that if things had gone wrong in the interim, it was not his fault. Over the preceding weeks, he had been advising patience and told the "fervid one" not to do anything until instructions arrived from Nérac. Their impulsive collaborator would not put up with any delays, however, and had excited those near him. Meanwhile, Antoine dithered, placing those who went ahead in a dangerous situation. Calvin acted on Beza's instructions of August 25 as soon as he got them, but their delivery had been held up for four days en route by a muleteer who had dallied along the road. Now many brethren were in great peril. It was essential that Beza multiply his exhortations to Antoine to act before it was too late. As for the money, he had sent all he could to Nérac as soon as possible. If he had not been able to raise more, it was not for want of trying, for he had written urging those in "Macropolis" (Paris), Provence, and "nearby cities" (probably Lyon) to contribute and had even stood as guarantor of a loan. Three weeks later, on October 1, Calvin explained to Bullinger that Beza had been sent to Nérac in late July to push Navarre not to be so sluggish to act and at the same time to try to temper the adventurism of the most turbulent.[138]

In light of Calvin's October letter to Bullinger and the information provided by de Ruble and Régnier de La Planche, Dufour convincingly glossed Beza's August 25 letter as follows. The "action" so optimistically and yet so cryptically evoked in that missive was an effort led by Antoine of Navarre to assert his authority to rule within a regency government, convoke the Estates, and displace the Guise. The equally vague "production" being prepared in the vicinity of Geneva by "the fervent one" was the plan commanded by Maligny to spur Antoine to act by seizing the city. Beza in Nérac was keeping Calvin abreast of Navarre's intentions and sending him instructions via courier about just what kind of an action to undertake and when to launch it so as to be assured of Antoine's support. Calvin was acting as treasurer for the venture and furnishing Maligny with money.

---

[138] *CO*, XVIII, cols. 177–80 and *Corr Bèze*, III, 67–70, Calvin to Beza, Geneva, Sept 10, 1560; *CO*, XVIII, col. 218, Calvin to Bullinger, Geneva, Oct 1, 1560; Dufour, "Affaire de Maligny," 273–74.

Calvin's 1563 request to Jeanne d'Albret for repayment of the 40,000 francs that he had raised to aid her husband amid his "*grandes perplexités*" of 1560 confirmed as much. He told Jeanne that a portion of the money had been transmitted to Maligny in Lyon at her late husband's request. Antoine had promised Beza that this would be repaid. "I can assure you, Madame, that I exhausted the little I had right down to the coins I use to buy my daily provisions. But . . . what I am asking for is not to reimburse a penny of what I contributed of my own, but to make whole what I owe the friends who helped me in this hour of need and so restore my good name."[139]

In Dufour's reading, although the Genevan reformer was considerably more deeply involved in this conspiracy than all previous historians other than Catholic partisans had allowed, he "did not direct the operation as Gabriel de Saconay suggested." Rather, the leading role belonged to Antoine of Navarre, even if events escaped his control to a degree because of his indecision and Maligny's eagerness to charge ahead in the hope that Antoine would be obliged to follow. Here Dufour's interpretation relied on Régnier de La Planche's account of how Maligny's mission came to be aborted at the last minute. According to this, Antoine initially believed that he could count on a degree of support among other grandees at court if an extraordinary meeting of the Estates were convened in a locality such as Lyon, but after the Assembly of Notables held at Fontainebleau between August 21 and 26 decided that the crown should convoke the Estates-General, he received a warning from a potential ally that going ahead with the action would expose him to accusations that he wanted to make himself king. He therefore wrote to Maligny telling him to drop the plan to seize Lyon and take his men instead to Limoges, where Navarre and those around him would meet up with him. Maligny, who had already infiltrated his men into the city, found himself in a bind. Ultimately, after stewing for about a week, he decided to cancel the plans for the uprising, but just as he was spreading the orders to that effect "an astonishing adventure happened"—the local authorities discovered the stockpile of arms, and he was forced to assemble his men posthaste and organize a military retreat from the city.[140]

---

[139] *CO*, XX, col. 36, Calvin to Jeanne, Geneva, June 1 1563, cited by Dufour, "Affaire de Maligny," 279–80.
[140] La Planche, 571–73, summarized by Dufour, "Affaire de Maligny," 276–78.

For those who encountered Dufour's article in the low-circulation regional history journal in which it appeared,[141] it clearly established how deeply involved Calvin and Beza were in the post-Amboise plotting, to the point of sending money to Maligny. Unfortunately, even the most meticulous and widely read of historians did not always come across it there. The article is noticeably absent from the 70-page bibliography of the authoritative *Histoire et dictionnaire des guerres de religion*.

Recent Work

The half century since the publication of Dufour's article has seen the appearance of several other, more modest, contributions to understanding the Protestant conspiracies. In 1973, Jacques Poujol directed the attention of historians away from the noble conspirators so emphasized by the prior historiography toward the several thousand ordinary Protestant believers that diplomatic sources suggest also gathered around Amboise. Poujol believed that they wanted to bring to fruition a long-standing Protestant desire to present their confession of faith to the king in order to show him they were not the heretics their enemies accused them of being. In his view, their involvement showed that the conspiracy was an *"attroupement d'exaltés"* atop which lesser noble zealots overlaid their plot to dispose of the Guises.[142]

In 1996, Elizabeth A. R. Brown reconstructed La Renaudie's earlier life with particular attention to the long family battles between and within the Du Tillet and Du Barry clans that led to La Renaudie's 1546 condemnation for introducing falsified documents in court. This legal vendetta did not cease in 1546. For a full decade thereafter, Jean Du Tillet continued to pursue La Renaudie and his relatives at law to get them to pay the compensation awarded him in the judgment. During the same years Du Tillet became an ever more trusted legal advisor to the Guises, while La Renaudie, once a Guise client, sought a new protector in Antoine de Bourbon. Régnier de La Planche, who

---

[141] Several currently ongoing historical journals bear the title *Cahiers d'histoire*. That in which Dufour's article appeared is further titled *"revue trimestrielle publiée par le Comité historique du Centre-Est."*

[142] Jacques Poujol, "De la Confession de Foi de 1559 à la conjuration d'Amboise," *BSHPF* 119 (1973): 158–77.

was related to the Du Tillets, had already drawn attention to the long legal battle between La Renaudie and Du Tillet. Brown's article suggested more strongly than La Planche that the scars left by this vendetta motivated La Renaudie's involvement in the conspiracy.[143]

Arlette Jouanna offered several vivid synthetic accounts of the conspiracies that were particularly sensitive to their legal–ideological dimension. The first came in her important 1989 *Le devoir de révolte. La noblesse française et la gestation de l'État moderne, 1559–1661*, a study of a moment in the history of French aristocratic political consciousness during which the nobility came to think of itself as having a special leadership role to play, by violence if necessary, in defending the interests of the various estates and the ancient legal order of the kingdom when evil advisors around the king rode roughshod over these. In her telling, the conspiracy of Amboise was a key early moment in the crystallization of this vision of politics among a fraction of the provincial aristocracy. Because the work focused on the intersection between aristocratic identity and the history of political thought, the nobility inevitably stood at the center of the story told about the Amboise enterprise, but the role of theologians and jurists in articulating the legal and political justification of the venture was also foregrounded.[144]

When Jouanna returned to the conspiracy of Amboise and examined the plotting of the summer and fall of 1560 as well in her outstanding work of reference and synthesis, *Histoire et dictionnaire des guerres de religion*, she took on more of the lessons of the past century's work than any previous author, drawing in particular on Romier and Naef. The involvement of ordinary artisans, the connivance of "merchants, artisans and occasionally even *échevins* and *consuls*" in several cities, and the engagement of several pastors were all noted. Still, she felt obliged to say that "the Protestants only took part on their own behalf without the backing of the churches or the pastors, and among these last one can scarcely count four who lent their

---

[143] Brown, "La Renaudie se venge: l'autre face de la conjuration d'Amboise" in *Complots*, eds. Bercé and Fasano Guarini, 451–74; La Planche, 129.

[144] Jouanna, *Le devoir de révolte*, esp. ch. 5, "Les 'ides de mars' (Amboise, 1560): la prise de conscience politique de la noblesse profonde." See also her "Le thème polémique du complot contre la noblesse lors des prises d'armes nobiliaires sous les derniers Valois" in *Complots*, eds. Bercé and Fasano Guerini, 475–90.

support." The group that drove the conspiracy, she once again asserted, was "the middling provincial nobility of the provinces touched by Protestantism." Following Romier, she said that mercenaries from Germany, Switzerland, Savoy, and Britain formed an important contingent.

> The source of the money [to pay them] remains a mystery in the current state of our knowledge. The Reformed churches, as the example of Nîmes shows, were reticent to contribute. Only some churches of Provence, Lyon's and undoubtedly some members of Paris' furnished subsidies and men. As for possible support from abroad, either from German Protestant princes or Queen Elizabeth of England, it seems to have been non-existent.

For the second phase of the plotting, having gone deeply into the primary sources of the period, she noted not merely Beza's trip to Nérac and the Maligny affair, but the evidence picked up by certain crown officials that armed men were converging on Poitiers and Orléans in September and October. "In the absence of solid studies of these movements as a whole, it is difficult to measure their precise scope, but it seems to have been considerable," she observed.[145] These pages reveal clearly both the extent and the limits of the change in historical understanding of the conspiracies of 1560 that took place over the course of the twentieth century.

At the moment of this study's writing, the most recent, authoritative extended treatment of both the Amboise conspiracy and the Maligny affair was Hugues Daussy's hefty, prizewinning 2014 *Le parti huguenot. Chronique d'une désillusion (1557–1572)*.[146] Although Daussy claimed to do no more than synthesize the available literature about

---

[145] *Histoire et dictionnaire*, 52–67, 72–75, quotations at 64, 63, 74.
[146] Pages 128–52 cover the Amboise conspiracy, pp. 172–77 the Maligny affair. There is no discussion of the movements of September and October mentioned by Jouanna. The 2019 Sorbonne doctoral dissertation of Sophie Tejedor, "A la croisée des temps. François II, roi de France et la crise des années 1559–1560," which I received as this book was entering final production, now provides an even more recent account of the conspiracies of 1560. Although traditional in its understanding of the plots and inattentive to the Calvin correspondence and the Genevan connection, it is exceptionally detailed and illuminating about the process and stages by which the court learned about the successive conspiracies, as well as about the measures taken by the authorities on receipt of this information. Also reaching me too late to be taken on board in this review of the state of the question was Serge Brunet's suggestive but often incomplete or unpersuasive "La conjuration d'Amboise (16 mars 1560), Emmanuel-Philibert de Savoie et Genève," in *La Maison de Savoie et les Alpes: emprise, innovation, identification XVe-XIXe siècle*, eds. Stéphane Gal and Laurent Perrillat (Chambéry: Publications de l'Université Savoie Mont Blanc, 2015), 293–329.

the conspiracies, the thirty pages that he devoted to them displayed an exceptional mastery of that literature and drew as well on many primary sources. Unlike Jouanna, he did not overlook Dufour's article. Since he conceived the book within the tradition of interpretation that can be traced back at least to Mariéjol's 1904 volume in the Lavisse *Histoire de France*, according to which the character of the French Reformation changed under Francis II, when noblemen began to convert in large numbers and transformed what had previously been a church into a political party, his treatment of these events nonetheless focused even more intently than Jouanna's *Histoire et dictionnaire* on the role of the aristocracy.[147] Little of the information found in her pages about the participation of ministers and urbanites reappears. Like Romier and Jouanna before him, Daussy began the tale of Huguenot plotting under Francis II with the Paris–Strasbourg–Geneva axis in which the constitutional argument undergirding the conspirators' actions was formed. He noted the leading role of the Paris ministers Morel and Chandieu and the Strasbourg jurist Hotman in first elaborating a legal argument justifying armed action to separate the king from the Guises and then in attempting to win Calvin's and Beza's support. "It is highly probable that the idea for this enterprise germinated in the little world of Paris's Reformed church." His close attention to identifying the noblemen who participated in the conspiracies led him to see that both Morel and an important nobleman from Saintonge known to have been a neighbor and friend of La Renaudie's, François Bouchard d'Aubeterre, married sisters from the same family; this connection, combined with the role of messenger between Geneva and Antoine of Navarre that La Renaudie had already assumed by 1558, may have led to La Renaudie's recruitment as the chief organizer of the conspiracy, as well as Bouchard d'Aubeterre's participation in it.[148] Yet although the role of ministers in the early stages of the conspiracy's development is noted, once La Renaudie takes the stage, the French pastors disappear from the scene. No mention is made of urban churches that provided men and money. Maillane's recruiting

---

[147] Mariéjol, *Histoire de France*, Vol. 6/1 *La Réforme et la Ligue*, 12–19, 25–26.
[148] Daussy, *Parti huguenot*, 132–33. The key source cited by Daussy that shows the bond among Morel, La Renaudie, and Bouchard d'Aubeterre is Bouchard's will naming Morel and La Renaudie as guardians for his children, preserved in AEG, notaire Jean Rageau 3, 368–77, published in 1879 in *FP²*, II, cols. 952–53.

efforts in Provence and Languedoc, duly noted, are said only to convince "several gentlemen" to go to the Nantes assembly. The section narrating the events around Amboise is entitled "a crusade of knights errant"—just the dismissive phrase used by Calvin in his self-exculpating letter to Coligny, and a remarkable illustration of the capacity for survival of the tropes of the post-Amboise Protestant depiction of the event. The book's treatment of the Maligny affair notes both Calvin's role in financing it and the pressure that he and Beza put on Antoine in the summer to step forward to claim more power, but once again the sole participants named in the narrative of the mobilization other than the two Geneva ministers are noblemen.[149] Although an important part of Daussy's research effort involved investigating the relations between the Huguenots in France and the various German Protestant princes with whom they attempted to build alliances, possible English connections received little attention and active support from Queen Elizabeth was ruled out on Sutherland's authority. How the troops that gathered at Amboise were supposed to have been paid was again said to "remain a complete mystery."[150]

* * *

History as an academic discipline rests on an idealized vision of collaborative scholarship. According to this legitimating myth, as successive generations mine new evidence from the archives, reconsider what was already known in light of the additional evidence, and look anew at events with the benefit of greater distance and new interpretive paradigms, they emancipate themselves from the blinkered, agenda-driven perspectives through which contemporaries view episodes of their own time and advance toward a fuller and more accurate vision of the past. Inspiring as this vision may be, the actual history of scholarship about virtually any given historical topic tends to reveal a far messier story of starts and stops, blind alleys, and the eternal recurrence of debates, interpretations, anecdotes, and topoi established early on. That is certainly the case of the story recounted in this chapter.

---

[149] Daussy, *Parti huguenot*, 139ff, esp. 141, 174–76.
[150] Daussy, *Parti huguenot*, 134n, 137n, 151n.

Although history may not repeat itself, historians repeat one another. Once events capture the attention of contemporaries and become enshrined as important links in a narrative chain, they continue to be foregrounded in subsequent histories, even when other events of the time may be equally significant for understanding either the broader story or the actions of important figures within it. Apologetic explanations of motive proffered in the immediate aftermath of events, partial or self-serving though they may be, often endure, especially when the vision of events that they promote remains important for the reputation and self-image of later generations that identify with participants in the original events. New evidence is discovered over time, but even the keenest within the community of historians may be unable immediately to see how that new evidence calls an old narrative into question, both because the broader contextual knowledge required fully to understand it may not yet be available, and because reconstructed accounts of complex events involving multiple actors typically rest on a multiplicity of clues and inferences, and so do not immediately unravel when contradictory evidence cuts one thread. Furthermore, new evidence or insights do not automatically accumulate steadily. What one generation of historians learns may be forgotten by the next, as old books are no longer read or interests shift. Long prior to our current era of academic hyper-specialization, the international community of historians was already divided into subcommunities organized around different national or topical foci. Historians have long had dozens of outlets in multiple languages in which to publish their findings. Important discoveries or insights pertinent to a subject are thus easily overlooked when they appear in obscure journals or studies seemingly located in another area of specialization.

The conspiracy of Amboise involved the massing of thousands of men around a royal castle and an attempt to seize the castle with the king in it. It was directly observed by numerous ambassadors at court, led to dozens of spectacular executions, and was reported to judges and officials throughout the kingdom in a letter by the king that soon found its way into print. Processions were staged in a number of cities to thank God for delivering the monarch from the threat. Apologists for the enterprise rushed their own version of what had been intended and what had happened into print. By contrast, the

Maligny affair involved little more than nocturnal alarms in a large provincial city. It eventuated in fewer executions of less prominent people and gave rise to no immediately published accounts. The crown's justified suspicion that broader new plots were afoot in the summer of 1560 was even less widely broadcast and known at the time, for it remained confined to the administrative, diplomatic, and ministerial letters in which it was expressed. In consequence, the conspiracy of Amboise rapidly assumed a prominent place in the many narrative accounts of the troubles of the era that soon followed. On the other hand, the Maligny affair was far less mentioned in these early histories, and the wider plots of the summer and fall less still. The same disproportionate attention has continued to be given to the Amboise conspiracy ever since, even though the evidence that has subsequently come to light about the Maligny affair and the broader plots of the summer and fall of 1560 logically prompts reconsideration of the two closely related questions that have been at the heart of research and debate about the Amboise conspiracy ever since its immediate aftermath, the extent to which the conspirators were driven by either malcontentedness or Huguenoterie, and the relationship of Calvin and Geneva to the plotting.

These questions were placed at the heart of discussion of the Amboise conspiracy by the initial perplexity of those inside the castle trying to understand the clandestine enterprise taking shape around them, by the manner in which the event was reported in the king's letter of March 31, by the responses to that letter that the defenders of the enterprise soon rushed into print, and by Calvin's denials of the rumors and accusations of his involvement. The early apologias cast the Amboise enterprise as a political enterprise of noblemen who were only incidentally Protestant. The first generation of Protestant historians, Louis Régnier de La Planche foremost among them, set forth many previously hidden details about the planning of that venture and even a few about the subsequent enterprises. They too, however, continued to cast noblemen as the key players, kept silent about possible links to Calvin or the Reformed churches, and rarely went into detail about the Maligny affair or the later plots. The vision and account of the plotting of 1560 that they set forth then proved to be astonishingly enduring over the subsequent centuries. The sheer mass of information available nowhere else that their accounts provided was the most fundamental reason why. Political and ideological reasons also played their part. A vision of history that foregrounded noble initiative and discontent rather than associating the Reformed churches with plotting appealed to the politique de Thou, writing in the wake of Henry IV's triumph over the League, through its suggestion that the existence of two faiths in the realm, one of them Reformed Protestantism, was not necessarily subversive of monarchical order. Even in the changed world of the nineteenth and early twentieth century, France's small but intellectually influential Protestant community was heavily invested in maintaining a positive image of their group as an innocent and long-suffering minority. Any revision of a by now long-established narrative of national history that ran counter to such an image had a very high barrier of resistance to overcome.

Although a surprising percentage of the basic information about the conspiracies of 1560 still to be found in the best recent histories of the subject can be traced all the way back to Régnier de La Planche or other historians of the late sixteenth century, the many man-hours that an ever-expanding and increasingly international community of historians has devoted since the nineteenth century to prospecting in archives, publishing sources, and rethinking received wisdom has certainly altered and enriched understanding of this topic. Clear movement can be observed on the question of English involvement toward a consensus that Queen Elizabeth did not promote or finance the conspiracies, even if the fullest and most recent reviews of this question do not take on board all of the pertinent evidence that shows that links existed between the conspirators and the Scottish Lords of the Congregation, that Elizabeth's ministers were aware that the conspiracies were afoot, and that Throckmorton in particular may have encouraged the French plotters and tried to interest Cecil and the queen in providing active support. Evidence has accumulated linking the Amboise conspiracy to the French Reformed churches, demonstrating the participation in it of a handful of French ministers and the support of a few urban churches, and tying Calvin and Beza more closely to the plotting than they cared to let on. In the long discussion of the relative mix of malcontentedness and Huguenoterie that has dominated reflection about the event, the importance of the latter component has increasingly come to be seen as central. Particularly important landmarks in the process of change were the publication of Calvin's correspondence and Roget's rapid grasping of its implications for the question of the reformer's involvement in the various conspiratorial enterprises of the year, de Ruble's discovery of the Triou deposition, Naef's rich trawls in the archives of Geneva and Bern, and Dufour's connecting the dots to see that Calvin was not just abreast of Maligny's enterprise but helped to fund it. Yet change has been anything but linear or immediately cumulative. Later historians soon lost sight of the Triou deposition. Dufour's article was often overlooked. The older paradigms and tropes of the Protestant apologetic tradition have shown a remarkable capacity for survival. Even historians who observe the role of ministers or urban groups in the events still cast noblemen as the central players in the ventures and insist on saying without firm evidence that the others acted without the approval of their church as a whole.

With this background in place, we can now turn to the testimony of Gilles Triou.

Three

The Testimony of Gilles Triou

The morning after Maligny and his men marched in arms through Lyon at midnight and then left town, the local authorities searched the houses from which they had emerged. There, they found hundreds of abandoned weapons and armored breastplates, lists of men and arms, and a number of mattresses, each large enough to sleep ten.[1] Two days later, on September 7, they arrested Triou. He was interrogated that day and the next two. The transcript of his deposition indicates that he provided all of the testimony that he ultimately was willing to swear to be truthful "in the torture room (*à la chambre de la question*)," but there is no indication that he was actually tortured to obtain it. It was after being led to admit that he had written part of a list entitled *"rolle d'armes en forme de bataillon"* that he spelled out what he knew about the plan to seize Lyon and Protestant plotting more generally. He confirmed his testimony in a further hearing on September 13.[2] The copy of his deposition that survives in the Archives Départementals des Pyrénées-Atlantiques is written in a clear hand but with frequent variations and possible errors in the spelling of names, erratic capitalization, and virtually no punctuation, rendering the understanding of certain passages difficult.

---

[1] AM Lyon, BB 81, fos. 306v–07v, published in Antoine Péricaud, *Notes et documents pour servir à l'histoire de Lyon, 1547–1560* (Lyon: Mougin-Rusand, 1841), 35.
[2] ADPA, E 582 (13), fos. 1–2v, 9v; Appendix, pp. 197–201, 211–12.

According to the biographical information Triou provided about himself, he led an itinerant life. After training for a while as a choirboy with a cleric in Normandy, he wandered through "many parts in Germany and elsewhere" before learning the cabinetmaker's trade in Bordeaux. He subsequently moved to Moulins. There, around 1552, he married a woman "of the same religion." (He does not specify the date of his own conversion to Protestantism.) They left Moulins for Lyon after three years because their neighbors started to complain that they never saw them at mass. Triou also briefly spent some time in Geneva in 1556. For two years prior to his interrogation, he served the Lyon church as a "distributor of the alms given ... to the poor faithful and others in need," a role for which he had been recruited by the wealthy *marchand libraire* Antoine Vincent, with whom he became acquainted because Vincent's wife was from Moulins. It is unclear whether he had the formal status of deacon in Lyon's church or was a sort of deacon's assistant to Vincent. In either event, his work in this capacity, done under the name "maître Gilles," was what led to his involvement in conspiracy.[3]

What Triou revealed about the conspiratorial activity in which he was involved in Lyon began with a meeting that took place in January 1560 in one of the upper-story rooms that the cloth merchant Pierre Terrasson rented in the house of the *marchand mercier* Jean Badieu. This would be one of the houses where arms and mattresses were found after the flight of the conspirators in September.[4] A small group of prominent Lyonnais and a minister then staying with Terrasson whose name Triou claimed not to remember gathered there after "there came (plural form *ilz vinrent*) [to town] *le* (italics mine) S^r de La Riviere de Chateau Neufz, who has some black taffeta on the tip of his nose where he cut it, who were lodged (plural form *estoient logés*) at the [inn of the sign of] the apple."[5] De Ruble read this passage to indicate that a single nobleman by the name of La Rivière de Chateauneuf summoned the meeting. Saconay wrote of two different

---
[3] ADPA, E 582 (13), fos. 2v–3, 9v; Appendix, pp. 201, 211.
[4] AM Lyon, BB 81, fo. 306v.
[5] ADPA, E 582 (13), fo. 3v; Appendix, p. 202: "par le moys de Janvyer dernier ilz vinrent le Sr de la Riviere de Chateau Neufz qui a du taphetas noyr au bout du nez qu'il a couppé estoient logés à la pomme firent assembler en la maison dudit Tarrasson en la chambre la plus haulte lesdits Vincent Constantin Nadard Claude Gousset."

individuals, the "Sr de La Riviere a Burgundian" and "Chateau-Neuf from Provence." I incline to reading the passage as referring to two individuals as well. Subsequent portions of the text refer nearly always to either "the aforesaid La Riviere" or "the aforesaid Chateau Neufz." The only further mention of "La Riviere Chateau Neufz" comes within a longer list of names not separated by commas. La Rivière [and?] de Chateauneuf was or were in Lyon to recruit for the enterprise of Amboise, and more specifically for the upcoming gathering at Nantes, just as Ardoin de Maillane was doing in Provence and Languedoc at the same time.[6] "La Rivière" spoke and urged those present to associate themselves with an assembly that "the churches of France" planned to hold to deliberate about unspecified "great matters." Thus, like Maillane, La Rivière presented the project as one of the churches. The Lyonnais responded positively, but with the caveat, so Triou said, that they did not want anything done contrary to the honor of God and the king.[7]

Who were the people at this meeting? "Chateau Neufz" can be confidently equated with the man whom Protestant historians from Régnier de La Planche to d'Aubigné list as one of the captains of the conspiracy for Provence and Languedoc under the name of "Chasteauneuf" or a variant thereof.[8] One would like to be able to say more about the background and subsequent life course of this mysterious man with the black nose patch who is one of the central characters in our story, but because Châteauneuf or its Occitan equivalent "Castelnau" was such a common name for a *seigneurie* in sixteenth-century France, it is impossible in the current state of knowledge to be sure which of at least two Provençal nobles who went by that name was the one at the meeting. Naef, and then Jouanna and Daussy, identify the captain and conspirator as Charles de Châteauneuf, seigneur de Mollèges, a Protestant conseiller in the Parlement of Aix

---

[6] See pp. 64–67.
[7] ADPA, E 582 (13), fo. 3v; Appendix, p. 202 "ledit de la Riviere propose que les eglises de france s'assembloient pour tenir journee et deliberer de grandz affaires. Requerat que les susdits declairassent s'ilz vouloient estre de lad assemblee et deliberation et s'i trouver, ce que les seigneurs assistans accordarent pourveu que ce ne fut contre l'honneur de dieu ny du Roy et qu'ilz n'en entendroient aultre chose jusques à ce que la journee se tiendront en laquelles s'ilz y vouloient venir y seroient receuz."
[8] La Planche, 134; La Popelinière, *Histoire de France*, I, 163; d'Aubigné, *Histoire universelle*, I, 271. Régnier de La Planche and La Popelinière call him "Chasteauneuf," d'Aubigné "Castelloux," and de Thou "Chateauvieux" at one point and "Chateauneuf" at another. Naef, 226n.

who was among the judges of that court who thought it prudent to leave Aix after a Protestant plot to seize it later in 1560 failed, and the same person as the Charles de Chasteauneuf who appears in Geneva's baptismal registers for January 1563 as the godfather of a child of one of the men whom Maillane tried in vain to convince to join him on his recruiting tour for the conspiracy.[9] Another plausible identification could be with Jean de Chateauneuf, *écuyer*, one of seventy Protestant refugees from Provence to sign a procuration in Lyon late in the First Civil War to raise money to carry on the fight.[10] Neither of these men is known to have been called "La Rivière." I have not been able to find evidence that either man, or perhaps still another Châteauneuf from Provence, lost part of his nose in a swordfight. Nor have I been able to learn anything at all about the Jean de Chateauneuf who took refuge in Lyon in 1562, determined to carry on the fight.

If La Rivière was indeed a second individual, an intriguing hypothesis would be that he was not a Burgundian noble—no Burgundian source of which I am aware mentions a Protestant nobleman of that name—but instead the young pastor of Paris Jean Le Maçon dit La Rivière, whose father, the *procureur du roi* of Angers, possessed the seigneurie of Launay, and who is variously referred to in the sources of the time as "Launaeus," "Riverius," and "La Rivière." A former law student disowned by his father after going to Lausanne and Geneva and embracing the Reformed cause, Le Maçon helped constitute the first church in Paris established on the Genevan model and was chosen as its pastor in 1555. He also laid the foundations of the church of Troyes when passing through that city in 1558 after a visit to Geneva.[11] It does not seem preposterous to link La Rivière to the Protestant conspiratorial activity of 1560, since he is known to have been involved in the communications among the Paris church, Hotman in Strasbourg, and Antoine, when the first appeals were made in 1559 to Navarre to step forward and claim a predominant role in the government.[12] Nothing in the current historiography offers cause

---

[9] Naef, 226n; Jouanna, *Devoir de révolte*, 139; Daussy, *Parti huguenot*, 143; Eugène Arnaud, *Histoire des protestants de Provence, du Comtat Venaissin et de la Principauté d'Orange* (2 vols., Paris: Grassart, 1884), I, 119.
[10] AEG, Notaires, Jean Ragueau 5, 731.
[11] *HE*, I, 118–20, 163; *LH*, I, 43.
[12] *CO*, XVII, col. 597, Morel to Calvin, [Paris], Aug 15, 1559; col. 609, Morel to Calvin, [Paris], Aug 23, 1559.

to suspect that a pastor might have been involved in recruiting for the conspiracy, but we will encounter other evidence of a minister doing just that in due course. In support of this hypothesis it can also be noted that no document shows Le Maçon to have been in Paris during the months when Triou's testimony places La Rivière in Lyon, although we have evidence for his presence there in 1557, 1558, 1559, and 1561. By contrast, he can be placed in Strasbourg in July 1560, together with his colleague Chandieu, a known conspirator. Both may have felt obliged to flee the capital after the Amboise conspiracy failed.[13] A year later Catherine de Medici would exclude both La Rivière and Chandieu from the colloquy of Poissy because she remained convinced of their engagement in the plotting against her son.

The six Lyonnais at this meeting who showed themselves willing to associate themselves with the conspiracy were (in addition to Triou) the *marchand libraire* and deacon Vincent; the *marchand orfèvre* Jean Constantin; Pierre Nadard or Nadal, known to be a *marchand épicier*; Claude Gousset, a velvet-weaver (*veloutier*); and Jean Bertrand, a papermaker. Triou specified at the end of his deposition that the *marchand drapier* Terrasson was not present, although he would later become deeply involved in the Maligny affair. So, too, would Jean Darut, who had been invited to this initial meeting but refused to come, saying that he did not want to hear anything about a matter of such grave consequence. Together with his two younger brothers, Darut ran one of the most important mercantile firms in the city, with a second base in Basel, that the trio had built up over thirty years after starting out as itinerant peddlers in Fétigny, Franche-Comté.[14] The owner of the house where the meeting took place, Jean Badieu,

---

[13] *CO*, XVI, cols. 425–26, Calvin to Reformed Church of Paris, Geneva, March 15, 1557; XVII, col. 110, Macar to Calvin, Paris, March 21, 1558; AEG, R Consist 17, fo. 11v (reference to an attestation signed by Jehan Le Maçon, minister in Paris, Aug 18, 1559); *CO*, XVIII, col. 143, Des Gallars to Calvin, London, July 1, 1560; col. 555, "La Riviere au nom de tous" to pastors of Geneva, Paris, July 14, 1561; col. 646, Merlin to Calvin, [Paris], Aug 25, 1561; Barbara B. Diefendorf, *Beneath the Cross: Catholics and Huguenots in Sixteenth-Century Paris* (Oxford: Oxford University Press, 1991), 119–20.

[14] Information about the occupational status, consistory membership, and other details of the life course of Constantin, Nadal and Darut generously provided by Natalie Zemon Davis, on the basis of her extensive research in Lyon's archives. The mercantile activities and involvement in the Reformed church of the Darut brothers also figure prominently in Richard Gascon, *Grand commerce et vie urbaine au XVIe siècle. Lyon et ses marchands (environs de 1520-environs de 1580)* (Paris: SEVPEN, 1971), 169, 213, 224, 322, 326–27, 442, 480, 521, 529. Claude Gousset's occupation is revealed by AEG, R Consist 17, fo. 206. Bertrand is identified as a *papetier* in the Triou deposition, fo. 9v.

fell under suspicion of being one of the ringleaders of the Maligny enterprise after some badly damaged armor and a bloody sheet were found in his part of the house, but he may not have been involved in either conspiracy. Triou was asked specifically about Badieu and replied that he had only seen him once in passing, although he had been told that he was a good man and charitable to the poor. Badieu does not reappear in the deposition.[15]

The best known and most intriguing of the Lyonnais at the meeting was Vincent, a friend of Calvin's and an important figure in a central episode in Protestantism's growth in France, the production in 1561 of thousands of copies of the metrical psalter by associated printers in Geneva, Lyon, Paris, Orléans, and Metz for distribution throughout the country. His participation in this project, which Eugénie Droz called "the largest publishing venture of the century," inspired her to reconstruct his background and career in detail for the 1957 volume *Aspects de la propagande religieuse*. Thanks to Droz's research, we know that Vincent's father was a consul and that he himself sat in the city council in 1543, 1551, and 1559. Even while maintaining his position in Lyon's governing elite, he began to move his family to Geneva and grew to know Calvin personally. Contracts show that he purchased a house in Geneva through an intermediary in 1557, set up a commercial partnership with two Genevans in March 1559, and had his daughter's marriage contract drawn up there in July 1559 in Calvin's own home with the reformer present. During the First Civil War, he would act in Geneva alongside Jacques Spifame, the wealthy former bishop of Nevers turned pastor and diplomat, as an agent for the Protestant-controlled *Echevinage* of Lyon to raise and pay for Swiss troops to come fight for the city. Despite apparently spending much time in Geneva, he was still a member of Lyon's consistory in November 1564 and so must have moved back and forth between the two cities.[16] On the basis of Triou's deposition, de Ruble and, after him, Romier, narrated the meeting in Terrasson's house, but neither was aware of Vincent's ties to Calvin or role in printing the psalter.

---

[15] Badieu's reputation as a leading conspirator is reflected in *La chronique lyonnaise de Jean Guéraud 1536–1562*, ed. Jean Tricou (Lyon: Imprimerie Audinienne, 1929), 126–27.
[16] Eugénie Droz, "Antoine Vincent. La propagande protestante par le psautier" in *Aspects de la propagande religieuse* (Geneva: Droz, 1957), 276–93, esp. 277–78.

Vincent was not the only person whom Triou's deposition would show to have a major role in the Maligny affair to occupy a leadership position in Lyon's church. Darut and Nadal also appear to have been deacons, as like Vincent they furnished Triou money to distribute to the poor on different occasions and attended meetings together. Constantin can be confidently identified as a Reformed elder in 1562–63; perhaps he was already one in 1560. If Claude Gousset was the same person as the Claude "Crouset" known to have sat in the Lyon consistory in 1564, he, too, had a leadership role in the church.[17] All were men of substance. This was unknown to de Ruble and Romier.

Despite their initial statement of interest in La Rivière's proposal, the six Lyonnais who met with him do not seem to have sent one of their own to the meeting at Nantes. Instead, they learned what happened there when "Chateau Neufz" returned from the meeting a month later. According to La Planche, at Nantes La Renaudie "and his companions" assigned Chasteauneuf the mission of "assembling the churches of Provence to determine who would be sent to carry out the Amboise enterprise and who would be given the task of leading everything in the province (*pays*) should it be necessary to preach publicly (*avenant qu'il falust prescher publiquement*)."[18] The pages of Regnier's history that follow this mention of Chasteauneuf offer the most intriguing, but perhaps also the least reliable, details about what might be called a provincial offshoot of the Amboise conspiracy found anywhere in that work. In the spring of 1559, Provence had already been the first province to experience noble-directed iconoclastic raids against Catholic churches, after Antoine and Paulon de Richieu, co-seigneurs of Mauvans, organized a band of marauders in reprisal for the violent disruption of a Reformed worship service held in their house in Castellane, which had been incited by a Lenten preacher. Antoine was subsequently ambushed and killed. Paulon sought justice for his death.[19] According to La Planche, Chasteauneuf's arrival in Provence led to a meeting being called at Mérindol at which "the

---

[17] Yves Krumenacker et al., *Lyon 1562, capitale protestante* (Lyon: Olivétan, 2009), 165; AD Rhône, E 171, fo. 22 shows Constantin already an elder in 1562 (reference kindly supplied by Natalie Zemon Davis).
[18] La Planche, 310.
[19] On the Mauvans brothers and the events in Provence in this period, the key sources are La Planche, 306–22; and "Mémoires de Claude de Cormis" in *Additions et illustrations sur les deux tomes de l'Histoire des Troubles de Provence* (2 vols., Aix: Charles David, 1680), I, 518–27.

deputies of sixty churches of Provence (for there were that many at the time)" chose Paulon to lead their "*gens de guerre*."[20] He undertook the organization of a force with such diligence that he was able to convince the churches to arm and equip two thousand men, "not counting the also numerous noblemen and volunteer soldiers." When the date of the Amboise enterprise approached, an advisory council created at the same time gathered with Mauvans and decided to seek to force their way into Aix to organize public preaching there. The plan was thwarted when those who were supposed to open one of the city gates from inside prematurely revealed their intentions. The provincial authorities mobilized a force larger than Mauvans's. He had to content himself with a new series of iconoclastic raids, almost certainly the incidents in Provence that Calvin called premature in his letter to Sturm,[21] which La Planche presents as being organized with exemplary discipline. In each town whose churches were cleansed of their idols, the most valuable church plate was melted down in the presence of the local *consuls* and the precious metal left in their care. In return, Mauvans received a receipt attesting that the community's property had not been carried away. Virtually no looting accompanied the expedition because all involved had been warned that any one guilty of the offense would be excommunicated by his local church and turned over to the secular authorities for appropriate punishment. That the destruction was quite as orderly as La Planche claimed may be doubted, and historians have never been able to find evidence of anything close to sixty Reformed churches in existence in Provence by early 1560. Triou's revelation of Chasteauneuf's passage through Lyon nonetheless fits with an itinerary from Nantes to Provence and would seem to corroborate at least that part of La Planche's narrative.

While in Lyon, Triou reported, Chasteauneuf met individually with Vincent, Nadal, and perhaps others of whom Triou was not aware, to explain to them the plan of action decided at the "journée" at Nantes "attended by several noblemen." The plan was that men would go in arms to court on March 10 or 12 to seize the Guises and hold them to account for the wrongs they had done to the king and the kingdom. The Estates would then be convened to put matters of

---

[20] La Planche, 310.
[21] See pp. 21–22.

both state and religion back into their proper order. Chasteauneuf also told them that Condé was the leader of the plot. In this, he was more forthright than Maillane had been when he recruited participants in Nîmes and Aix. His presentation of the goals of the conspiracy accords with the ample evidence from other sources that it aimed initially to displace the Guises and call the Estates, while also indicating that its larger goal was to restore the correct order in religion as well as the state.[22]

After hearing what Chasteauneuf had to report about the assembly at Nantes, Vincent and Nadal summoned Constantin, Darut, Gousset, and Triou to a new meeting. This time, Darut accepted the invitation. Collectively they decided to collaborate with the enterprise by sending twenty-five men and furnishing arms. Constantin and Gousset took charge of choosing the men and buying the arms with money provided by Nadal. Ultimately, they could only enroll ten men. A servant of Nadal's took twenty-five pistols to Orléans, a city known from von Mülinen's report and other sources to be one of the key staging points for the conspiracy.[23] Here we get a glimpse from one city of how the men who actually set forth for the Amboise enterprise were recruited, armed, and financed.

Shortly before the enterprise was supposed to be launched in the Loire valley, a military captain sent by Condé, the seigneur de "Goulayne," arrived in Lyon. He told the local co-conspirators that the prince had charged him with ensuring order, preventing pillaging, and seeing that "nobody budge (*nul ne bogeast*)" should the plot succeed. Once again, the contents of this deposition accord well with what La Planche's history would reveal sixteen years later. According to that work, the plan decided upon at Nantes was that as the captains from the different provinces led five hundred gentlemen to Blois to seize the king, other noblemen would go to the leading cities of the realm

---

[22] ADPA, E 582 (13), fo. 4; Appendix, pp. 202–03.
[23] ADPA, E 582 (13), fo. 4; Appendix, p. 202. On Orléans as a staging point, see p. 64; Paillard, 333, Chantonnay to Margaret of Parma, Amboise, March 20, 1560 ("Orléans n'est pas trop assurée, aiant donné passage aux conspirateurs pour deux ou trois cent au coup, à cheval et à pied, reçu et recellé les armes assemblées de tous côtés et bales et caises comme marchandises, afin que les mutins vinsent plus dissimulément sans armes, et ouvert nuitamment les portes pour embarquer icelles et les amener par la reivère jusques près d'icy, ce qui a été découvert et arrêté"); AS Mantova, Archivio Gonzaga 652, H. Strozzi to duke, Tours, April 6, 1560; Bernard de Lacombe, *Les débuts des guerres de religion (Orléans, 1559–1564): Catherine de Médicis entre Guise et Condé* (Paris: Perrin, 1899), 40.

to "assure that the populace only arose appropriately (*ne s'esmeust que bien à poinct*) and also to prevent the Guises from receiving any help or aid."[24] Goulaine also explained that he expected men to arrive soon from Piedmont, Provence, and Dauphiné to aid him. He stayed in the city for about three weeks, and left when it became clear that the enterprise had ended in failure.[25] The involvement in the conspiracy of a nobleman by this name has never been noted before. He was in all likelihood one of three brothers from an old noble family with substantial landed possessions near Nantes: Jacques, René, and François de Goulaine. The family was connected by marriage to that of François d'Acigné, seigneur de Montejean, the captain of the conspiracy for Brittany. All three of the brothers are known to have converted to Protestantism and one or more of them subsequently fought in the Huguenot armies.[26] That the planning for the Amboise enterprise included dispatching an experienced Breton captain to Lyon to command men brought in from surrounding regions indicates the national scope of its military operations.

The details of the portion of Triou's deposition that concern recruitment in an important city for the Amboise enterprise both accord well with and supplement those provided by Ardoin de Maillane.[27] Once again, we find the recruiting work done by a nobleman who presented himself as acting on behalf of the churches, although here a pastor may have accompanied him. Once again, the recruiter(s) contacted men with leadership positions in the local church of the localities visited. In Lyon, as in Aix, those contacted responded positively and ultimately agreed to raise men and arms, although the group of Lyon conspirators, unlike those from Aix, did not send one of theirs to the Nantes assembly. Although we can say with confidence that leading figures in the Lyon church took part in the conspiracy, we cannot assert that the consistory approved their actions in the

---

[24] La Planche, 134.
[25] ADPA, E 582 (13), fos. 5v, 9v–10; Appendix, pp. 205, 211–12.
[26] On the Goulaine brothers, see *FP¹*, V, 325–26; *Mémoires de Charles Gouyon, baron de La Moussaye (1553–1587)*, ed. G. Vallée and P. Parfouru (Paris: Perrin, 1901), 27; Roger Joxe, *Les protestants du comté de Nantes au seizième siècle et au début du dix-septième siècle* (Marseille: J. Laffitte, 1982), 111–14. Jacques would later be killed fighting for the Protestant cause at the 1569 battle of Jarnac. An "old captain named Golenes" who could be any one of these three led the Huguenot defense of the islands around Marennes in 1568.
[27] See pp. 64–67.

name of the congregation as a whole, because the full consistory probably included more men than just those named by Triou. Nor can we be sure whether the deacon who purchased arms used his money or the church's. It bears noting that in a city as large and rich as Lyon, only ten men were enlisted to go to Amboise. Arms were purchased and shipped off for just twenty-five. As there is no hint that the unnamed pastor at the January meeting dissented from the generally positive response to the appeals of the recruiter(s), Triou's deposition also provides evidence of another minister's at least peripheral involvement. Perhaps most noteworthy of all in this portion of the document is what substantial bourgeois the Lyon conspiracy leaders were. One was even close to Calvin.

Triou's involvement in affairs soon deepened. He remained in Lyon until late March, when "La Rivière" returned accompanied by a second man whose name is best deciphered as "Lagaret" or "Le Garet." In all probability, this was Charles Ferré, seigneur de La Garaye, a nobleman from the diocese of Saint Malo who took refuge in Geneva in 1556, was identified by La Place as the co-organizer with La Renaudie of the Nantes assembly, and would be arrested six months later in Bourg-en-Bresse by Savoyard officials and charged in connection with the plot against Lyon.[28] Both he and La Rivière were probably fleeing the debacle at Amboise. Condé was in great danger, they reported. Constantin, Gousset, and Triou should assemble more men to aid him. The Lyonnais said they lacked the means to do much but would go to Condé to hear his instructions. Those at the core of the Amboise venture clearly wanted to keep the enterprise going.

Gousset and Triou set out to track down the prince. Goulaine accompanied them on the first part of their journey by boat down the Loire before disembarking at Decize to seek Maligny in Burgundy. Triou went on to Orléans, then Paris, and finally to the town of Condé in search of the prince. He ultimately caught up with him at Etampes. By then, another person also looking for Condé had joined him, a nobleman from Champagne whose name he did not know but

---

[28] La Place, *Commentaires*, fo. 51; Naef, 200–06. The account of La Garaye's role in the events of 1560 provided by Clouard, "Protestantisme en Bretagne," 88, rests on a misreading of Triou's deposition and some false inferences therefrom.

whom he subsequently saw in Geneva. The two men got an audience with the prince. Triou explained that he had been sent by the church of Lyon to learn his will. Condé told the two that all troops had been dismissed, that he did not want to undertake anything against the king, and that he was upset by the ongoing campaign of denigration of the cardinal of Lorraine, which only increased the king's hostility to the faith. Triou then went to rejoin Gousset, who had remained in Orléans. There, the two met with two of the three ministers of that city's important church: "La Bergerie" and "La Fontaine." They "resolved to keep matters at peace." Triou and Gousset returned to Lyon and told Chateauneuf, La Garaye, and Constantin what Condé and the Orléans ministers had said. This trio of important decision makers—a Provençal nobleman, a Breton nobleman, and a Lyon goldsmith and (at least future) church elder—likewise decided against further action at the time. Triou then went to Geneva, perhaps fearing that it was not safe for him to stay in Lyon. His wife joined him there in June.[29]

What stands out in this portion of Triou's testimony is that both Condé and two Orléans ministers were sought out for consultation and urged the conspirators to stand down. It appears that in this period in late April after Condé had slipped away from court but before he joined his brother Antoine at Nérac, he still exercised a degree of strategic authority over organized oppositional activity. At the same time, he did not so tightly control affairs that he could prevent anti-Guise propaganda from being produced. Furthermore, his orders were not executed until more discussion had taken place with the Orléans ministers and among a troika of leading conspirators in the Southeast. Clearly, the two ministers also possessed some wider authority and must have been significant actors in the conspiratorial activities. It is worth recalling here that La Planche wrote that in the early months of Francis II's reign, ministers from not only Paris, but also Orléans, Tours, and other cities approached Antoine to urge him to embrace the Reformed cause openly.[30] Did these same ministers continue throughout the intervening period to play an organizational and even leadership role in the conspiracies? That Orléans was a key hub for the distribution of arms adds further plausibility to this hypothesis.

---

[29] ADPA, E 582 (13), fos. 4v–5v, 10; Appendix, pp. 203–05, 211.
[30] See p. 34.

The two Orléans ministers whom Triou knew simply by their pseudonyms can be identified as Pierre Gilbert, who operated under the name La Bergerie, and Robert Le Maçon, who also used the name La Fontaine. The former was an experienced pastor who had served for a number of years in Bernese territory before arriving in Orléans soon after the church's foundation in 1557. Calvin and Beza esteemed him sufficiently that they had him carry from Geneva to Paris the confession of faith that the Genevans rushed there when they learned of the meeting in 1559 that would subsequently be considered the first national synod. He fell ill and died in February 1561.[31] Robert Le Maçon was a young man of just twenty-six from the Beauce who would serve as minister of Orléans until the Saint Bartholomew's Massacre forced him to flee to London. There he would serve as pastor to the French Church for nearly forty years and act as a diplomatic agent for Henry IV during his wars against the Catholic League and Spain.[32]

For the next four months, from May to August, Triou heard nothing directly about further plotting, although he did pick up some interesting rumors going around Geneva. According to one report that he passed along to his interrogators, a new plan was hatched to seize Lyon. This time there would be no prior planning assembly, the better to preserve secrecy. Another had it that Calvin, Beza, Spifame, and a fourth man named "Pastereau"—perhaps the wealthy Bourges merchant and ex-mayor Jacques Pastoureau, known to have taken refuge in Geneva in 1559–60[33]—had delegated two nobles, "*le jeune Maligny*" and Robert Stuart, seigneur de Vézines, to raise fighting forces in Germany. For this purpose, the elder Maligny, Jean de Ferrières, had furnished his brother Edme 1500 *livres*. In the end,

---

[31] *HE*, I, 135, 183; *CO*, XVII, col. 526, Calvin to Morel, [Geneva], May 17, 1559.
[32] Charles G. D. Littleton, "Le Maçon, Robert [Robert La Fontaine] (1534/5–1611)," *Oxford Dictionary of National Biography*, Oxford University Press, 2004; online edn, Jan 2008 [http://www.oxforddnb.com/view/article/40600, accessed 14 June 2017].
[33] On whom see "Confiscation des biens de Jacques Pastoureau, de Bourges, retiré à Genève (1559)," *BSHPF* 45 (1896): 521–23; Henry Jongleux, *Archives de la ville de Bourges avant 1790* (Bourges: Jollet, 1877), 35. While in Geneva, Pastoureau's two daughters married the important refugee merchants and co-financiers of Geneva's first *moulin à soie*, Yves Camialle, from Orléans, and Louis Thézé, from Lyon and a member of that city's consistory in 1564. Thézé contracted his marriage "par l'advis de honorable Claude Le Maistre son amy bourgeois et marchand de Genève," whose involvement in the preparation of the Maligny affair and financing of the Huguenot war effort in the First Civil War we will soon see. AEG, Notaires, Jean Ragueau 3, 3–6, 103–07, 421–26; Liliane Mottu-Weber, *Economie et Refuge à Genève au siècle de la Réforme: la draperie et soierie (1540–1640)* (Geneva: Droz, 1987), 235; *Lyon 1562*, 165. Spifame, descended from a mercantile family of Lucca, was a man of considerable wealth himself, an old friend of Beza's from their Paris days, and a close neighbor and associate of Calvin. See *Corr Bèze*, III, 141–42 and the literature cited there.

however, Antoine and "those of Geneva" decided against having the mercenaries enter France, fearing that this risked letting loose too much destruction on the country.³⁴

As both the younger Maligny and Stuart would subsequently emerge as important figures in this second phase of Protestant plotting, these rumors may have had some foundation. We have already learned of the former's escape from Amboise after the failure of the conspiracy on one of Condé's best horses.³⁵ Stuart had recently had adventures even more worthy of a Dumas novel. Known to be in Condé's service, he was arrested in December 1559 in connection with one of the most shocking murders of the era, that of the president of the Parlement of Paris, Antoine Minard, shot returning to his house from the Palais de Justice as the trial of Anne Du Bourg neared its dénouement. Despite being subjected to torture so severe that his arm was broken, Stuart resolutely denied involvement. Soon after the initial warnings about the Amboise enterprise, the crown brought him from his Paris prison to Blois, hooded to conceal his identity and thwart rescue attempts, for questioning about that plot. Two months later, he escaped from the tower of the castle where he was detained, letting himself down with a bedsheet.³⁶

Needless to say, to the extent that Triou was well informed, what he had to say about these men being sent to Germany, that traditional recruiting ground of mercenary soldiers where we know that Hotman, Sturm, and the English agent Christopher Mundt were trying to create a wider Protestant military alliance, is also noteworthy with regard to the question of possible foreign involvement in the plots. If he was correct that Antoine and the Genevan quartet of Calvin, Beza, Spifame, and Pastoureau finally decided against bringing in any German soldiers, this has two significant implications. First, it offers more evidence that the international connections that unquestionably existed among Protestant activists in France, Germany, England, and Scotland did not eventuate in active foreign intervention or assistance

---

³⁴ ADPA, E 582 (13), fos. 6, 10v; Appendix, pp. 205–06, 212.
³⁵ See p. 27.
³⁶ *FP¹*, IX, 318; Paillard, pp. 91–92; *CSP For*, II, 437, Throckmorton to Cecil, Amboise, March 7, 1560; AS Modena, Ambasciatore Francia, 36 (II), fo. 25v, Alvarotti to duke, Amboise, May 6, 1560; William Monter, *Judging the French Reformation: Heresy Trials by Sixteenth-Century Parlements* (Cambridge, MA: Harvard University Press, 1999), 172–73.

for the plotters in France. Second, it suggests some sharing of the decision-making between Antoine and the Geneva group.

Then, on August 28, two men, Guillaume Trie, seigneur de Varennes, and Claude Le Maître, came to Triou's lodgings in Geneva and told him that he had to go to Lyon at once in conjunction with a plan to seize that city, although the text does not specify just what they asked him to do.[37] Once again, the identities of the men involved are worth considering. Both Trie and Le Maître were well-to-do merchants who had moved from Lyon to Geneva around 1550 and quickly integrated into its governing elite. Trie became one of Calvin's best friends, at once so close a theological and political ally that in 1553 he communicated to his brother in Lyon the key pieces of evidence that Calvin possessed demonstrating Michael Servetus' authorship of the *Christianismi Restitutio*, and so close a family friend that Calvin would oversee the care of his children after his death in 1561. Le Maître was a regular business associate of Trie's. That he also interacted with Calvin is proven by a notarial contract drawn up in Trie's house in the presence of Le Maître, Calvin, and another of Calvin's close friends, Germain Colladon. During the First Civil War, Spifame and Vincent would entrust Le Maître with handling some of the money to pay the Swiss they recruited.[38] That two such close associates of Calvin's communicated to Triou the order to go to Lyon adds a second key element to the evidence adduced by Dufour demonstrating Calvin's deep engagement in the Lyon enterprise.

Triou left for Lyon on August 30 and went to stay at Constantin's house. Also lodging there, operating under the name of "Saint-Cyre," was the "elder seigneur de Maligny the head of the aforesaid enterprise"—the key passage in the deposition showing that Jean de Ferrières commanded the operation, not his younger brother Edme, as so many historians have suggested in the wake of Régnier de La Planche's confusing prose.[39] Constantin told Triou that men would be arriving at the house from all parts throughout the week. Two days later Triou dined in the topmost room of Terrasson's house

---

[37] ADPA, E 582 (13), fo. 6; Appendix, p. 206.
[38] Doumergue, *Calvin*, III, 630–32; *Corr Bèze*, III, 140–41; Roland H. Bainton, *Hunted Heretic: The Life and Death of Michael Servetus, 1511–1553* (Boston: Beacon Press, 1953), 151–53, 156–58; LH, I, 8; AEG, Notaires, Jean Ragueau 2, 219; R Consist 15, fo. 52v; Droz, "Vincent," 289.
[39] See p. 35.

where the January meeting had taken place. Joining him were the goldsmith Constantin, the cloth merchant Terrasson, Maligny, "La Riviere Chateau Neufz," and another difficult-to-identify nobleman, the "seigneur de Bellimes" or "Belimour," whom Saconay identifies as an Auvergnat and may therefore have been either Claude de Veyny or his son Joseph, both seigneurs of Belime in Auvergne, about whose role in other events of this time I have not discovered any further information.[40] After supper, a tall nobleman with a dark beard whom Triou heard referred to as the seigneur "de Maleval" arrived and had Maligny step into another room for an urgent conversation, the contents of which Triou never learned.[41] The bearer of these important tidings I feel confident in identifying as a member of the large de Fay clan from the Rhône valley, Jean de Fay, most commonly known as the "seigneur de Virieu" after his heiress-wife's most significant landholding, but who also became lord of Malleval through his marriage to her. This identification is reinforced by the fact that Saconay and the many historians who have followed him mention "the Peyraud brothers of the Vivarais" as significant actors in the Lyon enterprise. Jean's brother, Antoine de Fay, was the seigneur of Peyraud in the Vivarais. Both of these experienced soldiers were known patrons of the Protestant cause who would play important roles in subsequent events in and around Lyon. A Reformed church had been founded in Malleval by 1561. A synod of the churches of Dauphiné, joined by those of Annonay (in the Vivarais) and Malleval (Forez), met in the chateau of Peyraud in September 1561.[42]

After Malleval delivered his message to Maligny, Triou returned to Constantin's house. The next day, the two drew up the rolls of men and arms that the authorities would later find. Tellingly, as they did this, Constantin told him not to say anything to the men in question about their mission, which would require them to form battalions at the gates and seize the leading figures of the city without pillaging anything. All Maligny had told them when recruiting them,

---

[40] On the family: P.-Louis Lainé, *Archives généalogiques et historiques de la noblesse de France* (11 vols., Paris: Imprimerie de Béthune, 1828–50), IV, 3.
[41] ADPA, E 582 (13), fos. 6v–7; Appendix, pp. 206–07.
[42] On these two brothers and their clan, see E. Nicod, "La maison de Fay-Peyraud (suite IV)," *Revue du Vivarais illustrée* 11 (1903): 315–38, esp. 320–25, which supersedes FP², VI, cols. 457–59; Benedict and Fornerod eds., *Organisation et action*, 96, 106.

he stressed, was that the operation aimed to have the Gospel preached in the city.[43] In other words, the rank-and-file were signed up for this mission with incomplete information about its nature—just as they may have been for Amboise, given the reports from there according to which many of those found in the surrounding woods either did not know why they were there or believed that they had come to petition the king to examine their confession of faith. Constantin also told Triou that the day for the operation had not been set in advance. Maligny was waiting for "news from the king of Navarre and prince of Condé that was slow in coming."[44]

Could Triou have been approached on the 28th by two of Calvin's associates and money-men and told to go immediately to Lyon because Beza's letter from Nérac canceling the Maligny affair had just arrived? Probably not, if we recall that Beza wrote to Calvin on August 25, that Nérac was several days' journey from Geneva, and that Calvin said that the muleteer carrying Beza's message inexplicably wasted four days en route.[45] It thus seems likely that the task Trie and Le Maître asked Triou to undertake involved carrying money for the Maligny mission to Lyon and helping to prepare it, as is also suggested by Triou's role in drawing up the list of arms per battalion. Because Malleval arrived late on September 2, the urgent message he delivered to Maligny might have been the instructions not to go ahead with the strike against Lyon. It would be helpful to find clues that might suggest in this instance whether Malleval is more likely to have arrived from Geneva, in which case we can presume he was sent by Calvin after receiving Beza's letter, or from Nérac, in which case he would have been sent by Antoine directly to Maligny, the scenario suggested by Régnier de La Planche. I have yet to discover any evidence that would support either of these possibilities. David Potter, who has studied the surviving muster rolls of Antoine's companies of *hommes d'armes*, tells me that Jean de Fay-Virieu-Malleval does not appear on the rolls of 1551, 1558, or 1561. A search of the index to Geneva's notarial records turns up no evidence of his having been there in 1560. Whatever Malleval told Maligny, the leader of the enterprise

---

[43] ADPA, E 582 (13), fos. 7v, 10; Appendix, pp. 208, 212.
[44] ADPA, E 582 (13), fo. 8; Appendix, p. 208.
[45] See pp. 70–71.

kept the content of the message to himself. While he brooded about what to do—for just two days, not a full week as Régnier de La Planche would later write—preparations went ahead for the planned attack. Then the arms were spotted and the militia came knocking at Constantin's door. The conspirators had to scramble to defend themselves.

Triou was able to provide relatively few details about what happened next, since he ran for the cellar when the trouble began. He was, however, able to see and hear enough to recount that Maligny and Belime rapidly organized the distribution of arms to their men "for the fear they had of being found out, and not to execute their enterprise, which they couldn't yet carry out." A few hours later, after the first skirmishing was over and Triou had come out of the cellar, Maligny, Belime, and Malleval returned to Constantin's house for one last deliberation about strategy. They ordered some arms to be hidden in Terrasson's house, where arms were indeed found by the authorities after the conspirators had fled.[46] Soon after that, everybody vacated the house, "even Constantin's wife carrying her child on her neck." Triou did not follow them.[47]

After learning all this, Triou's interrogators asked how many people had been expected to take part in the mission against Lyon. He replied that he could not provide an exact tally. All he could say was that the conspirators counted on aid arriving from several directions. A substantial contingent of reinforcements was expected from Provence and Dauphiné led by Paulon de Mauvans and Charles Dupuy-Montbrun, another noble captain who, like Mauvans, had already raised a band for armed action in his home province. In point of fact, the two had recently seized Malaucène in the Papal Comtat Venaissin, an ideal base from which to launch an intervention.[48] Triou had also heard that Robert Stuart was supposed to bring three hundred men whom he had raised in Geneva—secretly, since the city authori-

---

[46] We know this from the brief account in Lyon's municipal archives of "l'esmotion et eslevation faicte par certains estrangers appellez huguenaulx qui par subtilz moyens peu à peu seroient entrez dans la ville et soubz ombre de la religion se seroient esmeuz et levez en armes contre le guet de la ville," which corresponds well to several details of this portion of Triou's deposition. AM Lyon BB 81, fo. 307v.
[47] ADPA, E 582 (13), fos. 8-9; Appendix, pp. 209-10.
[48] After the thwarted seizure of Aix and the iconoclastic raids elsewhere in Provence in March and April, Mauvans had to flee to Geneva to escape a large force mobilized to apprehend him. Geneva's

ties did not want the city's defensive manpower reduced for fear of an attack by the duke of Savoy. Finally, he believed that Antoine of Navarre had men near him who might be sent if necessary. All of these fighters were supposed to be paid with a loan of 60,000 livres secured by Antoine. Triou had it on good authority, however, that Navarre's attempts to arrange this loan through the wealthy Lyon financier Georges Obrecht (who later would finance the Protestant cause in the First Civil War) fell through.[49] Other sources of funding had to be found. Constantin had to advance eighty livres to Maligny at one point to meet some expenses of the men in Lyon.[50]

Last of all, a roll of names written in a large Italian hand was read to Triou. He did not recognize the document itself, which must have been another list of participants in the enterprise against Lyon. He did, however, say that he knew eight of the men whose names were read from it, several of whom had recently come to the city after royal troops had been stationed in their home towns "for religion's sake": Jean Bertrand, Pierre Bussillon, Philibert Courtoys, Jean Doupoin, "le Petit Martin," Pierre Martin, "Maitre Quentin," and Pierre de Villeneuve.[51] From other contemporaneous Lyon sources,

---

authorities authorized him to reside in the city on July 9 (Naef, 226–27), but scarcely had he received this permission than he was back in the saddle in France, joining forces on August 7 with Montbrun to seize Malaucene. La Planche, 306–22; "Mémoires de Claude de Cormis," 518–27; Naef, 226–27. On the seizure of Malaucène, although omitting the wider context, the best account is Marc Venard, *Réforme protestante, Réforme catholique dans la province d'Avignon au XVIe siècle* (Paris: Cerf, 1993), 446–50. Montbrun would become one of the most storied Protestant captains of the Wars of Religion. According to d'Aubigné, he was the captain of the conspiracy of Amboise for Dauphiné. There is no evidence that he led troops to the Loire valley in the spring, however. Instead, like Mauvans, he militated in his home province. In April 1560 he was one of the noblemen bearing arms who protected the minister François de Saint-Paul as he preached from the porch of the Franciscan church of Montélimar. The incident brought the royal wrath down on all involved. Montbrun then refused a summons to appear before the Parlement of Grenoble, before attacking and humiliating the royal provost sent to apprehend him. For the next four months he was actively in arms between Dauphiné and the Comtat Venaissin before finally being forced to disband his forces and flee across the Alps to safety in Geneva. La Planche, 474–97, 569–91; *HE*, I, 400–14; Alexandra Lublinskaya and Vladimir Chichkine eds., *Documents pour servir à l'histoire de France au milieu du XVIe siècle. Début des guerres de Religion (1559–1560)* (Moscow, 2013), 170–71, 180–81; Lestocquoy ed., *Correspondance des nonces*, 251, Borromeo to Gualterio, Rome, Aug 21, 1560; Philip Benedict, "The Lesser Nobility and the French Reformation," in *Ritterschaft und Reformation*, eds. Kurt Andermann and Wolfgang Breul (Stuttgart: Franz Steiner Verlag, 2019), 349–50.

[49] Triou claimed to have learned this from a man named Florent who had lived in Obrecht's house and recently moved to Geneva. On Obrecht, see Henri Meylan, "Un financier protestant à Lyon, ami de Calvin et de Bèze, Georges Obrecht (1500–1569)," *Bulletin philologique et historique (jusqu'à 1610)* (1964): 213–20.

[50] ADPA, E 582 (13), fos. 7v–8; Appendix, pp. 208–09.

[51] ADPA, E 582 (13), fo. 10; Appendix, p. 212.

we know that two of these men, Boussillon, a gem-cutter, and Doupoin, a money-changer and silk manufacturer, were among those captured and executed in the days after the brief street fight.[52] Villeneuve, a merchant, escaped and would return after Francis II's death to become a leading voice in the Lyon consistory.[53] At the beginning of his interrogation, Triou had been shown other seized lists whose manner of identification in the record enables us to put names on four additional conspirators. One list that Triou recognized as having been written by Constantin began with the name "Me Pierre de Prouvence." This would be Pierre Bonnet dit de Provence, an eminent surgeon and another man identifiable as a leading figure in the consistory in subsequent years.[54] If he was already a consistory member, his place at the top of the list could suggest that at least certain elders or deacons also served as unit commanders for the planned enterprise. Another roll began with the name Guillaume Guay and ended with that of Claude Richard, neither of whom it has been possible to further identify with confidence. A third began "the *enseigne* of the well-armed velvet-weavers" and ended with the name Pierre Anthoine Rurcaille. This at least hints at Rurcaille's craft and suggests that the enterprise might partially have been organized around occupational groups. We will never know most of the names on these lists of men and arms seized by the authorities. Further information is lacking about some of those whose names we do know. But those whose occupations we can identify once again include substantial artisans and merchants, as well as a prominent member of the healing professions. At least two of these men also subsequently assumed leadership positions within the church and may already have occupied them in 1560, just like Vincent, Nadal, Constantin, and Darut. This was no purely aristocratic conspiracy.

The chronicle of the Catholic clothier Jean Guéraud identifies several other people arrested in the aftermath of the tumult, for the most part younger men: an unnamed servant living in Constantin's house; another servant, Antoine Dumas, who lived in Terrasson's

---

[52] AM Lyon BB 81, fo. 307v; *Chronique lyonnaise de Guéraud*, 126–28. Triou said about Doupoin: "on n'avoyt garde de tracter de telz affaires en presence de Jehan Du Poing parce qu'il estoyt legier de sens et parloit aussi tost pour luy que contre." ADPA, E 582 (13), fo. 9v; Appendix, p. 211.
[53] Information furnished by Natalie Zemon Davis.
[54] ADPA, E 582 (13), fo. 1v; Appendix, p. 199.

building; the ironmonger (*quincaillier*) Pierre de La Rivette; and an unnamed tutor who lived in Boussillon's house and who also doubled as an occasional Reformed preacher. Constantin's servant, La Rivette, and the schoolmaster-preacher all also met death. Dumas would gain his release—and thirty-seven years later would leave money in his very Catholic will for an anniversary mass to be said each year on September 5 to thank God for preserving him when he was imprisoned.[55] Guéraud also reveals that arms were found not only in Terrasson's house, but also in those of the Darut brothers and a "Mr Champier" who is hard to identify.[56] A still later source, Saconay's history, asserts that 66 lodgings had been prepared for the men infiltrated into the town.[57] The scale of the conspiracy was vast.

In sum, the Triou deposition offers a view of Protestant plotting from January through August 1560 from the vantage point of an actively involved Reformed artisan and deacon or deacon's assistant who moved between Lyon and Geneva. At one point Triou declared that "the enterprise was put together by noblemen who gave their word to one another," offering the perfect definition of a sworn aristocratic conspiracy.[58] Yet among the many revelations that it contains, one of the most important would seem to be that a core group of substantial Protestant merchants and artisans in Lyon, at least some of whom sat in the consistory, were continuously involved in what looks to have been an unbroken, far-from-exclusively-aristocratic sequence of conspiracies that ran from the beginning of 1560 through the Maligny affair. In February and March, they raised men and weapons for the Amboise enterprise. In August, they allowed their houses to be used as dormitories and arms depots for the planned seizure of Lyon. Furthermore, although Triou's testimony has the great interest of unhesitatingly naming Condé as the head of the Amboise venture from the start, and although it therefore probably played a role in confirming the suspicions of the prince that led to his subsequent arrest, it has the even greater interest of revealing as

---

[55] *Chronique lyonnaise de Guéraud*, 126–28; information provided by Natalie Zemon Davis. Dumas's will is AD Rhône, 3 H II, fo. 74v.
[56] One possibility suggested by Natalie Zemon Davis is Jacques Champier, seigneur de La Bastie.
[57] Saconay, *Discours des premiers troubles*, 32.
[58] ADPA, E 582 (13), fo. 8; Appendix, p. 208: "Se faisoit lad entreprinse par gentilzhomes qui se donneraient parolle de l'un à l'aultre."

important decision makers two Orléans ministers that historians have heretofore not even known to have been implicated in the conspiracies. This in turn suggests that we need to reconsider the nature of leadership within the sequence of plots.

Triou's testimony has other significant implications as well. It reinforces other pieces of evidence that suggest that the plotting was two-tiered, with the full political and constitutional ambitions of the core group of conspirators only being revealed to a fraction of urban leaders and noble participants, while rank-and-file recruits were told only of a narrower and more exclusively religious goal. It reveals that Maligny and his men expected reinforcements to arrive from a wide area. Foreign involvement was even considered, with Calvin, Beza, Spifame, and the merchant Pastoureau sending envoys to Germany to line up supporting troops. Ultimately, recourse to this aid from abroad was rejected. Nonetheless, a group of reinforcements from Geneva raised without the knowledge or approval of its authorities was counted upon to strengthen the forces in Lyon. The document clarifies the vexed question of which Maligny brother led the project, clearly specifying that the elder Jean was the "*chef de l'entreprise*" and also provided some funding, whereas his younger brother Edme acted as the key recruiter. In identifying Calvin and Beza's more than casual acquaintance Antoine Vincent as one of the central figures in the Lyon plotting from January 1560 onward, in relaying rumors of Calvin and Beza's involvement in delegating Robert Stuart and the younger Maligny to raise men in Germany, and in naming Calvin's close friend Guillaume Trie and his associate Claude Le Maître as key conduits between Geneva and the plotters gathered in Lyon, his testimony not only confirms and supplements what Dufour already deduced from the Calvin–Beza correspondence about the role of the two prominent reformers in supporting and financing the Maligny affair; it also reveals that people closer to Calvin than he cared to let on were also involved in the Amboise conspiracy. In so doing, it calls into question his subsequent claim that those who left Geneva to take part in that venture did so without his knowledge or against his urgings. Finally, if three hundred men from Geneva were indeed raised to offer reinforcements for Maligny's men in Lyon, might von Mülinen's report that four hundred took part in the Amboise conspiracy not also seem more probable than Calvin's claim that only sixty or seventy did so?

The Triou deposition thus illuminates the conspiratorial activity of the first nine months of 1560 from a strikingly different angle—if the cabinetmaker's testimony can be believed. Can it? Portions of what he said about events in Lyon that he directly witnessed can be compared with other local documents. These check out well. On the other hand, the first-hand narrative portion of his testimony skips from April, when Condé and the Orléans ministers told the Lyon-based conspirators to stand down, to August 28, when Trie and Le Maître came to see him and urge him to take a message from Geneva to Lyon. It ends, naturally enough, with his arrest. For the period between late April and August 28 it offers only hearsay and tells us relatively little about just how, when, and by whom the plotting of a new, ambitious enterprise resumed in this period. Inevitably, it is silent about whether conspiratorial activity of any sort continued after the interrogation. Furthermore, the cabinetmaker surely feared for his life when he faced his interrogators. He probably was threatened with torture. Régnier de La Planche, who knew about the arrest and interrogation of "Le Gantier," wrote that in return for a promise that his life would be spared, he "said more than he knew, accusing all those with whom he was acquainted from the enterprise."[59] The Catholic historian François de Belleforest echoed this.[60] Every uncorroborated detail provided by his testimony certainly cannot be assumed to be true.

---

[59] La Planche, 579–80. Farther along in the same work (p. 700), La Planche wrote that Le Gantier's was the only testimony that incriminated Condé but he "spoke merely from hearsay."

[60] Belleforest, *Grandes annales et histoire*, 1613. Belleforest wrote that a second arestee, Giuliano Calandrini, like Triou, "spoke more than they knew." That Calandrini was arrested and interrogated is confirmed by the arrêt du Conseil proclaiming Condé's innocence, which refers to his now lost testimony. Calandrini came from the prominent Lucchese international banking family and was another member of the Lyon consistory. He is mentioned in Triou's testimony as somebody with whom the cabinetmaker occasionally met in the presence of Nadal and Darut to identify possible recipients of alms. Nothing in Triou's testimony or the other Lyon sources of the time indicates his involvement in the conspiracies. He may have been arrested simply because his name came up in the course of the cabinetmaker's interrogation. Like Triou, he was not executed. After his release, he moved briefly to Geneva, whose Italian church received him as a member on November 9, 1560. He returned to Lyon by 1562. Still later, he lived in Paris and Sedan, where he died in 1573. Natalie Zemon Davis, "The Sacred and the Body Social in Sixteenth-Century Lyon," *Past & Present* 90 (1981): 48n; Vincenzo Burlamacchi, *Libro di ricordi degnissimi delle nostre famiglie*, ed. Simonetta Adorni-Braccesi (Rome: Instituto Storico per l'Età Moderna e Contemporanea, 1993), 107; Adorni-Braccesi, "*Una città infetta.*" *La repubblica di Lucca nella crisi religiosa del cinquecento* (Florence: Olshki, 1994), 315; Ole Peter Grell, *Brethren in Christ: A Calvinist Network in Reformation Europe* (Cambridge: Cambridge University Press, 2011), xv, 35–36, 41, 44, 50, 53–54, 58–59, 65.

Fortunately, a variety of complementary documents enable us to fill in some of the gaps in Triou's testimony about the resumption of conspiratorial activity between April and August and to see what transpired in the months after Triou signed off on his statement on September 18. These complementary sources also corroborate many of the largest implications of his deposition: that ministers and substantial urban-dwellers were deeply involved in the plotting alongside aristocrats, that the plotting was more closely linked to the leadership of at least some French Reformed churches than the post-Amboise pamphlets let on, and that among the participants in this conspiracy were men with very close ties to Calvin and other Geneva ministers. The plotting, it turns out, continued until the last days of Francis II's reign, with Calvin seeking anxiously throughout the last months to learn from afar whether Antoine would execute the plan that had superseded Maligny's enterprise and led to its last-minute cancellation. It is to this complementary evidence that we now turn.

Four

From Amboise to Lyon

The resumption of plotting after the debacle at Amboise is an aspect of the history of Francis II's reign that has not been much explored by modern historians.[1] Several sources enable us to observe it, if only through a veil. The first is Régnier de La Planche's account of this period of the reign. According to La Planche, the failure of the Amboise conspiracy did not discourage all those within the Reformed churches who wanted to bring their confession of faith before the crown or to summon a reunion of the Estates that would implement a change of government and government policy. When Catherine de Medici visited the abbey of Beaulieu near Loches in May, the son of a court furrier named Le Camus was able to present her with the confession of faith and a memorandum calling for the reformation of religion and the creation of a proper regency council in conformity with the ancient constitution. This was written by a young minister Charles d'Albiac dit Duplessis, under the pseudonym of Bordenave.[2] D'Albiac is known to have been been a scholarship student at the Academy of Lausanne from 1553 to 1558, who in 1557 was denied permission by the Bernese authorities to leave their territory to evangelize Gascony because they did not want those whose

---

[1] The ample pages of de Ruble, *Antoine et Jeanne*, II, 306–52, for all their copious documentation, are confused and often inaccurate. The relatively brief treatments in Romier, *Conjuration*, 217–22, 224–28; Jouanna, *Histoire et dictionnaire*, 72–74; and Daussy, *Parti huguenot*, 172–75, are better.
[2] La Planche, 337–57.

education they had subsidized running unnecessary risks.³ He left the Pays de Vaud the next year together with a substantial fraction of its pastors and professors following the discipline controversy. Not long thereafter, he was dispatched from Geneva to Tours. If he was the pastor of Tours who wrote to Calvin under the pseudonym "C. Riseus" in May 1559, as the editors of the Calvin correspondence speculate, he quickly established contact with both Antoine and the earl of Arran, taking shelter at one point on the earl's lands. Soon after the Amboise conspiracy, the Tours consistory thought it best for him to leave the city again for his safety, a fact that suggests some involvement in the enterprise.⁴ Le Camus and members of his family were arrested. Although the furrier claimed to know no more about the Amboise venture than that it sought to remedy "confusions" in the kingdom, he not only revealed d'Albiac's authorship of the subsequent memorandum, but also that the enterprise's organizers "had decided to rebuild it more securely than ever by seizing one of the provinces of the kingdom, fortifying themselves there, and circulating writings in so many languages that every nation would learn the merit of their cause."⁵

Around the same time (to continue La Planche's version of the story), Maligny was called to court for questioning in regard to the Amboise conspiracy. As has been mentioned, La Planche would have us believe that, unlike his younger brother Edme, Jean had not taken part in this first plot.⁶ On the other hand, Triou's report that Goulaine set off at Decize to seek Maligny in Burgundy might point to some sort of participation, if Triou had only specified here as he generally did elsewhere in his testimony whether he was referring to the elder or the younger of the two brothers.⁷ Whether, as La Planche's account would have it, an innocent Maligny was moved to gather some men in self-defense because he believed that the Guises could not be trusted, or whether he had some role in the Amboise conspiracy and was now judged a person who could rally new support if that first

---

³ Karine Crousaz, *L'Académie de Lausanne entre Humanisme et Réforme (ca. 1537–1560)* (Leiden: Brill, 2012), 298–99.
⁴ *HE*, I, 128, 344, 345; *CO*, XVII, no. 3054, Riseus to Calvin, n.p., May 16, 1559.
⁵ La Planche, 350.
⁶ See p. 2.
⁷ La Place, *Commentaires*, fo. 54; *MC*, I, 400, Francis II to Antoine, Marmoutier, April 9, 1560.

strike failed, it appears (returning again to La Planche's version of the story) that Maligny and his men then decided to send emissaries to talk with Condé and others "in all of the churches" to explain that if everybody thought only of their own safety, all would perish.[8] It would seem from La Planche's often confusing prose that Maligny met up with Condé at Poitiers. He certainly was with Condé and Antoine at Nérac after Condé got there. During their stay, a number of unidentified notable figures appealed to Antoine and Condé to act to deliver the king and kingdom from their oppression.[9] Further along in the narrative, La Planche tersely asserts that the Lyon enterprise was then organized by the younger Maligny, who went to Provence, and had so well organized it that everything was ready in Lyon when suddenly the letter arrived from the king of Navarre calling it off.[10] Here again Edme de Ferrières-Maligny is cast as a key recruiter and organizer, but his older brother initiated the affair.

Diplomatic and administrative letters meanwhile suggest that some involved in the Amboise enterprise reacted to its failure by seeking to carry on the struggle, identify a new leader, and gain aid from abroad. Eyes quickly began to turn to one or both of the Malignys as a possible new chief. Already on April 2, Mundt in Strasbourg conveyed word to Cecil that if Queen Elizabeth wanted to treat with those who were prime movers in the recent French plots, he could find agents who would put her in touch with them.[11] On April 12, Throckmorton notified Cecil from Amboise that he had been picking up word that "great offers" have been made to the earl of Arran by "Gascony, Poitou, Brittany and Normandy if he would descend into these parts."[12] The next day, the Florentine ambassador wrote Duke Cosimo, again from Amboise, that "the captain Maligny, one of the leaders who escaped from the rout," was believed to be assembling men for some new action, although his precise whereabouts were unknown.[13] The concern of some conspirators to solicit more aid at once accords well with Triou's assertion that La Garaye and La Rivière

---

[8] La Planche, 391.
[9] La Planche, 391–96, 406–74, where this remonstrance is reprinted in full.
[10] La Planche, 570–80.
[11] *CSP For*, II, 499.
[12] *CSP For*, II, 535.
[13] Desjardins ed., *Négociations diplomatiques avec la Toscane*, III, 415, Alfonso Tornabuoni to Cosimo I, Amboise, April 13, 1560.

asked the Lyonnais to provide more men when they passed through the city after the collapse of the Amboise enterprise. The suspicion that arose quickly at court that one of the Maligny brothers on the loose might be organizing a new plot receives a measure of confirmation from both La Planche's history and Triou's report that Goulaine, the agent initially dispatched by Condé to control Lyon if the initial plot succeeded, subsequently set out to find Maligny in Burgundy.[14] A fraction of the more ardent plotters was evidently committed to further action, whether because of belief in the rightness and urgency of the venture for which they had signed up, or because, once they had gotten involved and put their lives and estates on the line, they felt they had no alternative but to keep moving forward.

Administrative and diplomatic letters also point, like La Planche's account, to the Loire Valley as the region where conspiratorial activity first resumed. The provincial governor of Brittany in May reported rumors of new "follies" being planned.[15] That same month, a trusted informant told Throckmorton that some of those who had recently escaped from prison in Tours were gathering men. Six thousand met at Romorantin on May 19 "for the same cause that . . . this lent past . . . made all the stirre here." "Before th'ende of June he telleth me assuredly that there will eyther put down the house of Guise or lose their lives."[16] On June 7, the English ambassador reported that the leaders of the new "garboils" that were brewing had sent a summons to the king telling him to remove from authority the members of the Guise family and all who impede the progress of the Gospel. If he failed to do so, this would be done for him by force.[17] By this month, activity had also spread to the Midi. The Ferrarese ambassador claimed to have received news that four hundred noblemen in Provence had sold all their property and gone to England to "*guennegiar*" against the king, while in the Southwest a nephew of the executed Amboise

---

[14] Jean de Ferrières-Maligny's landed possessions are in fact known to have been concentrated in Burgundy. In January 1561 he would be reported to have taken refuge in one of his houses close to the border with Champagne fortified with enough men and artillery to make it impossible to capture him without siege guns and a large contingent of troops. L. Pingaud ed., *Correspondance des Saulx-Tavanes au XVIe siècle* (Paris: Champion, 1877), 60, Tavanes to Catherine, Dijon, Jan 18, 1561.

[15] Lublinskaya and Chichkine, eds., *Documents*, 72, Etampes to Guise, Lamballe, May 15, 1560.

[16] Forbes, ed., *Full View*, 468, 465, Throckmorton to Elizabeth, Amboise, May 22, 1560.

[17] *CSP For*, III, 105, Throckmorton to Cecil, Blois, June 7, 1560.

conspirator Castelnau was seeking to avenge his uncle's death and had raised a hundred men for this purpose, each of whom was in turn to raise another hundred.[18] Venetian and Florentine dispatches offered similar reports, with Duke Cosimo's envoy also mentioning large gatherings of noblemen in Normandy aching to avenge the blood of those executed at Amboise.[19]

Throckmorton's letter of May 22 also indicated that by that date key figures in Geneva were again pressing Antoine to openly promote the Reformed faith and to coordinate efforts in this direction with the Protestant princes of Germany:

> He [Throckmorton's unnamed source] informeth me also that the state of Geneva and Mr. Calvin, understanding the king of Navarre his slacknes, have sent unto him to charge him with his promis made unto them and the states of Almaine for religion: and had signifyed that whereas they have hitherto pray'd for him in their comon prayers by name; that in drawing back they will notify his doings to the world, and declare him *canem ad vomitum*, whereupon the said king, as he sayeth, hath caused reformation to be begonne throughe Gascoigne and Guyen, and hath abolished the use of the masse.[20]

From all that we know of the efforts of the Genevan authorities to keep a prudent distance from any political activity by members of the French refugee community, the informant's claim that the "state of Geneva" was pressing Antoine to keep his promises about religion must be dismissed as unlikely. His report that Navarre had abolished the mass in the Southwest was also surely exaggerated. At most, Antoine sheltered Reformed preachers, looked the other way as new churches took shape, and intervened occasionally to gain the liberation of imprisoned ministers. But it was the case that at this moment Hotman and Sturm in Strasbourg were renewing their diplomatic initiatives to the German princes as part of the wider effort to build an international political alliance to defend and advance the true faith in places where it had become implanted but faced persecution. Calvin

---

[18] AS Modena, Ambasciatore Francia, 36 (II), fo. 38, Alvarotti to duke, "Badia di Bellabranca," June 18, 1560.
[19] *CSP Ven*, 222, Michieli to doge, Châteaudun, June 16, 1560; Desjardins, ed., *Négociations diplomatiques avec la Toscane*, III, 421, Tornabuoni to Cosimo I, Chartres, June 18, 1560, both cited in de Ruble, *Antoine et Jeanne*, II, 308.
[20] Forbes, ed., *Full View*, 465, Throckmorton to Elizabeth, Amboise, May 22, 1560.

was in touch with them and inclined to collaborate. He promised Sturm and Hotman on June 8 that, in conjunction with their efforts, "We will do our best to prod the king of Navarre to claim the reins of state by putting forward in every way possible how the kingdom is being led to ruin by the disloyalty, arrogance and greed of the Guises." His assessment of the political situation in France was that the time was ripe for a bold stroke:

> If I am not mistaken, the king's Council will awaken to defend the general good once it sees the impasse it is in. Above all the queen mother will have to be led to cede by applying energetic pressure. Only force will detach her from the Guises, but in the end she will take the course that she thinks most helpful for her and her children.[21]

In the same month, Beza also expressed confidence that if the princes of the blood acted with sufficient boldness, the political nation would rally around them and the Guises would fall.[22]

We do not know whether, in addition to directly urging Antoine to act, Calvin and Beza sought to put further pressure on him by promoting the efforts in the Loire valley and elsewhere to gather men reported in the ambassadorial correspondence of May and June. It would seem more probable that what they learned about these efforts started by others inside France was what sparked their confidence that the Guise regime was vulnerable, whereupon they made contact with those involved to try to nudge them toward the course that they considered most legally and strategically appropriate. Their optimism about the situation then surely grew when, in late June or early July, in response to their solicitations, they received a request from Antoine that Beza be sent to his side. Beza left for Nérac on July 20. He would spend three months in Antoine's entourage.[23] When he arrived, Hotman was already there. If the rumors passed along by Triou were true, Calvin and Beza had probably also by then sent the younger Maligny and Stuart on their ultimately abandoned mission to raise

---

[21] *CO*, XVIII, col. 98, Calvin to Hotman and Sturm, Geneva, June 8, 1560: "Certe, nisi nos fallit opinio, regis consilium, ubi se tantis angustiis constringi sentiet, excitabitur ut publicae saluti consulat. Regina mater praesertim acerrimis punctionibus ad consensum trahenda erit, quia nisi coacta vix unquam a Guisianis poterit avelli. Sequetur tamen quod sibi et liberis utile esse persuasa fuerit."
[22] *CO*, XVIII, col. 121 and *Corr. Bèze*, II, 59, Beza to Bullinger, Geneva, June 26, 1560.
[23] Paul-F. Geisendorf, *Théodore de Bèze* (Geneva: Labor et Fides, 1949), 120–23.

men abroad. It was probably also by then that Calvin was imploring his contacts in Paris, Provence, Lyon, and elsewhere to contribute the money needed to mount a major mobilization.

Many others, too, went to Nérac to urge Antoine to act. Pierre Olhagaray, the pastor and court historian of Navarre who wrote at the turn of the seventeenth century, asserted that while Antoine, Condé, and Beza were at Nérac, Protestant nobles and *consuls* (town councilmen) came in numbers to ask him to sympathize with their suffering and defend their cause. He promised to do so in the presence of Beza and a second minister whom Olhagaray names "Antoine Barran"—almost certainly the same person as the Pierre Henri Barran, sometimes simply called "Maître Henri," an ex-Dominican "apostate and fugitive from France" who between 1556 and 1562 preached in various locations in Béarn and served for a while as minister of Pau.[24] The Reformed churches of the Southwest established a permanent delegation at Antoine's court around this time, as can be deduced from a decision taken by the churches of the *colloque* of the Condomois on August 1, 1560, to fund the expenses of "those deputized to be near the person of the king of Navarre as decided at the synod held in Agen."[25] Most striking, an undated memorandum by a crown spy with sources in Nérac suggests that the capital of the duchy of Albret became a hub for the raising of men and money during the spring and summer of 1560. This anonymous document, entitled simply *"Avertissement,"* appears from internal evidence to have been written in Toulouse in the week after September 12. It warns not of the plan to seize Lyon, which by then had been cancelled, but of "some sort of assembly" on Saint Martin's Day (November 11) the rendezvous for which would be Poitiers. What links it to the other pieces of evidence just discussed are its ample details about earlier recruitment

---

[24] Pierre Olhagaray, *Histoire de Foix, Béarn et Navarre* (Paris: D. Douceur, 1609), 526. Barran was also a poet and the author of a *Tragique comédie française de l'homme justifié par la foy* (1554). See Charles Samaran and Nicole Lemaître, eds., *Correspondance du Cardinal Georges d'Armagnac* (Paris: Comité des Travaux Historiques et Scientifiques, 2007), 378–79, 382–83, 450–51; *HE*, I, 129, 372.

[25] This decision is revealed by an extract from the now-lost church papers of Moncrabeau copied in the seventeenth century and provided to the commissioners charged with enforcing the Edict of Nantes. Archives Nationales (Paris), TT 254 (9). The document does not provide the date of the synod in Agen, nor is any other reference to this synod known. The meeting of the *colloque* of the the Condomois was likewise unknown to Nicolas Fornerod and me when we prepared the list of regional assemblies of the Reformed churches prior to 1563 in Benedict and Fornerod eds., *Organisation et action*, xx–xxiv.

efforts undertaken by a series of agents, several of whom it identifies by name.[26]

According to this document, the first such efforts began in May, when Boisnormand, "one of the leaders of sedition," took leave of the churches of the Southwest and went to Provence, where he "visited and suborned (*praticqua*) all he could" using the false name Sieur de La Pierre. He subsequently returned to Nérac accompanied by a companion "who used to be called La Fontaine and is now calling himself du Boys." They reported on the rapid growth the churches had experienced over the preceding months and brought lists of the number of men in each region they had visited capable of bearing arms, lists that the informant believed were deliberately inflated in order to bring even more people over to their side. (This is in fact a tactic that the Reformed used in this period.[27]) Meanwhile, the seigneur de Mesmy stayed for a long time in Nérac together with his wife "to visit the churches of the surrounding area." He was then named to lead the horsemen to be put in the field for the Poitiers rendezvous. Maligny the younger passed through Toulouse two to three months ago (i.e., in June or July) before setting out for Provence "to suborn many people of his affinity (*pour pratiquer beaucoup de gens de sa devotion*)." From there, he went on to Flanders and Normandy. On his way back south, he passed through Malaucène while Montbrun controlled it, receiving assurances that Montbrun could deliver 2,500 men as soon as Mauvans and his men arrived from Provence. He returned to Toulouse soon after August 20 accompanied by the seigneur de Cardet from near Nîmes and three other unnamed men who called themselves "captains of the religion." Last of all, the anonymous informant passed along recently arrived reports that Beza had just preached publicly in Nérac's church, and that "this past Tuesday the 12th of this month" a "*conseilh*" of some of those of the religion had decided that "if it was necessary to try something for their situation, this should not be done until the snow was on the Pyrenees, so that no aid could come easily from Spain, which is something they greatly fear."

---

[26] BnF, MS Français 15876, fo. 360.
[27] Philip Benedict and Nicolas Fornerod, "Les 2150 'églises' réformées de France de 1561–1562," *Revue Historique* 311 (2009): 529–60.

Who were these various recruiters? We know the younger Maligny was credited by La Planche with being the mastermind behind the recruitment and successful infiltration of so many soldiers into Lyon in early September. The nobleman who returned with him to Toulouse shortly after August 20, Raymond de Valette, seigneur de Cardet (a village near Anduze), was an experienced soldier whom we will shortly meet in another document at the head of an armed band that spent six weeks that summer in Nîmes providing muscle for the assemblies of that city's Reformed church.[28] One wonders whether either he or one of the three unnamed noblemen with him was not also the man "with a house near Nîmes" reported by the duke of Joyeuse on September 27 to have made three trips to Guyenne in the preceding three months to lead soldiers from there to Montbrun.[29]

Boisnormand could only be François Boisnormand dit Dugué, one of the best known of the early French ministers and one long known to have been involved in the conspiracies of this year. He was an ex-Franciscan who left the convent in Casteljaloux to go to Geneva in the 1540s. After teaching school and pastoring in the Pays de Vaud, he was sent to Béarn in response to an appeal for a pastor by the leaders of the fledgling church of Pau. On arrival, his first sermons and lodgings were in a manor house just outside the city belonging to the future captain of the Amboise enterprise, François de La Salle, seigneur de Mazères. The threat of arrest forced him to return briefly to Geneva, but he soon rejoined the entourage of the court of Navarre and would serve churches in the Southwest and Béarn for more than forty years of a long life.[30] He was one of the two preachers whom

---

[28] For the identification of Cardet's full name and military experience, see Yannick Chassin du Guerny, "Inventaire du chartrier du chateau de Cardet" (1970), typescript available on line at https://www.geneanet.org/archives/ouvrages/?action=detail&livre_id=540166&page=6&book_type=livre&name=Valette+de+Cardet&with_variantes=0&tk=77c4be39b02c828f (consulted Feb 10, 2018), 2, 16; idem, "Anduze, Durfort et Canaules. Inventaire des titres du notariat, XIVe-XVIIe siècles" (1970–98), typescript available on line at https://www.geneanet.org/archives/ouvrages/?action=detail&book_type=livre&livre_id=540199&page=83&name=Valette+de+Cardet&with_variantes=0&tk=e8767a1e7a6667a, 66, 82; Saint-Quirin, "Les verriers de Languedoc," *Bulletin de la Société Languedocienne de Géographie* 28 (1905): 56.

[29] Edouard de Barthélemy, ed., *Correspondance inédite du Vicomte de Joyeuse, lieutenant général pour le roi en Languedoc* (Paris: Techener, 1876), 71, Joyeuse to Montmorency, Joyeuse, Sept 27, 1560.

[30] On Boisnormand, see Nicholas Bordenave, *Histoire de Béarn et Navarre*, ed. Paul Raymond (Paris: Renouard, 1874), 53–57, 84–87; Olhagaray, *Histoire de Foix, Béarn et Navarre*, 517, 520; Kingdon, *Geneva and the Coming*, 10, 44, 61, 73–73, 76, 109; Benedict and Fornerod, eds., *Organisation et action*, 12–13n and the sources cited there.

Francis II ordered Antoine to detain in the wake of the troubles at Amboise.[31] On May 6 Antoine sent back his regrets that he had not been able to do so because Boisnormand had left the region two weeks before the king's letter arrived, having been tipped off by a servant of one of those executed at Amboise that he had fallen under suspicion; of course, Antoine promised, he would be sure to arrest the pastor if he returned.[32] Because the king of Navarre did nothing of the sort when Boisnormand came back to Nérac in late June but instead attended the sermons that he allowed the minister to resume, it seems more probable that Boisnormand only left in May, as the Avertissement states, after Francis II's orders arrived. In any event, it would have been during the period when Boisnormand was well advised for his safety to keep his distance from Antoine that he adopted his new pseudonym and headed off to Provence. Because the *Histoire ecclésiastique* places him back in Nérac in late June, his mission to Provence would have lasted about eight weeks.[33]

Boisnormand's companion formerly called "La Fontaine" and then going under the name "Du Bois" is harder to identify. Both La Fontaine and Du Bois were common names for families and seigneuries alike. Both were also common pseudonyms adopted by early French ministers. If this companion of Boisnormand's was also a minister, one would be tempted to identify him as another experienced pastor who had spent time in Bernese territory before going to the Southwest, Jacques Fontaine or de La Fontaine, who founded the church of Agen early in 1560 and subsequently served the nearby church of Gontaud—were it not for the fact that this La Fontaine appears to have been in prison between May and October 1560.[34] This makes one wonder whether Robert Le Maçon dit La Fontaine, the minister of Orléans mentioned in Triou's deposition, might not have made the long trip to Nérac.

Finally, the seigneur de Mesmy, Denis d'Aix (var. d'Aytz), also lord of La Cobre and La Feuillade, was a thirty-something ex-mayor of Périgueux variant spellings of whose name crop up recurrently in

---

[31] See p. 28.
[32] Paris, ed., *Négociations*, 371, Antoine to Francis II, Pau, May 6, 1560.
[33] *HE*, I, 368 places his sermon in Antoine's and Condé's presence on June 22, but de Ruble, *Antoine et Jeanne*, II, 310 notes that Navarre was in Bordeaux until at least June 25 before returning to Nérac.
[34] *HE*, I, 365, 372.

reports about Protestant militancy in the Southwest from 1560 to 1562. La Planche lists "Du Mesny" as the captain for Périgord and the Limousin in the Amboise conspiracy.[35] The Parlement of Bordeaux sent several letters to court in the summer of 1560 begging for guidance about how to respond to the "factions mounted in this *pays* by the sieur de Meymy, now calling himself the sieur de Lisle," whose "disciples . . . are so well armed and furnished with harquebuses that men of our robe cannot touch them."[36] A striking passage in the *Histoire ecclésiastique* identifies "le sieur de Mesmy de Perigort" as the leading figure in convincing Antoine's vast clientage network in the Southwest to assemble hundreds of cavalry and thousands of footsoldiers late in 1560 to oppose the troops of the maréchal de Thermes when they were sent to attack Béarn and then meet up with Spanish troops—an admission from a Protestant source twenty years after the fact that important troop-raising efforts were made in the region, even if skepticism is in order about the purposes for which the troops were said to be raised.[37] In January 1561, the sieur de "Memy" led a group of individuals who demanded the use of a church in Villeneuve-sur-Lot for the Reformed.[38]

The Avertissement thus reveals a vigorous effort involving several agents extending from May through August to determine how many men could bear arms and to prepare them to do so. Once again, as in Triou's deposition, at least one pastor occupied an important role in the process, alongside noblemen. Régnier de La Planche would later report that the younger Maligny went to Provence to prepare the groundwork for the Lyon enterprise. Triou passed along the rumor that he went from Geneva to Germany. The Avertissement has him going instead to Flanders. At first glance, this might seem decidedly less probable a destination for recruiting support for the Huguenot cause than Germany. As we shall see, however, the Ferrar-

---

[35] La Planche, 134; d'Aubigné, *Histoire universelle*, I, 271: "Mesni."
[36] BnF, MS Français 15873, Parlement of Bordeaux to Francis II, Bordeaux, Aug 18, 1560, published in *Archives Historiques de la Gironde*, 13, 122–23. Throughout the summer of 1560, the Agenais, Périgord, and the Bazadois saw armed assemblies for worship and raids to liberate prisoners. In one such raid a goldsmith by the name of Mathieu Le Fleur who had been held for interrogation in connection with an "enterprise against His Majesty" was freed from the chateau of Bergerac. BnF, MS Français 15873, Parlement of Bordeaux to Francis II, Bordeaux, Aug 23, 1560, published in *Archives Historiques de la Gironde* 13 (1871–72): 123–24; de Ruble, *Antoine et Jeanne*, II, 283–84, 288.
[37] *HE*, I, 441.
[38] BnF, MS Français 15871, fo. 115.

ese ambassador picked up rumors going around court at the beginning of September of armed men assembled in Hainaut as well as in Normandy, Guyenne, and Dauphiné.[39] With the exception of this discrepancy about the younger Maligny's foreign destination, its suggestion that he made a long loop that took him from Toulouse through Provence and then northward into other countries before returning via Normandy and the Comtat Venaissin is broadly compatible with the information provided by these two other sources, as well as being an itinerary that could easily have allowed him to pass through Geneva en route, as Triou's testimony also suggests he did. While the younger Maligny made this long voyage, Mesmy gathered support in the Southwest. Through their efforts, thousands of men could indeed have been readied to come to the aid of the elder Maligny after he seized Lyon, as Triou reported that the conspirators expected would happen.

Indeed, potential reinforcements were on the move toward Lyon even as Triou and Constantin drew up the rolls for distributing arms to those already in the city. On September 5 (the day after Maligny's men were flushed from their hiding places in Lyon and left the city), the crown's lieutenant in Languedoc, the duke of Joyeuse, wrote from his house in the Vivarais that over the past two weeks more than 1200 soldiers raised in the surrounding region had gone off in small groups heading north into the mountains of Gévaudan and the Velay. "I sent a man there to learn their plan but all they will say is that great things will soon be seen. I think they are heading for Lyon," he wrote.[40] Further news from Joyeuse followed three days later. Just in the last few days, eight hundred to a thousand soldiers armed with pikes, corselets, and harquebuses had marched out of Montpellier and Nîmes in broad daylight. Another group of three hundred was spotted around the same time near Valvignères in the Vivarais. Some now thought their destination was the court, others Lyon, and still others that they were going to fight the king's men under La Motte Gondrin, who

---

[39] See p. 132. AS Modena, Ambasciatore Francia, 36 (III), fo. 2, Alvarotti to duke, Paris, Sept 3, 1560.
[40] Barthélemy, ed., *Correspondance de Joyeuse*, 63, Joyeuse to Montmorency, Joyeuse, Sept 5, 1560. The movement of armed men in the direction of Lyon had already touched off enough concern about a possible plot against the city that on September 3, the day before the weapons were noticed in Constantin's house, its important community of foreign merchants offered to pay for an extra contingent of watchmen to protect it against the mysterious plans of "certain people called Huguenots." The échevins declined the offer. Timothy D. Watson, "The Lyon City Council c. 1525–1575: Politics, Culture, Religion" (unpubl. D. Phil., Oxford, 1999), 191.

were being mustered to confront Montbrun and Mauvans.[41] These two adventurers meanwhile left Malaucène around September 5. The baron de La Garde in Provence and the papal vice-legate in Avignon deployed troops along the Rhône to prevent them from meeting up with any of the bands marching out of Bas-Languedoc, whereupon the Huguenot units began to scatter. When some crossed paths with the baron de Castres, they told him that they had letters from the grandees, their superiors, ordering them to return to their houses and stand ready for an upcoming summons to execute the "great venture."[42] After the plan to seize Lyon was countermanded and the men assembled there marched out of the town by night, those coming to their aid were apparently told to reverse course.

Further details about the mobilization of men in the region of Bas-Languedoc and the Vivarais emerge from a 150-page register of a judicial investigation into heretical and seditious activity in those areas carried out several months later by officials of Parlement of Toulouse.[43] The judges were sent to the region in November at the behest of Honorat de Savoie, count of Villars, who himself had been dispatched from court in October with troops and instructions to put an end to the disorders of all sorts that had troubled the area for several months. During the summer of 1560, Reformed churches had begun to gather openly in many towns of Bas-Languedoc, often protected by groups of armed men. Incidents of iconoclasm and threats against clergymen multiplied. The register of the judicial commission's investigation, which was kept by the chief royal prosecutor, is often difficult to decipher. While primarily recording the daily movements and activities of the prosecutor and his colleagues as they gathered evidence and issued decisions, it also reproduces or briefly summarizes some documents that passed through their hands during

---

[41] Barthélemy, ed., *Correspondance de Joyeuse*, 64–65, Joyeuse to Tournon, Joyeuse, Sept 8, 1560, and Joyeuse to Francis II, Joyeuse, Sept 8, 1560.
[42] BnF, MS Français 15873, fo. 56, Baron de La Garde to Cardinal Lorraine, L'Isle-sous-Sorgue, Sept 9, 1560 (also cited in Romier, *Conjuration*, 226).
[43] ADHG, 51 B 66, "Registre de monsieur le procureur general du roy pour le voiage par luy faict au bas pays de Lenguedoc par commandement du Roy et de sa court de parlement de Thoulouse contre les rebelles et esmotionaires en l'an mil cinq cens soixante." This document, written in a difficult hand, is extensively summarized and quoted in François Loirette, "Catholiques et protestants en Languedoc à la veille des guerres civiles (1560) d'après un document inédit," *Revue de l'Histoire de l'Eglise de France* 23 (1937): 503–25. My decipherment of the original occasionally disagrees with Loirette's.

the two months of their investigation. These summaries are often broad and imprecise. Most frustrating, they rarely specify which individuals engaged in which actions when they report indictments or judgments against hundreds of people. Thus, a summons issued to 313 men and women of Montpellier indicts them collectively for staging and attending public preaching, celebrating communion openly in the Ecole Mage, petitioning the town's officers and the bishop for a building for their services, seizing the church of Saint Mathieu when this was not granted them, mounting their own night watch, introducing outside soldiers and vagabonds into the city, smashing the images in Saint Mathieu, disrupting the sermons of a Catholic preacher, attempting to break down the gate to the bishop's residence, and creating "captains and *centeniers* and mounted *enseignes* [the word meant both a military unit and the standard under which it marched], drums and fifes . . . to carry out their damnable . . . designs . . . and even to be present at the implementation of the accursed, pernicious and treasonous enterprise of Lyon, of which they were among the principals and where they went with a fraction of their henchmen having previously imposed dues and raised money."[44] For all of its frustrating imprecision, the register still indicates through general indictments such as this and through several nuggets of more specific testimony that organized contingents left for Lyon from Montpellier, Nîmes, Anduze, Pézenas, Montagnac, and Annonay.

Where further details about these mobilization efforts are provided, they often suggest that the troops were outfitted and paid by leaders of the local Reformed church. This is especially clear in the case of Montpellier, whose church rapidly emerged as one of the largest and most aggressive after its establishment on the consistorial–synodal model on February 8, 1560, just after Maillane passed through the region recruiting for the Amboise enterprise. The Montpellier indictment specifies that, "[Francois] Maupeau and [Claude] Formis were the deacons of the voyage of Lyon. [Pierre] Combes and Formis [furnished] the money and [Guillaume] Sandre distributed it to those who went there. . . . Sandre went there with Saint Jehan."[45] More central figures in the local church could not have been named than

---

[44] ADHG, 51 B 66, fo. 45; Loirette, "Catholiques et protestants," 510.
[45] ADHG, 51 B 66, fo. 16v.

Maupeau, a lawyer; and Formy, a medical doctor. They were the two most important deacons named when Guillaume Mauget came from Nîmes in February and established the congregation. Throughout the spring and summer of that year, they led services and exhorted the assembly when no pastor was present. When the *juge criminel* visited a public gathering of the congregation in July 1560 to warn it that it was violating the law, Maupeau rose and acted as the church's spokesman in requesting a building for its worship services. Both subsequently became pastors and helped found several churches in the region.[46] The wealthy Pierre Combes de Montaigu, seigneur de Combas and a bourgeois of Montpellier, also may well have been a member of the consistory; he certainly was by November 1561. If he was not already as important a figure within the Reformed church as Maupeau and Formy, he would become one soon. He represented the church at several important assemblies and negotiations in 1561–63. During the period of Protestant domination in the First Civil War, he was elected first consul of the city.[47] The two men who actually set off for Lyon thanks to the funds furnished by Combes and Formy— Guillaume Sandre, seigneur de Saint-Georges; and Louis Toyras, seigneur de Saint-Jean-de-Gardonnenque—were lesser noblemen from the surrounding area that other sources also identify as being among the leading fomenters of sedition in the region.[48] The heavy involvement of the church's leadership in raising men and money for Lyon and the large numbers of men reported by Joyeuse to have been mobilized in the city suggest that the Montpellier congregation went all in on the plotting not long after the church took shape in February 1560.

Less precisely, the list of Nîmes residents accused of involvement in the various disorders of the era identifies Guillaume de Sauzet as the "leader of the schemes and raids (*conducteur des menees et courses*)"

---

[46] *HE*, I, 248, 376, 378; Louise Guiraud, *Etudes sur la Réforme à Montpellier* (Montpellier: Valat, 1918), I, 129–33, 137–38, 146–48; II, *Preuves*, 38, 40, 256, 262, 351, 355.

[47] *HE*, III, 169, 201; Guiraud, *Réforme à Montpellier*, II, *Preuves*, 225, 262–64, 266, 374. Combes would still occupy an important place in the church in 1570. Ibid., I, 401.

[48] Guiraud, *Réforme à Montpellier*, I, 147; BnF, Nouvelles Acquisitions Françaises 7716, Villars to Constable Montmorency, Beaucaire, Oct 22, 1560, fo. 374v (reference to Saint-Jean and Cardet as "chefs et principaux fauteurs des emotions par deca"). Might these two and a third nobleman mentioned in this document, the baron de Fons, have been the three captains who, according to the Avertissement, visited Toulouse with Cardet and the younger Maligny?

in that city.⁴⁹ Sauzet, a lawyer, was a Nîmois counterpart to Formy, Maupeau, and Combes.⁵⁰ The local consistory register, which survives for 1561–63, variously lists him as an elder, a deacon and (in February 1562) "the longest-serving deacon in the church." He was so effective a spokesman for the church that the congregations of the region chose him as their deputy to court between May and September 1561. His name also appears in the Maillane deposition, which indicates that he was the deacon to whom Maillane made his recruiting pitch for the conspiracy of Amboise when he visited Nîmes in January 1560.⁵¹ How Sauzet responded to the appeal is not specified there, but since the minister Mauget confessed that he had a very hard time keeping church members from joining the Amboise enterprise even though Maillane only spoke to one deacon,⁵² it is hard to escape the conclusion that Sauzet not only supported the venture but deployed his powerful skills of persuasion to win people for it, before helping to organize the contingent that, according to Joyeuse, marched out of Nîmes in broad daylight hundreds strong in early September. The Toulouse register shows at the very least that the local authorities believed that he became the leader of some form of armed plotting at some point in the year. The very long list of men and women accused broadly of "sedition" in Nîmes also includes "two gentlemen of Mallane who are brothers of Mr de Mallane." Although their first names are not provided, these were in all likelihood Jean and Robert, who lived alongside Ardoin in Geneva for much of the 1550s. If so, we may wonder if their reappearance in their region of origin was not linked to the conspiratorial activity of the period and if they did not play some organizational role in it—a suspicion that would seem confirmed by a passing reference made by the sixteenth-century Montpellier-based historian Jacques de Montagne to "the two sons of the seigneur de Maillane of Beaucaire who went to Geneva to aid the enterprise against Lyon and then returned."⁵³ Ardoin himself, according to his

---

[49] ADHG, 51 B 66, fo. 11.
[50] Nicolas Fornerod and I provide a capsule biography of him with full references in "Les députés des Églises réformées à la cour en 1561–1562," *Revue Historique* 315 (2013): 330. This was written before I consulted the Toulouse register and so does not note this document's imputation to him of a leadership role in the tumults of 1560.
[51] Naef, 379–80.
[52] See p. 67.
[53] Claude de Vic and Joseph Vaissette, *Histoire générale de Languedoc* (Paris: J. Vincent, 1730–45), V, 196, citing "Montagne hist manus. de l'Europ, livre I, ch. 9," on which see Hauser, *Sources de l'histoire de France*, III, 16, 65.

testimony in Geneva, was also in unspecified parts of Languedoc from February through November.[54]

In Pézenas, too, the mobilization of men for the march northward can be connected to an important figure in the local church. Here foodstuffs to provision the soldiers sent to Lyon were reported as stockpiled in the house of the congregation's syndic (legal spokesman), a merchant by the name of Corbier, who then led the armed band that set off for Lyon.[55] In Anduze, another locality where the Reformed cause rapidly took deep root, testimony from the father superior of the local Franciscan monastery reveals that shortly before the seventeen soldiers raised and paid for by its Protestants set off northward through the mountains, a crowd came to the convent and demanded in the name of the Reformed assembly that he turn over church vestments and ornaments to be used to pay and clothe the men. "Oh what nice breeches, doublets and banners we can make!" some in the crowd exclaimed when they first glimpsed the clerical copes. In this instance, two civic officials served as spokesmen for the group.[56]

Very few of the rank-and-file who marched off are identified by name, but they appear to have been a mix of nobles and ordinary townsmen of diverse occupations. The information about Nîmes reveals that during the summer of 1560 a band of thirty to fifty soldiers raised by "seditious fellows," including the Seigneur de Cardet (mentioned in the Avertissement as arriving in Toulouse with the young Maligny), appeared in the city and regularly escorted the minister Arnaud Banc to his sermons. One suspects that members of this band, reinforced by others enrolled within the city, formed the core of the group that left from there. Leading one of the units was Jean Coderc, "an *enseigne* of the huguenots of Nîmes" according to the Parlement's register, further identified in another source of the period as a "cobbler who quit his trade to go fight." He would subsequently be arrested and face several months in prison under interrogation about the conspiracies.[57] The Parlement register also identifies ten

---

[54] Naef, 218, 376.
[55] ADHG, 51 B 66, fos. 51, 70; Loirette, "Catholiques et protestants," 514.
[56] ADHG, 51 B 66, fo. 35; Loirette, "Catholiques et protestants," 517. The spokesmen were "le baille nommé Vabres et un consul nomme Barthelemy qui est appothicaire." It is not known if they were also members of the consistory. For another instance of a church (Montagnac) outfitting recruits with clothing, see ADHG, 51 B 66, fo. 50; Loirette, "Catholiques et protestants," 521.
[57] ADHG, 51 B 66, fos. 12-13; Léon Ménard, *Histoire civile, ecclésiastique, et littéraire de la ville de Nismes* (7 vols., Paris: H. D. Chaubert, 1750–58), IV, *Preuves*, 2; *MC*, II, 392.

men from Annonay who allegedly set out for Lyon under the Reformed banner. Those for whom we have an indication of their status were the notary and *procureur du roi* Antoine Faure, the *greffier* Etienne Chaumet, Chaumet's nephew, the merchant Guillaume Cussonel, Cussonel's gardener, and a young barber whose name is not given. Faure is known to have allowed his house to be used for some of the first Reformed assemblies.[58]

Drawing together the administrative and judicial documentation from Languedoc, the diplomatic correspondence, Calvin's letters, and Régnier de La Planche, the following picture emerges of how the second round of plotting took shape during the months between April and August for which Triou's deposition offers only a few bits of hearsay evidence. Some of those who had been mobilized in March escaped from Amboise believing that they had to carry on the enterprise under a new leader. By May regrouping had begun on several fronts: in the Loire valley, with the drafting and surreptitious presentation to the queen mother of justificatory petitions, as well as the probable organization of groups of the discontented; in Provence, with Boisnormand's trip; and more broadly, with the elder Maligny's assumption of a leadership role whose precise character escapes us but looks similar to La Renaudie's before Amboise. Broadsides and pamphlets vilifying the Guise family in hyperbolic terms, some of them written by Hotman, also proliferated in April and May. As before, the goal of those involved in these clandestine actions remained twofold: to obtain some alteration of the religious situation, and to restructure the government by removing the Guises from power. But how, strategically, could this be effected? The initial tactics adopted by the more fervid conspirators are suggested by the statement of the court furrier Le Camus, quoted by La Planche, that they intended to seize one of the provinces of the kingdom, fortify themselves there, and circulate writings in so many languages that every nation would learn the merit of their cause.

---

[58] ADHG, 51 B 66, fo. 59v; Loirette, "Catholiques et protestants," 522; *HE*, I, 388; Eugène Arnaud, *Histoire des protestants du Vivarais et du Velay* (2 vols., Paris: Grassart, 1888), I, 22–23. The others named were Maître Noel Cousturier, Leonard Larmurier (*armurier* may be his occupation not his surname), Pierre Lebrun (or Labrut), and a certain Villefuesne, reportedly injured in the melee at Lyon and boasting of killing two Catholics.

By June, Condé had joined up with Antoine, while Calvin was promising Sturm and Hotman that he would push the elder Bourbon brother to stake the claim to power they believed he had. Calvin and Beza had also probably by then entered into contact with the Malignys, started to raise funds for a large new venture, and begun to debate with them just what form it should take. A month later Beza left for Nérac to be by Antoine's side. In his later apologia to Coligny, Calvin would write coyly "we have also heard talk of some sort of tumult that happened in Lyon." If it had been up to him, "that frivolity (*legereté*) would have been quietly allayed. Be that as it may, I never saw the person who is blamed for it." His reference to "the fervid one" in his September letter to Beza suggests that he had indeed tried to restrain Maligny but could not stop him from going ahead with his plan to infiltrate men into Lyon. And from what we know about Maligny's movements, it is possible that he never passed through Geneva, so Calvin indeed may never have actually laid eyes on him. What the letter does not say was that Calvin probably saw his younger brother and close collaborator, who did come through Geneva, and that even if Calvin never met the elder Maligny face-to-face, he had plenty of opportunity to communicate with him via letters. And not just to communicate, to collaborate. Even if Calvin and Beza thought that the Lyon venture was not the optimal plan, their ultimate willingness to work with the Malignys was shown by their financing of these efforts and the fact that Calvin's close friend Guillaume Trie sought out Triou when a man was needed to go to Lyon to help prepare the venture.

Meanwhile, that Boisnormand should have headed for Provence when he left Antoine's retinue ten weeks earlier is not surprising. He could expect to find allies for some sort of larger militant action there, since the province had seen an armed band under Mauvans take to the field at the same time that the main event of the Amboise conspiracy was supposed to occur in the Loire valley. Soon Dauphiné emerged as another province where local militancy arose. During the Easter season, the Reformed of several major cities took over churches or convents and, under the protection of armed nobles, used them for public Reformed preaching and the celebration of the Lord's Supper. When a crackdown followed, Montbrun resisted arrest, rallied supporters, and turned his chateau into an armed stronghold. Still later in the spring, as we have seen, newly founded churches in Bas-Languedoc and the Vivarais moved quickly toward ever more aggressive demands for recognition and displayed arms in public. As the younger Maligny, Mesmy, and perhaps others circulated around different parts of the country, it is easy to see how they could have drawn these groups into a larger common project and convinced them to provide men for it. The units that went out from the cities and towns of the area from Montpellier up through the Cévennes to the Vivarais were most often, although not always, led by noblemen, but the rank and file, as in Lyon, were townsmen of widely varying status recruited by leading members of the local Reformed churches, who in one instance even outfitted them with banners and cloaks made of recycled clerical vestments. Meanwhile, as the letters of the Italian ambassadors suggest, those at court feared, probably with good reason, that thirst for revenge among the kin and retainers of those executed at Amboise also spurred noblemen to associate with these efforts.

One of the most obscure aspects of this revival of Protestant plotting is whether organizational efforts similar to those that can be observed in the Midi were undertaken in the northern half of the kingdom as well, and, if so, just how geographically and socially extensive they were. As we have seen, Throckmorton in April mentioned Normandy, Brittany, and Poitou among the provinces where people were willing to make great offers to Arran if he would come lead them. The Avertissement reports the younger Maligny to have visited Normandy, a center of Reformed strength. Six months later, Calvin would be confident that the nobility of Brittany, Anjou, and Poitou would stand by Antoine.[59] The problem is that no record of a judicial investigation comparable to that for Bas-Languedoc survives for any other province, while surviving administrative correspondence from the northern half of the kingdom is also far less abundant than for the Midi.

Brittany is one important exception to this last statement, for a number of letters of its governor, Jean de Brosses, Duke of Etampes, have been preserved. Brittany was also the native province of both

---

[59] See p. 120.

La Garaye and Goulaine. An unspecified number of the province's noblemen fell under suspicion of having participated in the Amboise conspiracy after they left the region in March just prior to the scheduled strike. Over the next two months, Etampes and his subordinates watched these men closely when they returned and sent along warnings about the possibility of new "follies" and of communication between "those who made such a great scandal at Amboise" and Queen Elizabeth. They searched in vain for Maligny, Stuart, and Condé when ordered to arrest them after receiving incorrect warnings that they had taken shelter in the province.[60] In June and July, a note of genuine alarm crept into Etampes's letters, although he may simply have been trying to extract more money from the royal treasury. With the fighting going on in Scotland and a number of Breton ships having recently been seized at sea, he warned Guise on June 16 that the English had assembled so many men and vessels across the Channel that "I cannot think their enterprise is only against Scotland." Rumors were circulating that something was being prepared in Poitou and Guyenne. To protect the province, he said, he needed money to improve its coastal defenses. A month later, on July 20, his tone grew more beseeching. Warnings were coming "from all directions and even from those who trade with the [British] isles about the great preparations being made by the English and their determination to carry out their enterprise soon."[61] For all his alarm about preparations underway in England, Poitou, or Guyenne, however, calm seems to have prevailed within the province. His letters from the same two months report no worrisome signs of men on the march or incidents of trouble comparable to those in the Midi, with the exception of a purely local midsummer episode of religious violence in Rennes. At just the moment in September when Joyeuse wrote about the Protestant bands from Languedoc passing through the mountains of the

---

[60] Dom Hyacinthe Morice, ed., *Memoires pour servir de preuves à l'histoire ecclésiastique et civile de Bretagne* (3 vols., Paris: C. Osmont, 1742–46), III, col. 1234, 1244, Guise to Etampes, Marmoutier, April 23, "1559" (clearly misdated), Hierosme de Carné to Etampes, Brest, April 21, 1560; Lublinskaya and Chichkine, eds., *Documents*, 59–60, 71, 82–83, 111, Etampes to Guise, Lamballe, April 23 and May 15, 1560, Francis II to Etampes, Marchenoir, June 12, 1560, Etampes to Francis II, Lamballe, June 21, 1560.

[61] Lublinskaya and Chichkine, eds., *Documents*, 91–92, 143, Etampes to Guise, Montfort, June 16, 1560, Etampes to Francis II, Lamballe, July 20, 1560.

Velay and Gévaudan, Etampes reassured the crown, "I don't see anything moving," when told to be on the alert for new enterprises.[62]

Anjou, we will soon discover, witnessed arms stockpiling and concerted action by suspected veterans of the Amboise conspiracy in the fall. For every other part of northern France, no traces appear in the scanty evidence of organizational efforts like those in the South. Whatever the full geographic extent of preparation for a new enterprise over the course of the months from April onward, however, it was ample enough for Jean Sturm to inform the king of Denmark on August 19, "The Gallic conspiracy, suppressed in the first outbreak, seems to be secretly increased and strengthened, and what before was advanced by secret plots now seems ready to erupt into open war."[63]

If this well-informed schoolmaster–diplomat–activist was aware that a new eruption was brewing, just what form would it take? It seems clear that Maligny's planned strike was animated by the same general idea that Le Camus had enunciated several months previously. First, an area would be seized, fortified, and made a base from which to state the malcontents' case and organize a meeting that would be called an Estates-General. Then the Guises would be brought to justice and changes would be effected in both the government and religion. The strike also was meant to force the vacillating Antoine to declare himself for such an effort. All this can be inferred from several sources: Triou's explanation of the purpose of Maligny's plan to seize Lyon, Calvin's subsequent explanation to Bullinger that Beza had been sent to Nérac in part to push the sluggish and in part to restrain the turbulent, and finally the clear evidence from Calvin's correspondence that he was collaborating in the plans to launch the Maligny affair until he received Beza's instructions to call that enterprise off as an even better action now seemed possible. However, that aid was expected to come from Dauphiné, Provence, and Geneva hardly suffices to substantiate Romier's contention that Maligny

---

[62] Lublinskaya and Chichkine, eds., *Documents*, 116, Etampes to Guise, Quimperlé, June 27, 1560: "combien que de beaucoup de lieux je soys adverty qu'il y en a de maulvaise voulonté, si est ce que je n'ay poinct entendu qu'il y ait personne qui se remue pour faire aucune assemblee, au moins dedans ce pais"; 158, Etampes to Guise, Rennes, Aug 5, 1560; 219, 227, Etampes to Francis II and to Guise, Lamballe, Sept 15, 1560: "je ne voye qu'il s'emeve rien"; 260, Etampes to Francis II, Lamballe, Oct 15, 1560: "de sedition, s'il n'y a des voulontez bien couvertes, je n'en pense poinct ou bien peu qui y aient voulonté."
[63] *CO*, XVIII, col. 168.

sought together with Montbrun and Mauvans to make Lyon the capital of a canton allied with neighboring Geneva.

The new plan that superseded Maligny's operation against Lyon and about which Beza spoke so hopefully and yet so vaguely in his letter of August 25 is harder to reconstruct with confidence. De Ruble thought that:

> At the time of the Assembly of Fontainebleau, according to all indications, Antoine's plan was to touch off local insurrections from Bordeaux to Lyon to ignite the Midi, which would bring him soldiers and weaken royal power. With support from Provence, Dauphiné, Haut-Languedoc, Lyon and Geneva, he probably intended to assemble the units of the Count of Tende from Provence, Montbrun's and Mauvans' victorious bands, the Lyon conspirators and the seditious in Guyenne to march on Bordeaux and make it his *place d'armes*. With control of the sea and the possibility of receiving aid from the queen of England, he then could advance northward through cities won over to reform to the Loire and put pressure on the Constable Montmorency to join him. Squeezed into its last bastions, the court would soon have to capitulate.[64]

Romier, the other historian to think long and hard about this question, suggested a similar but not identical, plan:

> [Once the Bourbon brothers called off the plot against Lyon] they resolved to leave Guyenne when the moment was ripe . . . to carry their cause before the Estates General. Their plan can be inferred from the reports of the crown agents watching them and the avowals of their own servants. They meant to make the journey to the Estates a demonstration of their strength, traveling slowly to give their partisans time to join them. At each stop along the way, bands of soldiers and gentlemen would come augment their retinue, . . . [including] dissident nobles from Guyenne, Saintonge, the Limousin, and Poitou, contingents from the Southeast and others from Anjou and Brittany. When they finally reached the court, the Bourbons would find a large party of the great lords there, even in Francis II's immediate entourage, won over to their cause in advance. . . . But for this to work, the king of Navarre needed to have, even before leaving his *gouvernement*, a retinue large enough to intimidate whatever companies the Guises could quickly dispatch in his direction. This is why Maligny and Montbrun were ordered to head secretly for Limoges, of which Antoine was viscount through his wife. According

---

[64] De Ruble, *Antoine et Jeanne*, II, 335–36.

to warnings that Francis II would receive in early October, troops were also supposed to gather in Poitou.[65]

De Ruble's implication in the venture of the governor of Provence, Claude de Savoie, count of Tende, seems improbable in light of everything else known about his behavior in this period. I am unaware of evidence suggesting Bordeaux as a central rallying point or indicating that Montbrun was instructed to head for Limoges. With these exceptions, these two overlapping reconstructions accord well with what can be inferred from the surviving evidence. The core idea appears to have been to have Navarre and Condé proceed toward court with a growing retinue of horsemen and foot soldiers in the hope of appearing so powerful that all those who disliked or mistrusted the Guises would turn against them, agree to a restructuring of power at court, and consent to consult with the political nation about how properly to reform the kingdom. In light of what we have subsequently learned about Calvin and Beza's involvement with the Maligny affair, it seems important to point out that such a plan fits with the strategic analysis of the situation at the French court that Calvin laid out in his letter of June 8 to Hotman and Sturm in which he promised to prod Antoine to claim the reins of state. As we shall shortly see, it also fits with the contents of several letters of Calvin's over the subsequent months in which the reformer calls the strategy his and Beza's plan. Contrary to what de Ruble and Romier assert, the strategy may have been that of the Geneva reformers more than of Antoine and Condé.

---

[65] Romier, *Conjuration*, 230–31.

Five

From Lyon to Orléans

No sooner had Beza dispatched his letter of August 25 telling Calvin that the enterprise of Lyon needed to be called off, but that he hoped Navarre would embrace "our incomparably better plan," than two events at court completely scrambled the situation.

First, the Assembly of Notables that met at Fontainebleau between August 21 and 26 decided that the best way to address the serious problems facing the crown was to convoke the Estates-General. The decision, announced in letters patent dated August 31,[1] undercut any claim that Protestant conspirators might subsequently make that a gathering they assembled was a proper meeting of the Estates convoked because those around the king were ignoring their constitutional duty to summon a meeting when the monarch was underage.

Second, on August 26 or 27, a courier of Navarre's, Jacques de La Sague, was stopped near Etampes after leaving the house of François de Vendôme, Vidame de Chartres, the cousin of the Maligny brothers and also a relative of the baron of Castelnau. On La Sague were letters between the vidame, Navarre and Condé, some in cipher, whose contents aroused suspicion. La Sague was tortured and talked. The vidame was quickly arrested and placed in the Bastille. Couriers rushed the seized letters and information to Fontainebleau, where the king's council examined them at an urgent meeting on the night of August

---

[1] Théophile Boutiot and Albert Babeau, eds., *Documents inédits des archives de Troyes et relatifs aux États-Généraux* (Troyes: L. Lacroix, 1878), 25.

29.² The next day, the king's secretaries penned a letter ordering Antoine to bring his brother Condé to court. The king's missive only said that numerous mutually corroborating reports had reached him indicating Condé's involvement in "schemes and operations . . . prejudicial to my service and the safety of my state." He wanted to get to the bottom of the matter and believed that Navarre was the appropriate person to accompany his brother to court, since he had sway over him and had assured the king of his desire to serve him in any way possible just after the conspiracy of Amboise.³ A letter of the 31st to the duke of Savoy shows that the crown actually had more precise information and wider suspicions. It had been learned, it said, that captains had been induced in Condé's name to take up arms at the end of the upcoming month. Navarre was also reportedly implicated. Queen Elizabeth was suspected of providing some of the funds.⁴ Ambassadors' letters just after the vidame was arrested also spoke of fears that the sedition of Amboise was about to be renewed in many parts of the country, that Montbrun was headed for Lyon, that armed men were on the march in Guyenne under the leadership of the vidame's brother-in-law, Antoine de Grammont, and that more men were standing by in Hainaut and Normandy.⁵ Fearing that Antoine might not comply with the summons, the crown planned its delivery with minute care. The trusted courtier charged with the mission to Nérac, Antoine de Crussol, was told exactly what to say. Soldiers were stationed along his route in case armed backup was needed. The provincial governors deemed reliable were warned that a new conspiracy was afoot and ordered to mobilize their ordinance companies in strategic locations.⁶ After Crussol arrived, he instructed Antoine to

---

² *ADE*, I, 346, 357, 368, 379, Chantonnay to Philip II, Melun, Aug 31, Fontainebleau, Sept 1, Paris, Sept 8, 1560, Sebastiano Gualterio to Octaviano Rovere, Melun, Aug 31, 1560; *CSP Ven*, VII, 249–51, Michiel to doge and Senate, Melun, Aug 30, 1560; AS Modena, Ambasciatore Francia, 36 (II), fo. 66, Alvarotti to duke, Paris, Aug 29, 1560; Hector de La Ferrière, ed., *Lettres de Catherine de Médicis* (Paris: Imprimerie Nationale, 1880), I, 147, Francis II and Catherine de Medici to Crussol, undated; de Ruble, *Antoine et Jeanne*, II, 322–30; Romier, *Conjuration*, 215–16.
³ *MC*, I, 572–73, Francis II to Antoine, Fontainebleau, Aug 30, 1560.
⁴ Lublinskaya and Chichkine, eds., *Documents*, 185, Francis II to Emmanuel Philibert, Fontainebleau, Aug 31, [1560].
⁵ AS Mantova, Archivio Gonzaga 652, H. Strozzi to duke, Paris, Sept 2, 1560; AS Modena, Ambasciatore Francia, 36 (III), fo. 2, Alvarotti to duke, Paris, Sept 3, 1560.
⁶ Paris, ed., *Négociations*, 483–86, "Instructions de M. de Crussol allant par ordre du roi vers le roi de Navarre," Aug 30, 1560; Joseph Garnier, ed., *Correspondance de la mairie de Dijon* (3 vols., Dijon, 1868–70), II, 13–15, Francis II to bailiff of Dijon, Fontainebleau, Sept 1, 1560; de Ruble, *Antoine et Jeanne*, II, 358–64; La Planche, 564–66.

bring along as well four ministers: Beza, Boisnormand, Pierre Henri Barran, and the preceptor of the young Henry of Navarre, La Gaucherie.[7]

Within another eight days, the stockpile of arms was found in Constantin's house in Lyon, Maligny and his men were flushed from the city, those left behind like Triou were arrested, and their interrogation yielded more incriminating evidence of Condé's, Calvin's, and perhaps Antoine's involvement in conspiratorial activity. The situation facing those involved in Protestant plotting had changed in a fortnight. Plans had to be rethought.

As the information gleaned by the royal officials about the destination of the armed bands on the march has already suggested, plans indeed appear to have been rethought. On September 5, Joyeuse wrote from the Vivarais that he believed the men heading through the mountains were going to Lyon. Three days later, he was less certain; some of his informants thought they might be headed to Lyon, others that they were going to fight La Motte Gondrin in Dauphiné, still others that they were going to court. On September 9, the baron de La Garde sent along the baron de Castres's report that they were returning home to wait for further orders. The Avertissement of circa September 13–19 warned that a new gathering had now been decided upon for Poitiers in November. Letters from Villars in October appeared to confirm this. They reported bands of troops moving through the mountains of Forez and Auvergne for a rendezvous at Poitiers at the end of the month.[8]

When Crussol arrived in Nérac on September 8 and delivered the king's summons, the first prince of the blood and those around him were between a rock and a hard place. Antoine could obey the summons, go to the king with Condé and a small retinue, and attempt to establish his and his brother's innocence—or, if this was impossible, hope that the royal blood running through their veins would save them from severe punishment. Or he could do what those who had

---

[7] HE, I, 371. Nothing appears to be known about La Gaucherie other than his work as the tutor of the future Henry IV, which lasted intermittently for seven years. On this see Jean-Pierre Babelon, Henri IV (Paris: Fayard, 1982), 84, 99, 105, 111–14, 117, 134. For Barran, see p. 113.

[8] See pp. 118–19; BnF, MS 500 Colbert 27, fo. 51, Villars to cardinal of Lorraine and Guise, Beaucaire, Oct 12, 1560; BnF, MS Français 3157, fo. 147v (also MS Nouvelles Acquisitions Françaises 7716, p. 355, published in Paris, ed., Négociations, 657), Villars to Constable Montmorency, Beaucaire, Oct 12, 1560.

been pushing him to take the lead in demanding change in the composition of the king's council had urged him to do for some time: Gather the large number of men they claimed to be able to mobilize and try to force his way into a position of greater authority, after which the Guises could be put on trial and changes could be made in the king's policies. For this course of action to succeed, it had always been essential that the forces mustered outnumber those loyal to the existing government. Now, the crown would be on its guard. There would be no more chance of surprise.

Faced with this difficult choice, the partisans of action within the Protestant movement continued to push Antoine to make the bolder choice. The fullest evidence for this from a Protestant source comes once again from Régnier de La Planche. According to him, Beza, who remained by Antoine's side throughout September, urged him to do all he could to ensure that the meeting of the Estates-General brought the Guises to judgment rather than being manipulated by them to other ends.[9] Unidentified others told him that if he gave the word, "people would rise up from all parts to put him in a position of strength at this meeting of the Estates." The sudden developments of the preceding weeks nonetheless so frightened his chancellor Amaury Bouchard, who previously had urged inviting Beza to Nérac, that he now advised his master to obey the king's summons. Antoine decided to postpone making a decision for as long as possible. He set out for court with a substantial retinue and let it be known to those who urged action that he would not make a final decision until he reached Limoges. There, seven to eight hundred nobles "well mounted, armed and equipped" appealed to him to "declare himself and publish his intentions to all of the nobility of France, as he had so often given hope he might do." They told him that six to seven thousand foot soldiers from Gascony, Poitou, and the coastal areas around Marennes were enrolled under captains, another three to four thousand soldiers could be expected to come from Languedoc and Provence, and as many more from Normandy, all paid in advance. The strategy they proposed was to separate the king from the coun-

---

[9] Specifically, and in characteristically convoluted fashion, Régnier de La Planche wrote that Beza urged him "de faire en toutes sortes que la conclusion de l'assemblée de Fontainebleau touchant les Estats fust bien asseuree et executee contre ceux qui jamais ne l'auroyent accordee qu'en intention de s'en servir, au lieu de s'assujettir au jugement d'icelle." La Planche, 603.

cilors around him, take Orléans and hold the Estates there, and at the same time secure Bourges as a place of retreat in case the rest of the plan failed. The Guises were so detested, they assured Navarre, that the majority of the gendarmerie would swing around to his side if he just declared himself the protector of the king and the kingdom.[10]

The details furnished here by Régnier de La Planche are hard to corroborate. The considerable evidence available about the route that Antoine followed from Nérac to court does not indicate that he passed through Limoges. Where many subsequent Protestant historians bestowed credibility on what La Planche revealed about the conspiracy of Amboise by repeating it in their works, none reiterated these assertions about a meeting at Limoges or the number of men ready to march. On the other hand, we do have evidence of mobilization efforts in the coastal areas of Saintonge and Aunis. The governor of La Rochelle, Guy de Chabot, count of Jarnac, dispatched two letters in September reporting that several ministers "criss-crossed the region (*ont couru le pays*) to persuade people to act contrary to their duty to the king" before deciding at a series of night-time meetings to carry out their "intention" at the end of September.[11] The report that pastors were involved in the development of this plan is especially revealing in that its author was himself a Protestant who ordered the demolition of all idolatrous images in his town of Jarnac,[12] albeit a Protestant who would remain loyal to the crown throughout the years 1560–63; we are not dealing here simply with a hostile stereotype circulated by Catholic controversialists. On September 14 Sturm updated the king of Denmark: "I saw letters in which it is written that, if the King of Navarre is compelled to come [to court], he will come with troops of twenty thousand of the best soldiers, and if this should happen, we would hear of a bloody war."[13] Theodore Beza's treatment of this period in the *Histoire ecclésiastique des Eglises*

---

[10] La Planche, 600–05.
[11] Just one of Jarnac's two letters survives. It reveals the existence of the prior missive through its indication that the courier bearing that letter had been held up and relieved of his packet. Frustratingly, the second letter provides no details about what was planned, although it shows Jarnac to have been confident that he had learned the agitators' intent. Lublinskaya and Chichkine, eds., *Documents*, 249, Jarnac to Guise, La Rochelle, Sept 18, 1560.
[12] Philippe Vincent, *Recherches sur les commencemens et les premiers progres de la Reformation en la ville de La Rochelle* (Rotterdam: Abraham Acher, 1693), 79–80.
[13] *CO*, XVIII, col. 184.

réformées au royaume de France is also revealing by its very terseness. For the portion of that work devoted to the conspiracy of Amboise, he lifted whole paragraphs from La Planche. Since he was at Antoine's side in the summer and early fall of 1560, he could have provided an account of both the Maligny affair and any subsequent planned or proposed military operations that were even more detailed than La Planche's. But he did not say a word about the Maligny affair, and all that he wrote about Antoine's response to the king's summons was that "the king of Navarre with the prince his brother, *despite all they were urged (quoy quon leur allegast)* [italics mine], set out for the court toward the end of September."[14] Even twenty years after the fact, Beza did not want his counsel to be known, nor to implicate others. His phrasing nonetheless confirms that other courses of action were advocated.

The crown certainly continued to worry about a major operation such as that warned of by Jarnac and the anonymous Avertissement. In an emotional two-day meeting on October 4 and 5, the king and queen mother told the knights of the order of Saint Michael that a new plot was underway and had them pledge their loyalty. An ample contingent of troops was moved to Poitiers, where, according to a report passed along by the Spanish ambassador, forty to a hundred noble conspirators had already taken up lodgings. The king's lieutenants in other provinces were warned of the danger and told to keep their ordinance companies on alert. Efforts were launched to raise additional troops from Switzerland, prompting Bullinger to ask Calvin whether a treasonous conspiracy against the king was truly underfoot, as royal letters to the Swiss had asserted, or whether the Guise brothers were scheming to harm "the faithful . . . [who] want the ancient law of the kingdom restored," as many in the Protestant cantons suspected.[15] The king and queen mother set out for Orléans with a large

---

[14] *HE*, I, 371.

[15] AS Modena, Ambasciatore Francia 36 (III), fo. 22, Alvarotti to duke, Poissy, Oct 6, 1560; BnF, MS 500 Colbert 27, fos. 17–28, Francis II to nobles of Poitou, Lude, (published in "Lettres adressées à Jean et Guy de Daillon, comte du Lude, gouverneurs de Poitou de 1543 à 1557 et de 1557 à 1585," *Archives Historiques du Poitou*, 12 (1882): 94, Burie, Thermes, and Duras, Saint-Germain-en-Laye, Oct 6, 1560, Burie to Francis II, n.p., n.d. [c. Oct 7, 1560] (published in de Ruble, *Antoine et Jeanne*, II, 478–79); Paris, ed., *Négociations*, 642–45, 648–49, "Instructions pour le Sr de Montpezat allant devers la maréchal de Termes" and Francis II to Villars, Saint-Germain-en-Laye, Oct 6, 1560; Lublinskaya and Chichkine, eds., *Documents*, 260, Etampes to Francis II, Lamballe, Oct 15, 1560; Lestocquoy, ed., *Correspondance des nonces*, Gualterio to Borromeo, n.p., Oct 11, 1560; *ADE*, I, 437–38, Chantonnay to Philip II, Paris, October 8, 1560; *CO*, XVIII, col. 212, Bullinger to Calvin, Zurich, Oct 2, 1560; Romier, *Conjuration*, 234–47.

armed guard, sending Philibert de Marcilly, seigneur de Sipierre, ahead to secure the city. Whether they went there because additional letters, now lost, had tipped them off to a plan against it like that alleged by Régnier de La Planche, or simply as a precautionary measure to secure and overawe a city known to be a center of Protestant strength, as the Spanish ambassador thought, they entered the Loire valley metropolis on October 18. They would reside there for the next months with a reinforced guard and order the Estates-General to meet there under close watch. A new tone of firmness about how to treat Reformed gatherings also entered Francis II's letters around this time. The king declared that he was no longer prepared to endure the contempt of the law and of his instructions that too many throughout the kingdom had previously shown. He urged his officials to act firmly against illegal gatherings and dispatched not only Villars to Bas-Languedoc with orders to end all disorders and severely punish those responsible, but also Henri-Robert de La Marck, Duke of Bouillon, to Normandy and Paul de La Barthe, maréchal de Thermes, to Aquitaine.[16]

By mid-October, some Huguenots were also pursuing a new strategy. The summoning of the Estates-General offered an opportunity for the Protestants to make their concerns heard. At a significant minority of the first preliminary assemblies held in October to elect delegates and draft *doléances* for the Estates—in Paris, Blois, Angers, Châtellerault, Bourges, and Périgueux—spokesmen rose to argue for the adoption of demands for a reformation of religion and the state. Alarmed by these initiatives, the crown ordered its lieutenants in the provinces to prevent discussion of religious questions at the subsequent assemblies. Its agents were generally able to control these later meetings well enough to stop this.[17] The emerging synodal network of the Reformed churches then developed a parallel initiative according to which each synodal province would send a syndic on its behalf directly to the Estates-General carrying copies of the confession of faith, a common apologia, and procurations empowering them to speak in the name of the local churches.[18]

---

[16] Paris, ed., *Négociations*, 580–81, 651–53, Francis II to Thermes, Saint-Germain-en-Laye, Oct 1, 1560, to Aumale and Tavannes, Saint-Germain-en-Laye, Oct 9, 1560; *ADE*, I, 436, Chantonnay to Philip II, Paris, Oct 7, 1560; de Ruble, *Antoine et Jeanne*, II, 391–97.
[17] Romier, *Conjuration*, 263–66.
[18] Benedict and Fornerod, eds., *Organisation et action*, 12.

The statements made at the regional electoral assemblies generally took the form of peaceful petitioning, but the gathering of the Estates of Anjou at Angers on October 14 degenerated into shoving and fights after armed men wearing kerchiefs in their hats to identify one another packed the assembly room, cheered on calls for the toleration of Reformed worship and the redistribution of church wealth, ensured the election of delegates favorable to such goals, then refused to allow a motion to reconsider these decisions. The next day, they assembled several hundred strong and marched through the city. Just prior to this event, known to posterity as the "day of the kerchiefs," Angers' Catholic magistrates had warned that "survivors of the commotion at Amboise who have drawn to them all the depraved noblemen of the region" had infiltrated the city over the preceding weeks and made it their "arms depot." Here continuity between the mobilization of men in preparation for a second armed enterprise and the presentation of demands for change at the electoral assemblies seems probable. Such continuity is also suggested by the fact that the man whom those sporting the kerchiefs called upon to speak first in favor of their demands was the pastor Charles d'Albiac, the author of the memorandum slipped secretly to the queen mother back in May.[19] Another instance of continuity may come from Guyenne. At the provincial synod of the churches of that region held at Clairac on November 19, the individual chosen to collect the legal procurations from the churches of the synod that would be presented at the Estates-General along with the confession of faith and an apologia "in the form and style used by the other churches of France" was none other than Boisnormand. He was also elected *juré* (superintendant) of the churches of the area around Nérac. It is quite evident that neither his involvement in the prior conspiracies nor the fact that the crown had ordered his arrest was thought to disqualify him from a church leadership role.[20]

---

[19] Paris, ed., *Négociations*, 658, magistrates of Angers to cardinal of Lorraine, Angers, Oct 14, 1560; BnF, MS 500 Colbert 27, fo. 9, mayor of Angers to "Monseigneur à Nantes," Angers, Oct 14, 1560; La Planche, 650–51; *Remonstrance faite par M. Francois Grimaudet, advocat du Roy à Angiers, aux Estatz d'Anjou* (Lyon: Jean Saugrain, 1561). Laurent Bourquin, *Les nobles, la ville et le roi. L'autorité nobiliaire en Anjou pendant les guerres de Religion* (Paris: Belin, 2001), 43–46, offers a brief recent account of the day of the kerchiefs but does not set the event in its wider context or note d'Albiac's speech, which, unlike that of Grimaudet, has not survived. It is known through a brief summary in La Planche.

[20] Benedict and Fornerod, *Organisation et action*, 12.

For his part, Calvin dismissed from the start the Estates-General summoned by the crown as likely to be a sham assembly of Guise sycophants chosen at manipulated electoral assemblies. But little news from the entourage around Antoine and Condé reached him in Geneva throughout September and October. He could only watch anxiously from afar to see whether the Bourbon brothers pursued the course he hoped they would. On September 30, he wrote Bullinger, "Nothing yet from Beza, because his journey is secret." "The king of Navarre is quiet so far. But he is suspected of working at something great."[21] On October 14, he was able to report that Antoine and Condé were on their way to court. He believed that Antoine was determined to lay claim to the leading position in council to which his status entitled him and expected his brother soon to depart from his side, adjuring Bullinger to take care that nobody learn about this latter plan in advance. Antoine intended to stake his claim "without arms," so he asserted, even while indicating that his supporters might have to draw their swords in his defense. "Believe me, I declare for sure, there is no danger of an uprising, because nobody will budge unless Navarre is attacked, in which case I hope that many will block this."[22] After waiting a long time for more reliable information that never arrived, he finally wrote again on November 1:

> Things have come to a head. I don't know where Beza is or what he is doing. There are various rumors about Navarre. But I think that he has retreated, when he saw he would be coming into conflict with so many troops. Therefore there is civil war in France. The nobility of lesser Brittany ... will stand with him. The Angevins approach, as do a great number of Poitevins. Many will come together from Aquitaine.[23]

This was a mix of false reports and projected hopes that show not only Calvin's alarm that civil war might have broken out, but also his

---

[21] *CO*, XVIII, col. 207: "Pridem a Beza nihil, quia occlusum est iter." "Rex Navarrae adhuc quiescit. Suspectus tamen est ac si grande aliquid moliatur."
[22] *CO*, XVIII, cols. 218–19: "Crede mihi, pro certo assero, nullum esse periculum tumultus, quia nemo se movebit, nisi forte Navarrum hostiliter aggressi fuerint, pro cuius defensione, ut spero, multi se opponent."
[23] *CO*, XVIII, col. 230, Calvin to Bullinger, Nov. 1, 1560: "In Gallia res ubique turbulentae. Ad extrema ventum est. Ubi sit Beza vel quid agat mihi est incognitum. De Navarro varii rumores. Ego tamen existimo retrocessisse, quum videret sibi cum tot copiis esse confligendum. Ergo intestinum bellum in Gallia. Nobilitas minoris Britanniae (sunt veteres Armorici, nunc Britones) cum ipso stabit. Andegavi accedent, Pictonum magnus numerus. Ex Aquitania confluent multi."

continuing belief that Antoine was prepared to have recourse to arms if matters came to a showdown and his sense of the geography of support for armed action. In fact, no civil war was imminent. Two days before Calvin wrote this letter, Antoine and Condé submissively entered a heavily guarded Orléans.

As the day of the kerchiefs suggests, a concerted show of force by those recruited for some sort of coordinated armed action or those simply inclined to militancy remained a threat throughout October. As Antoine and his entourage traveled north, the royal minders warily watching his movements had a new scare around the 20th when they found evidence that they believed showed that the Huguenots still intended "to execute their enterprise."[24] On October 21, the count of Villars reported that the troop of a thousand foot soldiers and a hundred horsemen who had fled from Bas-Languedoc into the mountains of the Cévennes and Vivarais "boast of having an even larger enterprise than the two that failed that they hope to execute."[25] But the Guise-dominated government turned out to command wider legitimacy among the sword nobility than the conspirators had imagined. As Antoine advanced, he could observe how many ordinance companies were mobilized to oppose him if necessary and how slim the chances of success of any venture were. He reduced his entourage and allowed the ministers and firebrands accompanying him to slip away. Hotman is known to have returned to Strasbourg by October 17. Beza did not make it back to Geneva until the first week of November, a few days after Calvin wrote to Bullinger, although a month earlier he had been spotted a day's ride from Poitiers, perhaps in connection with the plan to mobilize men there, perhaps because by then he had already left Antoine's entourage for good.[26] Antoine and Condé reached Orléans on October 30. Condé was immediately imprisoned and placed on trial. Antoine was given the benefit of doubt and soon resumed attending meetings of the Privy Council. The next day, effigies of the younger Maligny and Montbrun were publicly decapitated and hung to display the king's resolution to punish those

---

[24] BnF, MS 500 Colbert 27, fo. 76, Thermes to Guise, Poitiers, Oct 23, 1560, published in de Ruble, *Antoine et Jeanne*, II, 487.
[25] BnF, MS 500 Colbert 27, fo. 100, Villars to Guise, Beaucaire, Oct 21, 1560.
[26] Kelley, *Hotman*, 123; Geisendorf, *Bèze*, 122; BnF, MS 500 Colbert 27, fo. 26, Burie to Francis II, n.p., n.d. [c. Oct 7, 1560], published in de Ruble, *Antoine et Jeanne*, II, 479.

involved in conspiracy. Also arrested and placed under special investigation was the wealthy *bailli* of Orléans, Jerome Groslot, in whose father's splendid town house (today the city's Hôtel de Ville), the king lodged during his stay. Groslot stood accused of involvement in the conspiracy of Amboise and plotting to turn the city over to Navarre.[27]

Antoine's refusal of confrontation disappointed those longing to force a change in policy, but even it did not stop a few die-hards from continuing to contemplate some sort of armed strike. "Those seeking novelties and hoping for some change are now deflated and feel as if their leader has abandoned them," the maréchal Biron wrote from Périgord on October 31. Some, "to give their deed the color of religion, say that they trusted too much in men and that God was now making them see that they should trust only in Him." Others now "propose to look for a turbulent leader of lesser cloth who has little to lose" "to see if they cannot better execute their bold and pernicious enterprise."[28] If a report of the Spanish ambassador unverified by any other source may be believed, a last attempt to get Antoine to lead an armed adventure was made as late as November 20–22. A *"desviado de Ginebra"* who had come to court on legal business approached Antoine secretly, revealed that 1800 men had gathered near Grenoble vowing to fight those who oppressed the Gospel, and asked him to protect and make use of them. Navarre was now eager to dispel suspicions about his loyalty to the government. He denounced the man, who was taken into custody and summarily tried.[29] By then, the illness that would soon kill Francis II had declared itself. Plotting, at least on a reduced scale, lasted until nearly the last day of his reign.

Meanwhile, in letters of November and December to Sturm and to ministerial colleagues in Zurich and Basel, Calvin spilled out both

---

[27] *CSP Ven*, VII, 264, Michiel and Suriano to doge and Senate, Orléans, Nov 1, 1560; Desjardins, ed., *Négociations diplomatiques avec la Toscane*, III, 447, Tornabuoni to Cosimo I, Orléans, Jan 10, 1561 (with a reference to "quel Maligny che fuggi a Amboise e che qui in effigie fu decapitato," showing that the younger Maligny was the brother symbolically decapitated here); Lacombe, *Débuts des guerres de religion (Orléans, 1559–1564)*, 72, 78–84.

[28] This sentence melds quotations from two different letters with similar but not identical content both written from Biron, Oct 31, 1560: *Letters and Documents of Marshal Biron*, 10, Biron to Queen Mother, and *Archives historiques de la Gironde*, 14 (1873): 2, Biron to Guise.

[29] *ADE*, I, 488, Chantonnay to Philip II, Orléans, Nov 20–22, 1560.

his bitterness at the refusal of the Bourbons to go down the path he had worked so hard to prepare for them and his anxiety about where this left the Reformed churches. Soon after Beza returned and could tell him all that had happened, he wrote to Sturm that:

> It was not possible to persuade [Antoine] to look out for himself, and he rejected the urgent offers of aid provided by many nobles. Let him die, he whom all know to be worthy of a wretched end! I feel no more compassion for his brother, who up until now I thought was different. But what will become of the unfortunate churches betrayed by his inconstancy? This worry crucifies me.[30]

A month later, stung by criticisms from "our neighbors" the true "fanners of sedition" that he and Beza were responsible for the unfortunate outcome of events—lapidary phrasing that I take to suggest that some in Lyon were second-guessing the last-minute cancellation of Maligny's enterprise—he explained to Bullinger:

> Those whom we wanted to save did not accept our counsel (albeit we did not work as much for their sake as for that of the entire church).... Beza did his duty not only faithfully but with incredible constancy. Plans changed a hundred times. Finally, as all can see, the king of Navarre and his brother chose to perish. If only we had been trusted, all this could have been resolved without a drop of blood spilled.[31]

The assertion that the plan could have been carried out without violence was reiterated to the Basel minister Simon Sulzer a few days later:

> [Antoine] always praised my counsels and Beza's, which were sure and safe, nor less suited to his dignity than to his interest and to the wellbeing of the entire church. We have always wished that his own grandeur would be ensured and that care would be taken that no drop of blood

---

[30] *CO*, XVIII, col. 232, Nov 9, 1560: "Quando persuaderi non potuit ut sibi consuleret, ac promptissima multae nobilitatis studia repudiavit. Pereat ipse quem omnes norunt esse dignum foedo exitu. Ne fratris quidem iam misereor, quem hactenus putavi alium esse. Verum quid miseris ecclesiis fiet, quas sua levitate prodiderunt. Haec me cura excruciat."

[31] *CO*, XVIII, cols. 254–55, Dec 8, 1560: "Non passi sunt sibi consuli quos voluimus esse salvos. Etsi non tam eorum causa laboravimus quam totius ecclesiae.... Praestitit Beza non modo fideliter sed incredibili constantia quod debuit. Centies mutata sunt consilia. Tandem accidit quod omnes vident, ut perire voluerint Rex Navarrae et eius frater. Si nobis creditum esset, ne gutta quidem sanguinis effusa facile transegissent."

be spilled, and thus plans were put together so that he might subdue his adversaries without force and disturbance.[32]

In light of what had happened between August and October, Calvin's continuing insistence that the course he and Beza had advocated could have avoided bloodshed seems almost delusional, but the alternative was to concede to himself and to others that the two bore a large share of the responsibility for a sequence of high-risk clandestine enterprises of questionable legality and considerable potential for violence that did not work out as they planned and badly weakened the situation of the Reformed churches. Believing that support for the Guises was more limited than it actually was, that the power of the house of Lorraine would crumble in the face of an impressive show of numbers, and that men could be raised from many parts of France to back Antoine in claiming what they believed to be his rightful leadership role in the king's council, they had thrown themselves into raising money for this project and urging Antoine to embrace it. When he initially hesitated, they were willing to provide some of the money to the Malignys for their plan to infiltrate men into Lyon and seize it to initiate the venture. When Antoine indicated to Beza that he was warming to their original course of action, the prince of the blood and the two reformers jointly canceled this operation at the last minute, leaving its leader and his men dangerously exposed. Then La Sague was arrested and Maligny's plot discovered. Beza and many others inside France still urged Antoine to press forward and call on the thousands of armed men they believed they could provide. Calvin hoped he would do this or, if he did not, that Condé would leave his side and initiate some sort of action. But neither Antoine nor Condé ultimately judged it prudent to do what Calvin and Beza thought they should.

Meanwhile, the tumult in Lyon, the agitation of the summer in the Bas-Languedoc, and the alarming movements of armed men through the mountains toward Lyon precipitated unprecedented repressive activity in the regions that appeared to be the most danger-

---

[32] *CO*, XVIII, col. 268, undated: "Semper mea et Bezae consilia laudavit, quae certe et tuta erant, nec minus ex dignitate quam in privatum eius commodum et totius ecclesiae salutem. Semper enim voluimus tam eius amplitudini esse consultum quam cavere ne gutta ulla sanguinis funderetur, et rationes sic erant compositae ut absque vi et motu adversarios subigeret."

ous centers of Protestant turbulence and sedition. Those dispatched with troops to these areas had been told to "punish well" any preachers they caught, to break up by force any assemblies they learned about, and to "thoroughly clean up the infinity of riff-raff (*canailles*) who serve only to trouble the region."[33] As Villars marched with his troops across Bas-Languedoc, scores of churches from Aigues-Mortes through Nîmes and Montpellier and up into the Cévennes ceased to assemble as he drew near. Hundreds of members, especially those most involved in the recent disturbances, fled. The minister of Aigues-Mortes was seized and hung before the building in which he had publicly preached. The judicial commissioners who followed in Villars's wake judged forty-eight leading figures of the troubles in Nîmes guilty in absentia of *lèse majesté divine et humaine*. As "rebels, seditious, rioters and disturbers of the public good, peace and tranquility," they were to be burned alive if ever captured. Their goods were ordered confiscated at once. A portion of the revenue thus obtained was to be used to raze ten houses in the city where the Reformed had worshipped and to erect on each site a chapel in which a regular mass would be said. A garrison of troops was stationed in Montpellier. To pay for it, a whopping special tax of 11,341 livres was imposed on the 817 households whose members had attended Protestant worship—although only 128 paid their share, the others having fled. Hundreds of Protestants also left both Orléans and Angers, whose churches were "*tout dissipé.*" Three Angevins were executed. Reformed churches ceased assembling across Rouergue and Quercy, in Castres, in Dieppe, and surely in many other cities as well. The churches that continued to meet redoubled their prayers and held fasts, as rumors circulated that everybody would be required to swear their assent to the Sorbonne articles of 1543 or face harsh punishment. In Paris, the prayer sessions, held in small groups to avoid detection, lasted up to two hours. Even places as far from the centers of agitation as Troyes felt the harsher climate. The chronicler of its Reformed church, Nicolas Pithou, wrote of this period, "The affairs of all the poor churches of France were then in a most pitiful state and marvelously troubled by the rigor of the edicts and investigations undertaken everywhere more rigorously

---

[33] Paris, ed., *Négociations*, 580–81, Francis II to Thermes, Saint-Germain-en-Laye, Oct 1, 1560.

than ever."[34] No wonder Calvin felt crucified by the situation of the Reformed churches.

In the end, miraculously, the entire dissipation of all of the church-building activity of the preceding years that he might have feared to be imminent did not come to pass. In what could only be perceived by the Reformed as a providential demonstration of God's solicitude for His children as they walked through the valley of the shadow of death, Francis II developed an ear infection that quickly abscessed and snuffed out his life. The political situation at court immediately changed, for it was universally agreed that a nine-year-old king was underage and required a formal regency government in which the princes of the blood exercised a significant role. In this new situation, Antoine was able to negotiate favorable terms for his brother and those hundreds or even thousands convicted of illicit assembly or sedition in return for his acquiescence to a power-sharing agreement that gave the preponderant role in the government to Catherine de Medici. Condé was liberated. A judgment proclaiming his innocence was issued. Most of the evidence against him was destroyed. The punitive sentences meted out for lèse majesté were annulled and those found guilty were allowed to return to the homes that they had fled. The churches that had been dispersed were able to assemble once again. The process of church-building resumed with renewed confidence.

---

[34] ADHG, 51 B 66, esp. fo. 42v; *HE*, I, 332, 345–47, 373–74, 383–86; Joseph Vaissete, *Abrégé de l'histoire générale de Languedoc* (6 vols., Paris: Jacques Vincent, 1749), V, 565; Ménard, *Nismes*, IV, 265–66; Guiraud, *Réforme à Montpellier*, I, 153–63 and II, *Preuves*, 337–78; Jean Faurin, *Journal de Faurin sur les guerres de Castres*, ed. Louis de La Pijardière (Montpellier: Firmin et Cabirou, 1878), 6; Guillaume and Jean Daval, *Histoire de la Réformation à Dieppe*, ed. Emile Lesens (Rouen: Esperance Cagniard, 1878), 17; La Place, *Commentaires*, fo. 119v (on the Paris prayer sessions, which were held between November 20 and December 1); Nicolas Pithou de Chamgobert, *Chronique de Troyes et de la Champagne durant les guerres de Religion (1524–1594)*, ed. Pierre-Eugène Leroy (2 vols., Reims: Presses Universitaires de Reims, 1998–2000), I, 298.

Six

Conspirators from Geneva: Men and Motives

Having to distance himself from a failed plot and insist that he had always sought to avoid bloodshed was nothing new for Calvin in November 1560. He had done the same after the initial Amboise conspiracy of March, convincingly enough that historians would repeat his assertions for centuries. During that same period, tracts by Huguenot publicists insisted that "*amateurs du bien public*," who were only coincidentally Protestant had undertaken the enterprise for chiefly, or exclusively, political ends. Together, these texts succeeded in erecting a wall of separation between the conspiracy and the Reformed churches and their ministers that would enduringly shape the historiography of the subject.

As we have seen, that wall has increasingly collapsed with each new generation's worth of discoveries. Already well before Romier wrote, the publication of Calvin's letters made it clear that Paris ministers participated in developing the legal argument undergirding the conspiracies. Here we have found pastors of other important urban congregations directly involved in the conspiracies themselves, issuing advice about strategy in the case of Pierre Gilbert dit La Bergerie and Robert Le Maçon dit La Fontaine of Orléans, and traveling to recruit for the plotting in the case of François Boisnormand and perhaps Jean Le Maçon dit La Rivière. Following Naef's work, it became impossible to deny that much of the organizing of the Amboise conspiracy went on in and around Geneva, even if Calvin might have disapproved of the plan and its leader. It also became known that the noble recruiter for the Amboise enterprise, Ardoin de Maillane, claimed to act in the name of the Reformed churches and directed his recruiting efforts at ministers and deacons of the congregations in the towns he visited. The first historian to discover the Triou deposition, Antoine de Ruble, already grasped that it showed the active involvement of a group of merchants and artisans in at least one major city in helping to organize and raise funds for the Amboise conspiracy, and that these same men played an even more important role in lodging men and procuring and distributing arms for its would-be sequel, the Maligny affair. Now that we can better identify those named in that document, we can see that a majority of the core group of the most active Lyonnais organizers were members of the local consistory. Those on their muster rolls were ordinary townsmen of a range of occupations. The Languedoc judicial investigation shows that leading figures in several churches there also directed the raising of hundreds or even thousands of men for the second enterprise. There, too, men from a wide range of trades marched off alongside noblemen. Following Dufour's article, it was clear to those who read it that during the summer of 1560 Calvin and Beza became directly involved in financing and trying to guide this second possible show of force. Here we have discovered that Calvin's close friend Guillaume Trie was the man who approached Gilles Triou to go to Lyon to help prepare the muster rolls for planned seizure of the city. We have also learned that among the chief Lyon participants in the Amboise venture was the prominent printer and friend of Calvin's, Antoine Vincent, who divided his time between the two Rhône cities. This cannot but prompt us to question Calvin's claim that the Amboise conspirators who left Geneva did so without his knowledge or against his urging. More broadly, it is clear that at the level of the leadership, Huguenoterie was central, not incidental, to the conspiracies, whose strength derived from their capacity to generate collaboration among nobles, urban elements, and ministers.

If it now is clear that a number of ministers and prominent figures in important urban churches helped to organize the conspiracies together with noblemen such as La Renaudie, La Garaye, the Maligny brothers, Maillane, and Chasteauneuf, one would like to know more about how significant religious conviction may have been in motivating the rank-and-file participants in the conspiracy, *roturier* and noble alike. Were the ordinary men who set out for Amboise in March or Lyon in September dedicated adherents of the new faith or men on the margins of the church community recruited for pay from the large population of underemployed craftsmen and day laborers found in every city at the time? Were the majority of aristocratic participants committed Reformed believers or "libertines" who bore no love for the pastors and their strict morality but were drawn to the plotting by thirst for adventure, resentment at mistreatment by the Guises, or the desire to avenge a relative's death? Of course, several different considerations can enter into play in any individual's decision to join a perilous political enterprise. Parsing the relative weight of multiple motives is difficult even for prominent individuals about whom copious documentation survives. It is impossible for most of the obscure men caught up in the ventures examined here. Still, some evidence does survive that sheds a measure of light on these questions.

To find this evidence, we need to return to Geneva. As two centuries of research has shown, when seeking to discover biographical details about otherwise obscure early French Protestants, no place is as rich in accessible documentation as the "Protestant Rome," with its published *Livre des habitants* and registers of the Company of Pastors, its indexed notarial archives, its full set of council records now available on line, and its ample consistory records currently in the course of being published for Calvin's lifetime. Already discovered documentation from these archives, notably the Morély and Maillane investigations, enable the identification of fifteen probable or certain participants in the enterprise of Amboise who either lived in city and its surrounding rural areas for some time prior to the expedition or passed through it just before the event. Naef followed up his discovery of these documents by mining a great deal of complementary biographical information about those mentioned in them. But it turns out that even he did not unearth every document in the city's records that identifies participants in the Amboise conspiracy. Jeffrey Watt, current head of the team editing the consistory records, kindly brought to my attention an entry in the register for 1560 that provides the name of nine heretofore unknown participants, eight of whom have the added interest of being commoners rather than nobles. Some of these men appeared before the church morals court on other occasions as well. By linking the evidence about these men, it becomes possible to say more about their past behavior and religious engagement than is normally possible for ordinary men and women of the sixteenth century. Furthermore, the evidence about the noblemen already identified by Naef also illuminates the religious convictions of many of them while allowing us to discover that some had close personal ties to Calvin or other prominent Genevan ministers, but others had been subjected to their censure. This evidence speaks suggestively to the question of how much Calvin might have known in advance about the Amboise conspiracy and how actively and successfully he tried to dissuade participation in it.

The first reaction of many Genevans to the news of the Amboise enterprise's failure was concern for the safety of acquaintances who had set forth to participate. When it was learned that several inhabitants of the city were among those executed in its wake, this concern would intensify.[1] By the third week in May, however, enough of those who had gone to Amboise had returned alive that the city's pastors began to worry about something quite different, namely, that some who had been arrested had made a Catholic confession of faith to gain their release. Such a possible violation of their obligation to profess Christ and Christ alone required looking into. On May 23, the consistory issued a summons to two specified individuals, Claude d'Anduze, seigneur de Veyrac, and Guillaume Souchet. At the same time, it called on the elders to bring in "all of the others who were in France for the recent agitation, some of whom got away through means that we do not understand [and] others of whom were taken prisoner but gained their liberation by vowing to be eternally faithful to the king and to live according to the catholic faith."[2] Five days later, nine men appeared before the consistory on suspicion of having made an "unchristian protestation."[3] In addition to Veyrac and Souchet, they were (to use the spelling of the document) Claude Abry, Jacques Baillet, Jean Barsonnay, Pierre Bataille, Jean de Conames, Pierre Garraut, and Pierre Vigner.

---

[1] Naef, 122–23, 316.
[2] AEG, R Consist 17, fo. 80v, entry of May 23, 1560. Guillaume Souchet is here called "Guillaume le guennier." He can be identified as the Guillaume Souchet named in the entry five days later thanks to *LH*, I, 20: "Guillaume Souchet, guenier, natif de Paris."
[3] AEG, R Consist 17, fo. 82, entry of May 28, 1560.

The *Livre des habitants*, the *Livre de bourgeoisie*, and the matriculation register of the Geneva Academy permit the probable identification of eight of these nine. Their occupations varied, but they do not appear to have been destitute, desperate, or marginal men easily recruited for any adventure. Most of the eight had been in the city for anywhere between three and ten years. Five had settled in and prospered enough to be part of the swell of immigrants allowed to purchase rights of bourgeoisie in the aftermath of the 1555 triumph of the pro-Calvin party. Others had children. Before fleeing to Geneva, two had not been subjects of the king of France. One had come from ducal Lorraine. The other left papal Avignon.

The longest-standing Genevan among them was Bataille, a cobbler who was one of eight inhabitants of Bourges to emigrate in 1550 after a proto-church there was discovered and broken up. He never became a bourgeois, but had been mature and prosperous enough to have had a servant or apprentice in Bourges.[4] Abry, a sword-polisher (*fourbisseur*) from Vézelise in Lorraine, arrived in 1551 and purchased rights of bourgeoisie for the relatively substantial sum of eight *écus* in 1555.[5] Souchet, a maker of leather carrying cases (*gainier*) from Paris, also arrived in 1551 and became a bourgeois in 1557.[6] The noble Veyrac came to Geneva from his patronymic Cévenol town of Anduze in 1553 and purchased rights of bourgeoisie in 1556.[7] Pierre Garraut was either the man listed in the *Livre des habitants* as "Pierre Dollet dict Garrot," a velvet-weaver (*veloutier*) from Avignon who arrived in 1553, or his young son of the same name. The elder Pierre and his three sons all became bourgeois in 1557.[8] Vigner (or Vignier, Vinay) was a Parisian bookseller who arrived in 1555 and became a

---

[4] *LH*, I, 9; AEG, R Consist 17, fo. 126v, entry of August 1, 1560. As AEG, R Consist 15, fo. 53v, entry of March 30, 1559 shows, Bataille had an adolescent son in 1560, so must have been at least forty years old. I owe the information from Geneva's consistory registers cited in this and other notes to the vast data base of linked transcriptions and biographical information compiled by the editors of these documents, which Jeffrey and Isabella Watt generously put at my disposition.
[5] *LH*, I, 18; *LB*, 243.
[6] *LH*, I, 20; *LB*, 257.
[7] *LH*, I, 26; *LB*, 249.
[8] *LH*, I, 25; *LB*, 257. Other entries in the consistory register that seem clearly all to refer to the same man identify him on three occasions as "Pierre Garrot" and once as "Pierre Du Laict, dict Garrault," giving reason for confidence in the identification of the "Pierre Garraut" convoked in 1560 with either the "Pierre Dullet dict Garrotier, velostier, natifz d'Avignon" listed in the *Livre des habitants* and the "Pierre Du Lect, dict Garret, filz de feu Pierre, d'Avignon, Gaspard, George et Pierre, ses filz" listed in the *Livre de bourgeois*, or the last-mentioned son of the same name.

bourgeois two years later.⁹ If Jacques Baillet was the same person as the Jacques "Baillart" received as an inhabitant in 1557, which also seems likely, he was a lace-maker (*passementier*) from Melun not known ever to have become a bourgeois.¹⁰ Finally, Jean de "Conames" was in all probability Jean de Cenesme, a young Parisian matriculate in the recently founded Academy of Geneva and the "Cenamus noster" who carried messages between Geneva and Paris, including the legal opinion about the question of the regency drafted by Hotman in 1559.¹¹ Although it has not been possible to slot this future pastor precisely into Léon Mirot's history of the branches of the wealthy Cenami banking family of Lucca that moved to Paris or Lyon and ascended through financial offices into the nobility, he almost certainly came from this illustrious stock.¹² In 1561 he would be dispatched by the Company of Pastors as a minister to an unspecified church in France.¹³ The group thus included six artisans of some standing, a nobleman, and a soon-to-be-ordained student from a wealthy family known to Morel, Calvin, and Beza as "our Cenamus."

When they came before the consistory, only one of these men, Veyrac, confessed to having made an "unchristian" profession of faith to get out of prison. He was told that his cowardly behavior constituted "a great scandal and it would have been better had he died." To set an example, he was suspended from communion. Abry, Baillet, Bataille, Bersonnay, Garraut, Souchet, and Vignier all insisted that they had done nothing improper. Some had "answered according to God" when briefly asked about their faith. Others claimed not to have been questioned about religion at all. They were allowed to continue to

---

[9] *LH*, I, 51; *LB*, 259; H. J. Bremme, *Buchdrucker und Buchhändler zur Zeit der Glaubenskämpfe. Studien zur Genfer Druckgeschichte, 1561-1580* (Geneva: Droz, 1969), 238.

[10] *LH*, I, 104.

[11] *CO*, XVII, col. 502, Morel to Calvin, n.p., April 23 1559; Dareste, "Hotman, d'après sa correspondance inédite," 50-51; Naef, 142, 165-66.

[12] Léon Mirot, "Etudes lucquoises. Chapitre IV. Les Cename," *Bibliothèque de l'Ecole des Chartes* 91 (1930): 100-68, esp. 127-28. Several members of this large clan are known to have been drawn to Protestantism in France. Francois de Cenesme, from the branch of the family that established itself in Paris in the fifteenth century, was seigneur de Luzarches, close to Paris, and a lieutenant in the ordinance company of the admiral Coligny until his death in 1557 or 1558. That a Reformed church was established in Luzarches by 1561 suggests support for the cause from him or his heirs. His brother Pierre, seigneur de Trossy, prior of Nemours and an apostolic protonotary, converted to Protestantism, married, and settled in Sedan. Neither are known to have had a son Jean.

[13] Peter Wilcox, "L'envoi de pasteurs aux Églises de France. Trois listes établies par Colladon (1561-1562)," *BSHPF* 139 (1993): 359. I have not been able to corroborate Naef's statement that he was sent to Lyon.

receive the Supper but were nonetheless admonished "to be wiser next time and not consent to a foolish enterprise." Cenesme was let off without even this reprimand after telling the consistory that he had been unarmed when captured, had informed his captors where he was from, and had been released without having to make any sort of profession of faith. The good will he had earned from the ministers by carrying messages between the Geneva and Paris churches might explain why the consistory spared him an admonition.

Six of these participants in the Amboise conspiracy appeared before the consistory on other occasions as well. In some instances they were summoned to answer for their own behavior; in others they acted as witnesses. Their testimony suggests that they ran the gamut from committed Calvinists to just the kind of men Calvin would have considered "artisans of the lowest sort," to recall his characterization of the craftsmen involved in his letter to Blaurer.[14]

Two of those who appeared on other occasions before the consistory emerge clearly from their encounters with this body as good Reformed believers. The nobleman Veyrac was the first of these, to judge not only by his confession of his own wavering when imprisoned, but also by the fact that he had previously denounced to the consistory a man he overheard blaspheming. He also had close connections with the most high born of Geneva's ministers, Pierre d'Airebaudouze, seigneur d'Anduze, whom he must have known since boyhood and under whose roof in Geneva he lived. He might have confessed his moment of weakness to d'Airebaudouze on returning to his house. The two men would remain close over the subsequent years. Eight years later Veyrac left bequests in his will to three of the pastor's daughters.[15] Claude Abry, the sword-polisher from Lorraine, was also an active promoter of the Genevan reformation of manners. In 1556 he complained to the body that two of his fellow craftsmen who saw him working on Christmas spoke sharply and blasphemously to him for doing so. In 1561 he brought in for admonition a servant of his who had recently arrived from Lyon and wanted to celebrate Carnival

---

[14] See p. 25.
[15] *RCG*, VIII, 91; "Chartier de Chambonnet (Ponteils et Brésis, Gard): Inventaire," https://fi.geneanet.org/archives/ouvrages/?action=showdoc&book_type=livre&livre_id=540170&name=andus&page=75&search_type=livre&tk=3c71aabbbfc1acb7&ts=1433033831 (last consulted January 16, 2018).

rather than work on Mardi Gras.[16] In addition to these two, we can certainly also judge Cenesme, who did not reappear before the consistory, an upright man in that body's eyes. His ordination a year later is prima-facie evidence of this.

The disciplinary record of two other Amboise conspirators was more mixed, but they, too, displayed clear signs of piety and commitment to the Reformed cause. The cobbler Pierre Bataille, like Abry and Veyrac, testified against individuals accused of blasphemy. He also often argued heatedly about politico-religious issues, which sometimes brought him to the consistory's attention. In 1557 he had to answer to an accusation that he had called Calvin "the biggest hypocrite in Geneva." He denied that he had uttered such a "scandalous proposition"; he had simply said that this is what Papists might say. Two months later, following a sermon in which Calvin said that there had never been as much "brigandage" anywhere in the world as in Geneva when the Perrinists were in control, a man with whom he was talking opined that such remarks were neither "godly (*selon Dieu*)" nor pertinent to the Biblical text for the day's sermon. Bataille defended Calvin. His son developed a reputation as a "*mauvais garçon*" and became so disobedient and given to drink that he was sent to the Hospital in 1559 for a whipping, but it seems unfair to blame the father for the sins of his child.[17]

Similarly, it would seem harsh to judge the bookseller Pierre Vignier too severely for the actions that led to his only other known appearance before the consistory, even if it did lead to his being suspended from communion. This came ten years later, in 1570, in a case well known to historians of the book. It started because Lucas Cop, son of the late pastor Michel Cop, had turned into a notorious sinner who declared that *Pantagruel* was his "vademecum" and eagerly shared his copy of Rabelais's work with friends. The Council imprisoned him at the instigation of the pastors for theft, owning forbidden books, having had sexual relations with a serving woman, and lying to the consistory. Vignier became involved when it emerged that he had bound the young man's copy of *Pantagruel*. Furthermore, he got

---

[16] *RCG*, X, 276; AEG, R Consist 17, fo. 222v, entry of Feb 20, 1561.
[17] *RCG*, XII, 17, 191, 194, 202–03, 212–13, 277, 300, 308, 343; AEG, R Consist 15, fo. 53v, entry of March 30, 1559.

in a spat with Lucas's mother when he crossed paths with her. She called him "a wicked man for having bound the ... book," then, as the words grew angrier, told him "he should eat his shit." Summoned by the consistory and asked why he had helped to preserve a book notoriously filled with bad words and atheistic ideas, he indicated that the pastor's son had told him he would not misuse the book and he believed him. Whether for this mistake in judgment or for having allowed himself to be drawn into an argument with the foul-mouthed pastor's widow, Vignier was forced to sit out the next Lord's Supper despite his prompt appeal to be allowed to participate.[18]

By contrast, Guillaume Souchet's recurrent brushes with the consistory prove that the *roturier* conspirators of Amboise were no uniform band of saints. Between 1555 and 1561 Souchet was summoned before the consistory several times for mistreating his wife, once after she called him a drunkard. He also had to answer to a charge of putting his hand up the skirt of another woman.[19]

The four cases of Abry, Bataille, Vignier, and Souchet constitute a tiny sample on which to build a large generalization, but they are of exceptional interest as they speak to the behavior and degree of religious zeal of the hundreds or even thousands of commoner participants in the conspiracies of 1560 about whom we know nothing. They show that these ranged from strong supporters of the Calvinist reformation of morals to violent men who recurrently fell afoul of the consistory.

Of the fourteen noble conspirators or possible conspirators other than Veyrac identified to date as living in or around Geneva or passing through the city shortly before the enterprise of Amboise, complementary information illuminating their religious convictions, personal networks, or behavior is available for nine. In eight of these cases, as for Veyrac, the evidence suggests strong religious commitment and/or close ties to prominent ministers. These eight can in turn be divided into two equal groups. The first consists of those with strong but

---

[18] AEG, R Consist 27, fos. 32, 52v, 81v; Marcel Grève, *Etudes rabelaisiennes*, vol. 3, *L'interprétation de Rabelais au XVIe siècle* (Geneva: Droz, 1961), 211–12, esp. notes 129, 132, and 134, which reproduce key passages from the consistory records; Bremme, *Buchdrucker*, 238; Ingeborg Jostock, *La censure négociée. Le contrôle du livre à Genève, 1560–1625* (Geneva: Droz, 2007), 181–84.
[19] RCG, X, 213; XI, 163, 171; AEG, R Consist 14, fo. 2v, entry of June 23, 1558, 17, fo. 210v, entry of Jan 9, 1561.

independent religious convictions that occasionally set them at odds with Geneva's ministers over details of discipline or worship. The second is made up of those with clear links to Calvin or other prominent ministers for whom no hints of deviationism survive. Only one of the four in the first group, it must immediately be noted, can be said with complete confidence to have been a conspirator; for another this is highly probable, for the last two the connections are merely suggestive.

The most certain conspirator in the first group was Ardoin de Maillane, whom we have encountered so many times before as the recruiter for the Amboise enterprise in Provence and Languedoc. He lived just outside Geneva in Bernese territory but often came into the city, not least to attend church services, and qualified as a *habitant de Genève*. Again like Veyrac, he was close to d'Airebaudouze, who hailed from the same region in France, acting as godfather of one of the pastor's children.[20] But he was not an unqualified admirer of Geneva's church order or all of its ministers, even if he was deeply interested in religious questions. In May 1558, the consistory learned that he, his brother Jean (whose participation in at least the enterprise of Lyon also seems highly probable), and other acquaintances frequently talked at the dining table about sermons or other details of church services they had just attended, and not always approvingly. On one occasion, the Maillane brothers reportedly said that "when ministers were appointed it wasn't meet that three or four people choose them," a phrase that suggests they may have been partisans of wider congregational participation in the selection of ministers. On other occasions, they criticized a pastor's remarks or what they believed to be an ill-formulated prayer.[21] When the consistory got wind of this, it turned to the secular authorities to ask whether it was appropriate for Bernese subjects to express their views on such matters and to urge that the Maillanes be told that when in Geneva, they should just listen to the

---

[20] Kingdon, *Geneva and the Coming*, 72, 77.

[21] AEG, R Consist 13, fos. 47v–48v, entry of May 12, 1558, partially reprinted in *CO*, XXI, col. 691: "M. d'Agnon depose que par cy-devant il a ouy tenir propos aux seigneurs de Mailliannes qu'il avoyt de l'erreur aux prieres, là où il dit: 'Nous avons une alliance beaucoup meilleur que celle'.... Le seigneur Jehan Gillard, seigneur d'Aguylle depose que ... led. Mailliane disoyt que l'on avoit dit à Nycod, lorsqu'on le mennoyt exequuté qu'il estoyt reprouvé. Dont il trouva cela estrange, et que l'on ne pouvoyt jugé de cela synon Dieu."

preachers and keep their thoughts to themselves.[22] Several days later, Ardoin and Jean were called before the Council, as was Calvin, who labeled them as "displeasing (*deplaisans*)." They were ordered to go before the consistory to "show repentance for their thoughtlessness (*legiereté*) and temerity" and to reiterate their desire to live according to the "Christian reformation and order observed in this city," which they did.[23] It will be recalled that Ardoin later told some in Nîmes whom he was trying to convince to join the conspiracy that Geneva's ministers were not the only ones with the Holy Spirit.[24] One suspects that he still resented his and his brother's encounter with Calvin and the consistory. When recruited for the conspiracy, he and his brother were likely the sort of men who would have made up their own minds about whether or not to get involved without seeking out or deferring to Calvin's advice.

At the same time that the Maillane brothers were denounced, the consistory also learned something even more alarming: "there was someone named Monsieur de Sainct-Germye who was supposed to compose a collection of errors in the doctrine that is preached that they would present to the Council." The suggestion that people in Geneva who regularly talked about doctrinal issues intended to compile a list of alleged errors to be referred to the secular authorities got the immediate attention of the consistory and Council alike. Still more disquieting, the man designated to make the list was one of the most prestigious French refugees to Geneva, Antoine de Lautrec, seigneur de Saint-Germier, a former *conseiller* in the Parlement of Toulouse. He was summoned at once to appear before the Small Council, even before the Maillanes. On examination, he admitted to the magistrates, "It is true that in talking with those close to him and with friends he said that there were a few things that he would have liked to see in this church and in the others that had undergone a reformation." However, this was "not in doctrine—God forbid that he should think such a thing—but instead touching the church order." Specifically, he thought that excommunication should be pronounced

---

[22] *CO*, XXI, col. 691. See also Naef, 218; Kingdon, *Geneva and the Coming*, 72.
[23] *CO*, XXI, cols. 694–95.
[24] See p. 66.

by the entire church with the elders presiding, as in the apostolic era. The magistrates then summoned Calvin to join the hearing. He expressed his extreme displeasure that, "given their familiarity," Lautrec did not come to consult with him or other ministers when he had doubts or questions about church affairs. Lautrec protested his respect for Calvin and begged for reconciliation. The Council was able to get them to shake hands, but only after issuing a stern remonstrance to Lautrec to avoid such potentially divisive initiatives in the future. He was then ordered to go before the consistory and assure the full body of ministers of his agreement with them.[25]

From the point of view of the history of ecclesiological ideas, this episode is significant in showing that a small group of nobles and legists in Geneva discussed and shared in 1558 some of the ideas that Morély would set forth in his *Traicté de la discipline et police chrestienne* of 1562. From the point of view of the history of Protestant conspiratorial activity, Morély is not usually categorized as one of the conspirators of Amboise, but at the very least he was on the fringes of the enterprise. While living in Paris in 1558, he was involved alongside Hotman and Sturm in the effort to win support for the Protestants of Metz and of France from the Lutheran princes of Germany.[26] On January 1, 1560, he asked leave of the Council of Geneva to go to France. After his return in April, he testified somewhat coyly "that he wanted to go for his private affairs; he didn't want to say any more, but it was principally for that." Might it also have been conspiracy-related? François de Bordon, subsequently arrested in Savoy on charges of involvement in the Lyon enterprise, approached him as soon as he returned, "to learn how things went in France" and what had become of several mutual acquaintances. Morély's trial testimony revealed him to be well informed about the attitudes of different ministers toward the conspiracy and the contacts between Beza and La Renaudie. At the very least he should be placed in the immediate orbit of the conspirators. One of the men who accompanied him on his trip back to Geneva was Lautrec, evidently a friend since a year later he would stand as godfather for Morély's son. The other was Adrien de Saint-

---

[25] *CO*, XXI, cols. 691–93.
[26] Philippe Denis and Jean Rott, *Jean Morély (ca 1524–ca 1594) et l'utopie d'une démocratie dans l'Eglise* (Geneva: Droz, 1993), 41–43.

Amand, seigneur de Vellut, whose estate outside of Geneva is known to have been visited at different times by La Renaudie, La Garaye, Maillane, and Veyrac.[27] This arouses suspicion that Lautrec and Vellut were also returning after having played some role in the Amboise conspiracy.

It is unfortunate that Lautrec's involvement in the conspiracy of Amboise cannot be verified, for here is a man who professed his respect for Calvin and was recognized by the reformer as having a certain "familiarity" with him, but who also displayed an independent mind and had incurred Calvin's disapproval and the Small Council's censure for contemplating requesting changes in church government and the liturgy. If he, Morély, and Jean de Maillane all took part in the conspiracy, we could conclude that one group of noblemen among whom La Renaudie had particular success in finding willing collaborators were those who, although deeply engaged with religious questions, did not always defer to the views of Calvin and the larger body of Genevan ministers. That would, of course, seem logical in light of Calvin's skepticism about La Renaudie and his plan, as well as his assertion to Coligny that he tried to dissuade those whom he knew to be "mixed up in this fantasy."[28]

A point worth noting here is that after Maillane signed on to the conspiracy, he took care to shroud in secrecy the recruiting work he did for it in Geneva, albeit unsuccessfully. This is revealed by the testimony in his case offered by three refugees from Provence, François de François "dit Sr de Gardanne," the noble Joseph Pinchenat from Aix, and Antoine Digne "dit Sr Bargemont."[29] According to this trio, "around the time of the assembly [of Aubonne] held for going to Amboise" Maillane set up an evening meeting with them at Digne's house. On arriving, he prayed them not to communicate what he was going to say to anybody else. He then told them that an "opportunity for serving God's church had presented itself that merely required them take arms to subdue the tyranny of the Guisards and agree to go to a place that would be designated." If they were willing to take

---

[27] Naef, 130–31, 143, 219, 379; Denis and Rott, *Morély*, 44n.
[28] *CO*, XVIII, col. 428.
[29] Naef, 372–73. The claims to nobility of François and Bardanne reflected in the wording of this document seem tenuous. Their registration in the *LH*, I, 64, 195, simply lists them as hailing respectively from Gardanne and Bargement.

up the challenge, they should "swear to obey he who would take command, who would come," whose identity Maillane said he did not know. They replied that they needed to think it over before making any commitment. They then sought the advice of an unnamed individual, who told them that "these affairs were not well founded and they could not in good conscience get involved." Why the interrogating magistrates did not ask, or the scribe did not see fit to record, the identity of the person whom the three men sought out for advice is unclear. It might have been Calvin. It might have been somebody else. Whatever the case, we can see that even in Geneva, where it was presumably less dangerous to recruit for the conspiracy than elsewhere, this was done *sub rosa*, at once to hide what was being done from Calvin, from foreign spies who might betray it, and from the civic authorities who had to protect the city's reputation as a good neighbor of the French crown. Nevertheless, word of the venture would have reached persons of moral authority who were opposed to it through the questions of men like François, Pinchenat, and Digne who sought their advice. Their opposition swayed these and presumably others as well who considered signing on.

The question of whether or not to participate in the conspiracy was a difficult ethico-legal question with possible life-or-death consequences. It must have divided noble refugees in Geneva and led to intense discussions among them. Yet those like Maillane whose beliefs or experience distanced them from Calvin were not the only noblemen of strong religious convictions to agree to participate. In addition to "Cenamus noster," the conspirators from Geneva included several of the reformer's closest neighbors. One of them was one of the most central figures in the enterprise, Charles Ferré, seigneur de La Garaye. He arrived in Geneva in 1556 after removing the images from his family's chapel in Brittany and burning them. In 1557 he acquired the status of bourgeois. Until he sold his large house to Jacques Spifame in December 1559 (to raise money for the enterprise?), he lived on the Rue des Chanoines in close proximity to Calvin. Present at the house sale were Francois Budé, seigneur de Villeneuve, from a family intimately linked to Calvin, and Guillaume Prevost, seigneur de Saint-Germain, Hotman's brother-in-law and also a man known to associate with Calvin.[30]

---

[30] Naef, 200–05; Romier, *Conjuration*, 49.

Even more tightly connected to Calvin's inner circle was his other neighbor, Villemongis, who fled France in the 1540s, initially acquired a seigneurie in Bernese territory, and then moved to the Rue des Chanoines in 1558. He acted as godfather for a son of Laurent de Normandie, the impresario of the Genevan propaganda network and Calvin's close friend, served at least twice as a witness to legal documents concerning the Estienne printing family that were drawn up in Calvin's house, and is known from a letter of Calvin's to have dined there in the presence of both the reformer and Guillaume Trie.[31] He perished memorably on the executioner's block at Amboise, so memorably that two different legends about his last seconds circulated after his death. One tale that went around Geneva said that an inexperienced executioner so botched the immediately preceding beheading that when Villemongis's turn came, he indicated to the executioner just where to strike the blow so that only one swing of the broadsword was required.[32] The other story, first told by La Place and included in all editions of Crespin's martyrology from 1570 onward, recounts that when he knelt to be executed, he dipped his bound hands in the blood of those decapitated before him, lifted them, and cried "Lord, here is the unjustly spilled blood of your children, avenge it"[33] (Figure 6.1.) It seems highly probable that Villemongis was the "one who can now testify for me before God whom you know but who it is not necessary to name" that Calvin mentioned in his letter to Coligny. This person came five or six times to discuss with Calvin whether or not to join the conspiracy. Calvin claimed that each time he sought to talk him out of going and wrested from him a promise that he would not, only to have him come one last time and say that he could not rest easy until he found out whether or not the Admiral supported the enterprise and wanted him to join it.

If Villemongis and La Garaye lived close to Calvin and had often knocked on his door, one or two other conspirators had close ties to other ministers. François Bouchard, vicomte d'Aubeterre, who came from the same region of France as La Renaudie and associated with

---

[31] Naef, 102–05; Jean-François Gilmont, *Insupportable mais fascinant. Jean Calvin, ses amis, ses ennemis et les autres* (Turnhout: Brepols, 2012), 106.

[32] François Bonivard, "Advis et devis de noblesse et de ses offices ou degrez des iii estatz monarchique, aristocratique et démocratique" (a text of ca. 1565), published with *Advis et devis de l'ancienne et nouvelle police de Geneve*, ed. Gustave Revillod (Geneva: J.-G. Fick, 1865), 317.

[33] Crespin, *Histoire des martyrs*, III, 69; Benedict, *Graphic History*, 248.

Figure 6.1. Detail from Jean Perrissin, *The Executions at Amboise Done on March 15 1560*, woodcut, [1570], 32 x 50 cm, collection of the author. The kneeling Villemongis with the blood of his previously decapitated co-conspirators dripping from his raised hands has been placed at the focal point of this woodcut, the second of the two images of the events around Amboise produced for the print series of *The Wars, Massacres and Troubles of Our Time*. Surrounding Villemongis and the executioner are other scenes from the repression. The caption accompanying the print identifies the heads at the bottom of the trestle and the bodies beneath it identified by the letter B as those of Castelnau and his companions. La Renaudie's corpse hangs from the gallows facing Villemongis on the left (A). On the right atop a post behind the executioner (E) are the exposed heads of several unidentified conspirators, whereas at the top (D) likewise unidentified victims are thrown from the battlements and left to hang from them. Contemporaries who escaped the scene or passed by Amboise and other towns in the region in the following weeks remembered particularly vividly the bodies still hanging from the walls. Contrary to what is suggested by the title given the print, the executions depicted took place at different days over the course of two weeks after March 15, not on that date alone. The artists responsible for this print series imagined the scenes on the basis of accounts provided by oral informants and subsequent Protestant histories. From specific details in the wording of the caption to this woodcut, the key source used by the artist in conceiving this scene can be determined to have been the *Commentaires* of Pierre de La Place, whose account of the event was also reproduced in the 1570 edition of Crespin's martyrology.

him when both men were in Geneva, drew up a will in the city on February 17, 1560—in other words, just before setting out for Amboise—that named as his children's guardian in the event of his death the minister and probable conspirator François de Morel, who was married to his wife's sister. The document was redacted in the presence of Jean Guagnon, a minister in nearby Bernese territory, and Germain Colladon, the leading judicial advisor to the Genevan government and Calvin's close friend. The will testifies to Bouchard's commitment to the Reformed cause, most notably in its provision that disinherits any of his three children, David, Martha, and Sara, if they quit the Reformed church and "pollute themselves in papistic idolatries."[34] Bouchard would be captured outside Amboise but was of such high birth and enjoyed such powerful protectors that his life was spared, probably at the behest of the maréchal Saint-André.[35]

The same notary who recorded Bouchard's will took down a second one later that day for the Angevin nobleman Guillaume Morice, seigneur de La Ripaudière. The timing of his will-making suggests that he, too, may have been an Amboise conspirator, although this is the only evidence that links this future minister to the conspiracy; the timing of his will-making may have been purely coincidental. The Genevan minister Raymond Chauvet was among the witnesses. Pierre Viret was the godfather of one of La Ripaudière's sons.[36]

As with the *roturiers*, however, there was at least one black sheep among the noble conspirators. François de Bordon, seigneur de Compeys, the man who visited Morély just after his return to Geneva to ask whether he knew anything about the fate of several friends or acquaintances, would be arrested in Bourg-en-Bresse five months later in the company of La Garaye on suspicion of having participated in the Lyon enterprise. He was detained in a Savoyard prison for five months and only released when it was clear that the new regency

---

[34] AEG, Notaires, Jean Ragueau 3, 368–77; *FP²*, II, cols. 949–53; Daussy, *Parti huguenot*, 132–33.
[35] Brantôme, who clearly knew and disliked Aubeterre, attributed his release to the intervention of the duke of Guise. Brantôme, *Oeuvres complètes*, IV, 251. De Ruble, *Antoine et Jeanne*, II, 185, credits Saint-André. A 1559 contract in Geneva (AEG, Notaires, Jean Ragueau 3, 131) in which Anne d'Aubeterre cedes part of her inheritance to Saint-André for the sum of 36,000 livres confirms the d'Aubeterre family's connection to the powerful marshal and argues for de Ruble's theory.
[36] AEG, Notaires, Jean Ragueau 3, 377–83. La Ripaudière is known to have been sent as a minister to France in 1561. He served the church of Noyen-sur-Sarthe in late 1561 and 1562. During the First Civil War he took refuge on the Isle of Jersey. He would remain there and serve as a pastor until his death around 1583. Benedict and Fornerod, eds., *Organisation et Action*, 214–15n.

government acting in the name of Charles IX did not wish to prosecute those involved in the September disturbance. Unlike all of the other conspirators we have met so far, de Bordon was a second-generation Genevan. His father, a weaver, had moved from Lyon prior to the Reformation, purchased rights of bourgeoisie in 1512, and ascended in time to a seat in the Council of Twenty-Five. François, a *marchand drapier*, acquired the seigneurie of Compeys in 1542. Soon thereafter, he became a *banneret* of the militia company of the Arquebusiers, a group known for its rowdiness and its inclination toward the anti-Calvin Perrinist faction. On the former score, at least, Bordon did the company proud. Unlike his three brothers, who all married into leading local families, he never wed, but he still fathered three children, in 1545, 1548, and 1552, the first of whom was baptized "*à la papisterie*." All three cases earned him the stern attention of the consistory. Over time, he mellowed and grew respectable enough to be admitted to the Council of Two Hundred. It seems that he supported the pro-Calvin party in the 1555 showdown with the Perrinists.[37] But to judge by his inquiry to Morély about what happened to "M. du Crest," he was still keeping company with some seriously unreformed people in 1560, since the man who three years previously had made homage for the seigneurie of Crest, situated close to Bordon's property of Compeys, was Jacques de Savoie, the illegitimate half-brother and trusted agent of the duke of Nemours, prior of Talloires, and himself the father of two illegitimate children born of a relationship with the widow of the previous seigneur de Crest that began while the man was still alive after he had invited Savoie to live in their chateau.[38]

In 1570 the Roman Inquisition examined Gian Galeazzo Sanseverino, count of Caiazzo, an officer in the French crown's Italian infantry who had recently returned to the peninsula to take possession of an inheritance. Protestant preaching had been briefly tolerated at

---

[37] Naef, 115–19, 123, 200–08.
[38] Naef, 123–24n; *RCG*, VIII, 185, 189, 214; IX, 56; X, 89, 286; Matthew A. Vester, *Jacques de Savoie-Nemours. L'apanage du Genevois au coeur de la puissance dynastique savoyarde au XVIe siècle* (Geneva: Droz, 2008), 56, 157, 173n, 190, 216. Could this Savoyard prior with a concubine also have taken part in the Amboise conspiracy, as Bordon's inquiry about him might seem to suggest? Noblemen shunted into clerical livings for which they felt no calling are not unknown among the turbulent Protestant captains of these years. An example revealed by the investigation of the Toulouse judges sent to Bas-Languedoc in 1560 is the abbot of Valmagne, Robert de Lauzun, from an important Gascon military family most of whose members remained Catholic. The judges ordered him arrested after receiving reports that he had returned with a band of fighting men to his abbey

the French court when Sanseverino was there in 1561, and the inquisitors suspected that he had attended some sermons. He freely admitted that he had indeed heard Protestant preachers, but he told his interrogators that he didn't remember a thing they said, just as he didn't remember anything from the many Catholic sermons he had heard in his lifetime. "At court nobody talks about religion or argues about such matters.... Arms and love are discussed, nothing else."[39]

The image of aristocratic priorities encapsulated in Caiazzo's reply is a familiar one that many historians who have written about the conspiracy of Amboise appear to have shared, but it clearly does not apply to the majority of noble refugee conspirators from Geneva whom we have just observed debating fine points of the liturgy and denouncing blasphemers, even if it might aptly characterize de Bordon's priorities. The important contingent of aristocratic conspirators that went out from the city included some with strong religious commitments but a past history of disagreement with Calvin, others with close ties to the city's ministers. Among the artisans who made the voyage, upright believers committed to the Genevan reformation of morals mixed with rougher men.

So what then are we to make of Calvin's statements that Amboise was a conspiracy of foolish knights errant, that he had no idea what was being secretly brewed, and that those who left the city either did so without his knowledge or against his urging? The evidence about how men were recruited for the conspiracy and the connections that can be established between certain conspirators and the city's ministers at once provide some support for these claims and show where they are misleading or implausible. Recruitment in the city was done secretly. Some who responded positively to the appeal were men who

---

in the coastal plain near Montagnac in December. According to these reports, he had spent two thousand écus in the recent "emotions," still had a further thousand to spend on future enterprises, and since his return had encouraged public psalm singing and stripped a traveling judicial official of the papers he was carrying. ADHG, 51 B 66, fo. 32v, 38v; Jean de Carsalade du Pont, "Jean de Lauzieres la Chapelle," *Revue de Gascogne* 24 (1883): 301–28, esp. 307–08. In the case of Jacques de Savoie, seigneur du Crest, however, I suspect that he left the Geneva region in March 1560 for reasons other than to take part in the conspiracy. His half-brother Nemours protected the king at Amboise and arrested two leading captains of the enterprise. Vester provides enough evidence of cooperation between the protonotary and the duke at scattered dates between 1555 and 1567 to make it seem unlikely that he would have gotten involved in an adventure his half-brother opposed.

[39] Quoted in Alain Tallon, "*Fuoriuscitismo* et hérésie: le cas des Sanseverino," in Giovanni Ciapelli, Serena Luzzi and Massimo Rospocher eds., *Famiglia e religione in Europa in età moderna. Studi in onore di Silvana Seidel Menchi* (Rome: Edizione di Storia et Letteratura, 2011), 68.

were not likely to let Calvin know what they were up to. He tried to dissuade the "one who can now testify for me before God." He or others dissuaded François, Pinchenat, and Digne. But try as he might, Maillane could not keep his recruiting efforts confidential. Veyrac, Villemongis, Bouchard, La Ripaudière, "Cenamus noster," and Antoine Vincent all had close ties to Calvin or other ministers. Are we to believe that he and his colleagues tried to argue them all out of participating as strenuously as he claims to have done for the unnamed one now dead and incapable of contradicting his assertion, or that all of these men other than Villemongis kept their involvement in the venture secret from their pastor friends? The consistory informed itself well about goings-on in Geneva. A fairly clear idea of what was being planned must have made its way to Calvin through one channel or another. His statement to Coligny that he had no idea of the conspiracy being secretly brewed by some in the city would have to be deemed unbelievable even if we did not have his letter to Sturm written when the outcome of the enterprise was unknown. This, as has already been highlighted, indicates that he was advising people in Provence how to coordinate their actions with what was planned at Amboise and hoped that the larger enterprise would turn out well. Given the stature of his acquaintances known to have been involved, Calvin also surely knew that the conspiracy involved more than foolish knights-errant. His dismissal of it as such in his letter to Coligny looks more like a strategy for covering up the participation of at least some of his ministerial colleagues and a feeble excuse to explain why he did not more actively try to stop it than the accurate characterization of the sociology of the conspirators that too many historians have taken it to be.

Seven

Conclusion: Rethinking the Nature and Significance of the Plotting of 1560

The discoveries and rediscoveries reported here offer a moment to fundamentally rethink the story of the conspiracies of 1560. From the time of the events onward, the telling of this tale has been marked by an overwhelming concentration on the Amboise enterprise, to the point that many historians and Calvin biographers seem entirely unaware of the Maligny affair or the efforts made for six months after Amboise to push Antoine or Condé to lead an armed cavalcade to court. The evidence adduced here makes it clear that these were successive phases of a single larger project marked by considerable continuity of personnel. Any account that ends the story with Amboise underestimates the scale and persistence of Protestant conspiratorial activity, yields an incomplete picture of Calvin's involvement in it, and invites misjudgments of his political sagacity and views on armed resistance. Furthermore, little doubt can remain anymore: Not only did considerably more Huguenoterie than discontentment animate the plotting, its organizers and financiers included ministers and leading townsmen as well as nobles, all of whom claimed to be acting in the name of the Reformed churches when they recruited participants. The scale of these enterprises, like the success of the Protestant movement in general in these years, derived from their ability to inspire collaboration among nobles, urban elements, and ministers, although in this case the collaboration almost brought the larger movement to ruin.

How does the story of the conspiracies of Francis II's reign look if we escape the shadow of the Protestant apologetic tradition, recognize that 1560 was one long season of Huguenot conspiracies, and use the evidence from the later phases of the plotting to get a better sense of how the first phase might have been organized and who might have been involved? Historians have known for some time that the constitutional argument that would structure and justify the successive enterprises was worked out by a group of young lawyers and pastors communicating among Paris, Strasbourg, and Geneva in the first months after the adolescent king's accession. Within a month of Henry II's death, the Paris church, desperate to obtain a moderation of the enforcement of the laws against heresy, sent La Roche Chandieu to call on Antoine, the great nobleman who had until then shown himself the most inclined to protect Reformed pastors and churches. The purpose of his visit was to remind Antoine of his rights, as this group understood them, and to "let him know our will and that of all the nobility."[1] Calvin was kept apprised of the effort. When Antoine responded passively to their appeal, some within the church, although not Calvin, began to maintain that the support of any prince of the blood or simply of the various estates sufficed to justify action to restructure the composition of the royal council. Hugues Daussy recently called it "highly probable" that "the idea for the enterprise germinated in the little world of Paris's Reformed church." The circle in which the plotting began probably should be widened, given that Régnier de La Planche indicated that ministers from Orléans, Tours, and other places also approached Antoine early on, and that we have seen pastors from these churches reappearing in significant roles at later moments in the story.

At some unknown point in the fall of 1559, Condé and La Renaudie made known their willingness to lead a concerted action. Were they approached and convinced to assume their roles by the ministers and intellectual activists who elaborated the general idea for the conspiracy, or were they part of the circles in which the plotting was elaborated from the start? We will probably never know for sure. La Renaudie had already carried a message from those seeking to mobilize support for the Protestants of Metz to Antoine in 1558, so this could already have stimulated the Bourbon brothers to begin to

---

[1] *CO*, XVII, col. 590, Morel to Calvin, Paris, Aug 1, 1559.

think about how the Protestant movement both inside and beyond France might be used to advance their interests, just as it could have made La Renaudie known as a man with the skills and motivation needed to take on a key role in the enterprise. Another possible scenario is that the pastor François Morel used his family connections with La Renaudie to contact the Saintongeais nobleman in 1559 and convince him to take on the task.

Whichever way the initiative flowed, it clearly is misleading to shunt the ministers offstage from the moment of La Renaudie's appearance on the scene and tell the story thereafter with reference just to noble actors. Chandieu as well as La Renaudie journeyed to Geneva to urge their project on Calvin. The men dispatched by La Renaudie to recruit participants for the Amboise venture after the Aubonne meeting may have included not merely the two noblemen, Ardoin de Maillane and Châteauneuf, but also the Paris minister Robert Le Maçon, who often operated under the pseudonym "La Rivière." An unnamed pastor was present at the initial meeting in Pierre Terrasson's upper room at which "La Rivière [and?] de Chateau Neufz" presented the plan to several leading members of Lyon's church. When the earl of Arran in Scotland was apprised in January that a Protestant action led by "one of the gretest princes of the realm" was imminent, the information arrived in letters from several ministers. Three pastors were captured and executed around Amboise. After the debacle in the Loire valley, the Lyon conspirators Gilles Triou and Claude Gousset went to consult not only with the prince of Condé, but also with the Orléans ministers Pierre Gilbert dit La Bergerie and Robert Le Macon dit La Fontaine, about whether to continue in arms. In May, the minister Boisnormand left the Southwest for Provence to see what forces could be assembled for a new venture. Charles d'Albiac, the pastor of Tours, wrote a memorandum advocating changes in religion and the regime in the context of the revival of agitation in the Loire valley. Pierre Desprez, seigneur de La Cour de Chiré, was both a preacher and the captain of the conspirators for the region of Châtellerault who carried a message to the earl of Arran. Several months later, several ministers crisscrossed the coastal regions of Saintonge and Aunis recruiting men.

While ministers, nobles, and legists took the lead in elaborating, justifying, and organizing the Amboise enterprise, as it grew in scale church elders, deacons, and many ordinary townsmen were drawn in as well. The Triou deposition showed us how "La Rivière [and?] de Chateau Neufz" successfully recruited a core group of six Lyonnais merchants and artisans, three of them certain or probable deacons or elders. They in turn organized the recruiting of a contingent of ten men who set off from Lyon for Amboise, while also paying for arms to be shipped to Orléans for use by the conspirators. Over the subsequent months, the core Lyon group added new collaborators of wealth and prominence in the church. They would enroll, shelter, and provide arms and supplies for the hundreds or even thousands of men readied in the city or infiltrated into it for the Maligny enterprise. We cannot put names on the counterparts of Triou, Gousset, Vincent, Constantin, Nadal, Bertrand, Terrasson, and Darut in Aix-en-Provence, but we know from Maillane's deposition that they existed, that they sent a deputy to the Nantes assembly, and that they, too, provided men and money for the enterprise. In Nîmes, a number of church members, probably including the influential deacon Guillaume Sauzet, were drawn in despite the minister Arnaud Banc's opposition. If we had evidence comparable to the depositions of Maillane and Triou for places other than Lyon, Aix, Nîmes, and Mérindol, who knows how many other comparable situations might be revealed? A refrain owing a clear debt to the Protestant apologetic tradition that runs through the literature is that the ministers or church members who got involved in the Amboise conspiracy did so on their own without the backing of the local church. Not a single consistory register has survived from the period prior to January 1, 1561, that allows us either to prove or to disprove this claim. What we do know is that in the second phase of the plotting, as in the first, individuals occupying local positions of church leadership, such as the lawyer François Maupeau and the doctor Claude Formy in Montpellier or the merchant Corbier in Pézenas, can be identified as the key organizers and outfitters of the groups of conspirators that set out from those cities. Although most of the captains who actually led them whom we have been able to identify were drawn from the nobility, Corbier marched at the front of the Pézenas contingent. The ex-cobbler Jean Coderc commanded an *enseigne* from Nîmes.

As for the rank-and-file urban participants, we have been able here to put names on nearly fifty roturiers from Lyon, Annonay, and Geneva. They came from a wide range of urban occupations. If the small sample of those known to have set out for Amboise from Geneva is at all representative, most were relatively substantial, well-established householders, some of them zealous partisans of the Calvinist reformation of manners, others less so. It seems highly probable that many of the artisans who participated were not apprised of the full nature of the enterprise, but simply told that they were going to present the king with the Reformed confession of faith or acting to obtain freedom of worship. The sources examined here have only permitted us to identify by name one student among the town-dwelling conspirators, the Parisian Jean de Cenesme, enrolled at Geneva's new Academy, but students may have constituted another urban group that provided a significant number of participants. One of the fullest contemporary accounts of the situation around Amboise written in the immediate aftermath of the events reported "many artisans and students" alongside "numerous gentlemen" in the "world of people of all sorts" recently apprehended.[2] An entry in the chronicle of the German nation of the university of Orléans suggests that this university may have been a particularly fertile recruiting ground.[3]

That the prosperous core group of conspirators in large, wealthy Lyon could only raise ten men to send to Amboise might seem to argue against according urban contingents too much of a role in the first round of plotting, especially in light of the reports and rumors that the number of men involved ran into the thousands or even tens of thousands.[4] But perhaps too much should not be made of this small

---

[2] BnF, MS Français 3158, fo. 55, Claude de L'Aubespine to constable Montmorency, Amboise, March 19, 1560, published in de Ruble, *Antoine et Jeanne*, II, 458–59.
[3] Jean-Eugène Bimbinet, *Chronique historique extraite des registres des écoliers allemands* (Orléans: H. Herluison, 1875), 25.
[4] The report from one participant passed along to Bern by the bailiff of Gex (see p. 64) that three to four thousand people from all parts of France and beyond arrived in the vicinity of Amboise is perhaps the most reliable contemporary report emanating from the side of the conspirators. The most detailed estimate from the government side of the number of men actually arrested or spotted around Amboise comes in Claude de L'Aubespine's letter of March 19 (De Ruble, *Antoine et Jeanne*, II, 458–59), but it only provides numerical estimates of the size of the noble contingents. According to it, two hundred horsemen were involved in the attack on the Bonshommes gate, twenty-two "captains and soldiers" had previously been arrested along with Castelnau and Mazères at the chateau de Noizay, more had subsequently been taken, and it was feared that a thousand to twelve hundred horse were still in the vicinity. It must be noted that this letter was written nearly two weeks after the first bands of men, some armed, others unarmed, had already been apprehended in the woods around Amboise, and several days after seven to eight hundred horsemen, "both masters and valets," had entered Tours where many were taken prisoner (on which see Naef, 258). La Planche, 133, states that five hundred of the best horsemen were selected for the raid that sought to enter the

contingent. Lyon was far from Amboise. According to the Mantuan ambassador, most of those arrested around the city and castle came from Touraine, Poitou, and Gascony.[5] In the second mobilization in the Midi, urban contingents were clearly fundamental. As reliable sources indicate that in this phase of the plotting the Reformed of the small towns of Bas-Languedoc raised bands numbering in the dozens to go to Lyon, while their counterparts in the region's largest cities, Nîmes and Montpellier, organized units mounting into the hundreds, it does not seem impossible to imagine city-based groups of conspirators in the Loire valley, Poitou, and Aquitaine raising men in similar numbers six months earlier, while noble participants from these regions rallied their friends and kinsmen to compose the units of horsemen. The important contingents from the Loire valley and the Southwest would also have been joined by a substantial group from Geneva, the estimate of whose numbers is probably still best placed, as by Naef, anywhere between seventy and four hundred. Among those who gathered around Amboise may also have been mercenaries, but of all the groups said by at least one contemporary source to have been involved, the British, Swiss, Savoyard, and German troops mentioned by the Venetian ambassador and so emphasized by historians from Romier onward find the least corroboration in other documents from the time. Other ambassadors' dispatches say that only Frenchmen were involved. The report passed along by the bailiff of Gex that the thousands who gathered around Amboise arrived there without a clear idea of what to do and found no captains to lead them does not sound like the behavior of mercenary contingents. Nor does the report of the Habsburg ambassador Chantonnay that many of those taken walked straight into the arms of their captors in the woods around Amboise as if enchanted because communication among the

---

city through the Bonshommes gate. The rumors circulating on both sides in advance of the strike spoke of much larger numbers. René de Daillon wrote to a friend on March 7 from Amboise that three to four thousand horsemen and twelve to fifteen thousand foot soldiers were feared to be en route to kill the king and those around him. Archives du Palais, Monaco, J 121, fo. 23, René de Daillon to Antoine de Matignon, Amboise, March 7, 1560. Both Chantonnay's correspondence and a manuscript news report preserved in the Bernese archives speak of up to thirty or even forty thousand men. *ADE*, I, 208, 214; Naef, 259. Hotman wrote excitedly to Calvin in February of word reaching him from multiple directions of over forty thousand men in arms. *CO*, XVIII, col. 19; Dareste, "Hotman, d'après sa correspondance inédite," 23.

[5] AS Mantova, Archivio Gonzaga 652, H. Strozzi to duke, Tours, April 6, 1560, cited on p. 15.

conspirators was so poor that nobody warned them that the plot had been discovered.⁶

If mercenary troops were indeed marginal in the Amboise conspiracy, the question of how thousands of men might have been financed becomes less of a mystery. Many of those involved may have been volunteer soldiers like the ones Régnier de La Planche mentioned in Provence. Noblemen surely supported the bands of retainers they mobilized. To be sure, the weapons shipped off to Blois or Orléans cost money. Although the Lyon conspirators sent arms for just 25 men, a Lorraine arms-dealer delivered 150 harquebuses to "our men" in Châlons-en-Champagne, Hotman reported to Calvin. Sustenance for participants who could not pay their own way to the gathering spots also had to be provided. A different letter of the Venetian ambassador reporting the detention and release of sixty commoners taken near Amboise states that if they were partly moved to rise in arms by friendship for the captains they served, they also received a small bit of earnest money as was typical when soldiers were raised for companies without knowing the exact site or purpose of their service.⁷ We have repeatedly observed church deacons or wealthy converts drawn into one or another of the plots providing essential funding—not simply the Lyon conspirators paying for the men they sent to Amboise, but also the ex-bishop Spifame and the Bourges merchant Pastoureau subsidizing the voyage of the younger Maligny in the summer to recruit men, the leading figures in several churches of Bas-Languedoc financing the contingents that left for Lyon at the end of August, perhaps from church funds, and the wealthy Jean Constantin stepping up to provide emergency funds to cover immediate expenses for Maligny's men in Lyon. We also have Calvin's own word that he raised money for the second round of the plotting from "friends" in Paris, Lyon, and Provence—friends who could have included Guillaume Trie and Claude Le Maître. At least so long as too many costly mercenaries did not come from afar, it does not seem far-fetched to imagine sources like these sufficing to provide much

---

⁶ AS Modena, Ambasciatore Francia, 36 (I), fo. 66v, Alvarotti to duke, Amboise, March 23, 1560; Paillard, 316; also *ADE*, I, 216.
⁷ *CO*, XVIII, col. 19, Hotman to Calvin, Feb 26, 1560; Dareste, "Hotman, d'après sa correspondance inédite," 23; *CSP Ven*, VII, 159, Michieli to doge and Senate, Amboise, March 16, 1560.

of the funds immediately needed for the successive enterprises. Furthermore, those who advanced money may have expected that the Bourbon brothers would ultimately reimburse them from their landed fortunes for acting on their behalf, as is suggested by the fact that Calvin later convinced Jeanne d'Albret to repay him for the sums he relayed to units inside France that he said was done at the behest of her late husband. In addition, the organizers of the conspiracies may have expected to tap into other sources of funding if their venture succeeded. The Habsburg ambassador Chantonnay was astonished to learn that among the papers seized from the arrested conspirators at Amboise was one that computed how much it would cost to pay the men raised for the venture for an entire year.[8] The cardinal of Lorraine told him that the deciphered document showed that their expectation was that they could gain access to royal tax revenue and the wealth of the Church to maintain them for so long. This may have been misinformation spread by the cardinal to make the conspiracy appear more seditious than it actually was, but such a plan would not have been incompatible with what we know about the juridical ideas legitimating the enterprise. Because the conspirators saw themselves as acting in defense of the king and the ancient constitution, they could have believed that their forces deserved some sort of public funding if the proper order of affairs was restored. Finally, if the English agent Tremayne's mission on his trip to Brittany in February 1560 was indeed to meet with the conspirators gathered at Nantes, as Poujol speculated, the English might have secretly channeled some money to the Amboise conspirators, even if they kept their distance from the later ventures.

A fundamental mystery about the conspiracies that the evidence reviewed here has not fully dispelled concerns their exact aims and ambitions. As we have seen, the letters of well-placed ambassadors from the weeks immediately after March 17, sometimes even successive letters from the same envoy relying on new information or disinformation, differed wildly in their diagnoses of what the Amboise

---

[8] "Est venu cette folie si avant que jà est comprise la somme totale à combien il pourra monter l'an, comme si le pouvoient maintenir." Chantonnay to Margaret of Parma, Amboise, March 18, 1560, quoted in Paillard, 105.

enterprise was all about. One reported that the mobilization was directed against the Guises and sought freedom of worship; another that the conspirators intended to take Francis II under their control and make him live as a Protestant; a third added that if the king balked, he would be removed and a new monarch put in his place; a fourth said the goal was to kill the king and his council and establish a republic. These last fears seem overheated, as does the assertion in the royal letter of March 31 that the Amboise conspiracy aimed at nothing less than a complete subversion of the state, even if a few bits of evidence suggest that the latent radicality detected within the broader Protestant movement by Denis Crouzet may have manifested itself among some of the conspirators. Thus, an ecclesiastical judge acquainted with La Renaudie told the Parlement of Bordeaux in September 1561 that in a private conversation two years prior the Saintongeais ringleader had said that it was folly for a kingdom like France to be governed by a single king and had revealed a plan to divide it into cantons, one of which he hoped to lead.[9] A report brought to court asserted that the most heavily Protestant towns of the Southwest aspired to establish their own military defense forces supported by ecclesiastical revenues.[10] The possibility of a measure of truth in such reports cannot be ruled out. At the very least, they help explain the fears expressed about subversion. It nonetheless seems clear that the collective ambition of the main body of the Amboise conspirators was what Châteauneuf told the Lyon group that the Nantes assembly had decided to do: Bring the Guises to justice and convene the Estates to put matters of both state and religion back into their proper order. We can be reasonably confident, too, that Maligny also aimed to spur the summoning of an assembly that could claim the status of an Estates-General. The ideal scenario under the plan that Calvin and Beza advocated in the summer and fall was to assemble such vast backing for Antoine's claims to power that Guise influence would

---

[9] C.-B-F. Boscheron des Portes, *Histoire du Parlement de Bordeaux depuis sa création jusqu'à sa suppression (1451–1790)*, (2 vols., Bordeaux: Charles Lefebvre, 1877), I, 130; Georges Weill, *Les théories sur le pouvoir royal en France pendant les guerres de religion* (Paris: Hachette, 1891), 34; Denis Crouzet, *Les guerriers de Dieu. La violence au temps des troubles de religion (vers 1525–vers 1610)* (2 vols., Seyssel: Champ-Vallon, 1990), I, 741–62.
[10] See p. 12.

simply collapse when the first prince of the blood and his supporters neared court.

Once the leading members of the house of Lorraine were removed from power, and if they were taken alive, what body would then administer justice to them? The likely answer is suggested by Régnier de La Planche's explanation that the princes of the blood as legitimate magistrates could take up arms at the request of *sanior pars* of the Estates to oppose an improper seizure of power and then assemble the Estates to make those responsible "render account for their administration." At the time, the Parlements normally pronounced judgment in treason trials after a special handpicked commission assembled the relevant evidence. In this instance, however, it is likely that the conspirators expected that a body that declared itself a duly constituted meeting of the Estates would organize a trial for corruption and fiscal mismanagement. This would have been in keeping with ideas already germinating in Hotman's mind and given their clearest expression a few years later in the *Francogallia*, according to which the extensive jurisdiction of the Parlements was a recent perversion of the proper judicial order and the highest administrative authority in the kingdom lay with the assembly of the three estates, especially during a regency.[11]

If the optimal plan was to displace the Guises without a shot being fired and have them judged by the Estates, those who hoped to fight their way into Amboise could not have been so unrealistic as to imagine that the brothers would meekly surrender. Calvin certainly envisaged a scenario in which the Guises and their backers resisted. Most of conspirators aware of the full political and military goals of the plots must have been prepared to slay members of the Guise family if necessary. A goldsmith from Geneva arrested near Amboise is reported in one local history to have told the cardinal of Lorraine when interrogated that he had come to do just this. The loose-lipped

---

[11] La Planche, 126–27; S.H. Cuttler, *The Law of Treason and Treason Trials in Later Medieval France* (Cambridge: Cambridge University Press, 1981), passim, esp. 55–115, 242–43; Hotman, *Francogallia*, ed. Giesey, 21, 291–93.

Hotman boasted in Strasbourg that all of the males of the family would soon be dead.[12]

The hope was then that the Estates would effect a reformation of religion and the state, but what precise measures did the conspirators have in mind? Here is where evidence from the year 1560 is the sparsest, but a document from a few months later may offer an answer. The document in question is the set of proposed demands circulated among the Reformed in March 1561 together with instructions about how to get them adopted as *doléances* at the upcoming electoral assemblies for the second meeting of the Estates-General that ultimately met at Pontoise in August 1561.[13] We do not know who drew up these secret instructions, but their survival in two distinct copies and the fact that they served as the basis for demands made by delegates from regions as distant from one another as Languedoc and Touraine indicates broad distribution. In the domain of religion, they called for the repeal of all laws governing religious practice or belief except those condemning Anabaptism, libertinism, and atheism; the granting of churches or other places of assembly to those who could not in good conscience participate in the ceremonies of the Roman Church; and the rapid convocation of a national council to determine the proper contours of the true religion as defined by God's word. In the domain of government and the constitution, they demanded a central place in the regency government for the princes of the blood, a role for the Estates in naming the members of the Privy Council that would govern together with these princes until the king reached the age of eighteen or twenty, meetings of the Estates every two years throughout the regency to allow the different groups within the kingdom to voice their grievances, the exclusion of all ecclesiastics from the Privy Council, a limit on membership within that council to a single member of an given family except for princes of the blood, and a careful audit of the recent management of the royal finances. In an intermediate sphere, they demanded the abolition of Church courts

---

[12] See above pp. 45, 139; Bonivard, *Advis et devis*, 316–17.
[13] Benedict and Fornerod, eds., *Organisation et action*, xiv, xcii–xcv, 25–32, 193.

and a significant role for the Admiral Coligny in the education of the young king and his brothers, so that they might be instructed "in the fear of God." This was a period when many Protestants hoped that the king and queen mother might be won over to Reformed Christianity.[14] If the identity of those charged with bringing up the young members of the royal family could be dictated and ecclesiastics removed from the entourage around them, the chances of effecting their conversion, or at least winning toleration, would greatly increase.

It must be stressed that the account of Protestant plotting provided by this volume is by no means the full story of the growth and activism of the French Reformed churches during the seventeen-month reign of Francis II. Prior to the adolescent king's accession, barely a hundred clandestine Reformed congregations were established. In 1560 alone, 169 more took shape. Most were created in the spring and summer of the year, a time of explosive growth when certain of the largest and strongest churches dared to assemble in public and, on occasion, as in Montpellier, even seize churches or public buildings for their use. Local or regional histories of the Reformed churches for the reign of Francis II focus overwhelmingly on the details and difficulties of local church growth. Institutional developments, the arrival and departure of pastors, arrests, executions, the moments when the congregation was able to assemble with regularity and when its meetings were forced to cease—these are what fill the pages of such histories. Connections to the conspiracies traced in this monograph are scarcely ever mentioned.

What has been examined here are the actions of what we might call the "action faction" of the Huguenot movement, those willing to organize a sworn conspiracy and mobilize in arms to advance the cause. We will never know what percentage of church leaders or ordinary converts aligned themselves with this faction. By no means did all. Examples of Protestants who refused to get involved in the conspiracies whom we have encountered include the three refugees

---

[14] Philip Benedict, "The Dynamics of Protestant Militancy: France, 1555–1563," in *Reformation, Revolt and Civil War in France and the Netherlands, 1555–1585*, eds. Philip Benedict, Guido Marnef, Henk van Nierop and Marc Venard (Amsterdam: Royal Netherlands Academy of Arts and Sciences, 1999), 38; Daussy, *Parti huguenot*, 99–06.

from Provence who declined Maillane's invitation to join him on his recruiting voyage to that province; the Nîmes minister Arnaud Banc, who opposed Maillane's efforts to convince that church to commit to the Amboise venture; and the governor of La Rochelle Guy de Chabot, count of Jarnac, who was even prepared to denounce to higher authorities the role of ministers in recruiting for the conspiracies.

If the story of Protestant plotting was hardly the whole story of the French Reformed churches during the reign of Francis II, the events recounted here nonetheless constituted a more important part of that larger history than has previously been recognized. Francis ascended to the throne amid a period of intensified repression that continued for the first six months of his reign and culminated in the execution of Anne Du Bourg in December. Counterintuitively, the initial events around Amboise three months later, far from intensifying suspicion of heresy in all of its forms, changed the dynamic by encouraging the crown to differentiate between sedition and heresy. Doubt had already been growing at court about the efficacy of repression. Now the interrogation of those captured around Amboise revealed how many simple people strongly committed to the new faith could be led by persecution into a dangerous enterprise whose full contours they did not understand. New policies were quickly formulated that focused on sedition or illicit assembly while scaling back prosecution of simple heresy. An edict of March 8 amnestied all prisoners throughout the kingdom detained on suspicion of religious deviance except those thought to be involved in conspiracies against the king, those who had helped free co-religionists from prison or seized royal packets, and the ministers who organized the illicit congregations and assemblies. A second measure nine days later pardoned those who had come to the vicinity of Amboise to present their confession of faith provided that they left within forty-eight hours in groups of three or less. This measure also sought to show that the king was not deaf to the concerns of his subjects if presented in properly deferential fashion. Those who had come to Amboise were told that once they returned home, they could send unarmed representatives back to court with their requests and remonstrances. This was an implicit invitation to structure themselves as formal associations with designated syndics. In indicating that the king would receive these spokesmen, a path was opened for something very close to legal recognition of the Reformed churches as corporate bodies.[15]

While those who had come to petition peacefully were pardoned, the repression of those captured and found guilty of trying to fight their way into Amboise castle was harsh. About thirty men were publicly executed. Up to fifty more were secretly drowned. Still others were taken away yoked together by the dozen to row in the galleys.[16] Corpses of many of those executed were left hanging for days from the battlements of Amboise or other nearby cities. The theater of horror thus created profoundly impressed contemporaries. Yet in the weeks that followed, dozens of prisoners for crimes of religious belief were set at liberty by courts around the kingdom. The edict of Romorantin of May significantly restructured the overall system of repression by giving ecclesiastical courts, which could not pronounce capital sentences, exclusive jurisdiction over the crime of heresy, while leaving the secular tribunals to deal with the distinct offense of illicit assembly. The relaxation of pressure was such that by the summer, vendors of Protestant propaganda dared openly to peddle placards against the mass at the Norman trade fair of Guibray. The Protestants also began to avail themselves of the right of petition offered by the measure of March 17. At the August Assembly of Notables at Fontainebleau, the admiral Coligny presented two requests that he asserted were backed

---

[15] *Edict du roy contenant la grace et pardon pour ceux qui par cy devant ont mal senty de la Foy* (Paris, 1560; copy in BnF, MS Nouvelles Acquisitions Françaises 7176, fo. 174); MC I, 9–14; Fontanon, ed., *Edicts et ordonnances des rois de France*, IV, 229, 261–63; François-André Isambert, A. J. L. Jourdan and Decrusy, eds., *Recueil général des anciennes lois françaises: depuis l'an 420 jusqu'à la Révolution de 1789* (Paris: Belin-Leprieur, 1821–33), XIV, 22–26, 31–33; *ADE*, I, 231–34, 290–94; Sutherland, *Huguenot Struggle*, 104–05; Eric Durot, "Le prédicant, hérétique et séditieux. De l'édit de Compiègne (1557) à l'édit de janvier (1562)," *Revue Historique* 649 (2009): 39–64, esp. 53, which is to be preferred to Sutherland on the dating of the first edict; Romier, *Conjuration*, 167; Olivier Christin, "Compter, se compter, escompter: la formation de la cause protestante, 1561," in *La religion vécue. Les laïcs dans l'Europe modern*, eds., Laurence Croq and David Garrioch (Rennes: Presses Universitaires de Rennes, 2013), 27–44; Daussy, *Parti huguenot*, 180.

[16] These estimates of the scale of the repression rely on the reports found in the contemporary diplomatic correspondence, which do not always entirely agree but suggest approximate orders of magnitude. AS Mantova, Archivio Gonzaga 652, H. Strozzi to duke, Blois, March 18, 1560, Amboise, March 29, 1560; Lestocquoy, ed., *Correspondance des nonces*, 229, 230, Lenzi to Borromeo [Amboise], March 25, 26 and March 31, 1560; Paillard, 336–37, Chantonnay to Margaret of Parma, Amboise, March 28, 1560; *ADE*, I, 223, Chantonnay to Philip II, Amboise, March 30, 1560; *CSP For*, II, 488, 505, Throckmorton to Elizabeth, Amboise, March 29 and April 6, 1560; de Ruble, *Antoine et Jeanne*, II, 184–85, 196.

by more than 50,000 signatures asking the king to protect "the faithful of France who wish to live according to the reformation of the Gospel." The requests went on to urge him to restore the true service of God as David and Josias had done in the time of Israel, and to grant them churches in which they could assemble for worship.[17] Even though it remained against the law to assemble for Reformed worship, the Protestant movement had a greater margin of liberty within which to expand during the late spring and summer of 1560 than ever before. Growth in the number of churches structured along Genevan lines took off.

The improving situation of the Reformed churches in this period makes Calvin's decision to align himself with the action faction at some point around May or June all the more remarkable. Indeed, it leads one to question his political acumen and the quality of the information he was receiving. In the period leading up to Amboise, he was certainly aware of many details of what La Renaudie, Chandieu, and the others most deeply engaged in the preparations for Amboise were up to. He even appears to have urged coordination between some planned actions of unknown character in Provence and what he knew was about to happen in the Loire valley. Still, we must take the exasperated and dismissive remarks that he made about La Renaudie in the letter that he wrote to Sturm even before the outcome of the venture was known as confirmation of his later claims that he kept his distance from the boldest adventurers, did not approve of the Amboise enterprise, and tried to talk certain close acquaintances out of participating in it.

Why then at some point around May or June did he begin to raise money for men and arms to be put at Navarre's disposal for a second venture, start working together with Beza to convince Antoine to lead a major display of force, and even get involved in furnishing aid for Maligny's plan to seize Lyon? The confidence that he and Beza expressed that the Guises could be displaced by a sufficiently

---

[17] *CO*, XVIII, cols. 662–70; "Une Mission à la Foire de Guibray," *BSHPF* 28 (1879): 455–64 (incorrectly dated 1561 rather than 1560 in both of these editions, as first noted by Gabrielle Berthoud, *Antoine Marcourt Réformateur et Pamphlétaire du 'Livre des Marchans' aux Placards de 1534* (Geneva: Droz, 1973), 161); *MC*, II, 654–59; Bernerd C. Weber, "The Council of Fontainebleau (1560)," *Archiv für Reformationsgeschichte* 45 (1954): 43–61.

impressive show of force suggests that reports from the Paris pastors or other informants may have led them to overestimate the degree of hostility toward the house of Lorraine at court and to underestimate Guise support among key lieutenants in the provinces. May was also the high point of an ultimately futile diplomatic offensive by Duke Emmanuel-Philibert of Savoy to induce France, Spain, Venice, and the Papal States to join him in a Catholic alliance to reassert episcopal and Savoyard authority over Geneva. As rumors about his efforts and reports of troops assembling in nearby France and Savoy multiplied, fear arose in Geneva that an attempt to reconquer it could be imminent.[18] In this context, Calvin may have felt that the best defense was a good offense. His sermons in these months, Willem Nijenhuis noted some time ago, denounced kings and the "monkeys" who surround them with unprecedented vitriol. Although he continued to emphasize as before that ordinary believers facing persecution could only pray for patience and leave the taking up of arms to those legitimately empowered to use them, he now suggested for the first time that private persons, especially those granted certain rights that they had not been able to exercise, could on occasion receive a special call from God to deliver their people.[19] A combination of hope and fear may have undergirded his rapprochement with the action faction.

The launching of a second round of conspiracies and the active involvement of Geneva's leading pastors in them at the very moment when the still clandestine, still outlawed Reformed churches inside France were beginning to discover that they could multiply with unprecedented rapidity proved disastrous. Calvin's and Beza's initial willingness to support Maligny's enterprise despite some apparent reservations on their part about "the fervid one of ours," then the last-minute cancellation of that venture, left the men who had been infiltrated into Lyon in a dangerously exposed position. After their

---

[18] Naef, 170–90; Serge Brunet, "La conjuration d'Amboise (16 mars 1560), Emmanuel-Philibert de Savoie et Genève," in *La Maison de Savoie et les Alpes: emprise, innovation, identification XVe-XIXe siècle*, eds. Stéphane Gal and Laurent Perrillat (Chambéry: Publications de l'Université Savoie Mont Blanc, 2015), 306–16.

[19] Willem Nijenhuis, "The Limits of Civil Disobedience in Calvin's Last Known Sermons: The Development of His Ideas on the Right of Civil Resistance," in *Ecclesia Reformata: Studies on the Reformation*, (2 vols., Leiden: Brill, 1972–94), II, 82–84; *CO*, XXIII, cols. 643–45, "Premier sermon de l'histoire de Melchisedec."

arms were spotted, most were able to extricate themselves safely from the city thanks to quick action by their commanders, but the arrests that followed led to the execution of at least six conspirators and the interrogation of Triou. This yielded convincing evidence of both Condé's and Calvin's involvement in the plotting, which in turn intensified the fear of a new armed enterprise that the prior week's discovery of the suspicious papers on La Sague had already aroused at court. The monarch and those around him were now on their guard. They quickly convinced a larger number of loyal lieutenants in the provinces to mobilize their ordinance companies than Calvin and Beza had thought possible. These were deployed around the kingdom in strategic places for opposing any action that Navarre might undertake.

In abandoning the Maligny enterprise for an alternative plan to be led by Antoine, Calvin and Beza also chose to believe that they could now rely on an individual who was known for his accommodating personality and who had on prior occasions already disappointed Reformed hopes that he would emerge as a forceful advocate of their cause. The events that immediately followed placed their would-be champion in a far stickier situation than ever before. Once the crown got wind of the possibility that he might lead a new enterprise, the element of surprise was lost. Ordinance companies on the ready were now arrayed against any move he might make. Calvin judged Antoine's ultimate decision to submit meekly to the king's summons to court a cowardly dereliction of his duties to God and man. His refusal to mobilize his supporters would have looked very different to Machiavelli. In the chapter of *The Prince* that explores how to acquire new princedoms through arms and *virtù*, a chapter that would have been especially apposite for Antoine and one that he could well have known since several French translations of the work had already been prepared for high French aristocrats, the importance of finding the right opportunity (*occasione*) to strike is emphasized.[20] That opportunity, if it ever existed, was lost once La Sague was arrested and the Lyon enterprise discovered. In the cold, hard light of princely political calculation, advancing submissively to court with his brother in tow was probably the only way for Navarre to avert even greater disaster

---

[20] I owe this important point to Mark Greengrass.

for himself and his retainers, even if it disappointed and left exposed all who had placed themselves and their fortunes at risk by mobilizing on his behalf.

Meanwhile, the crown's discovery that hundreds or even thousands of armed men had successfully infiltrated Lyon, the reports it soon received of armed bands on the march elsewhere, and the fear of still further enterprises that was periodically renewed throughout September and October brought renewed repressive activity of unprecedented vigor down upon the Reformed churches in the regions that appeared to be the centers of Protestant turbulence and sedition. If Calvin wrote that he was crucified with worry about the churches of France in this period, he had good reason to be. Many ceased to assemble. Believers fled Nîmes, Montpellier, Orléans, and other cities by the hundreds. His own optimistic misreading of the political situation in the kingdom and active engagement in the financing and planning of a second round of conspiracies had contributed to sparking a crackdown, not on heresy so much as on sedition, that wiped out most of the church-building successes of the spring and summer.

Then within weeks "again the hand of God flashed forth."[21] The young king fell ill and died. The politico-religious situation was scrambled anew. Despite Calvin's bitter remark of November that he would not care if Antoine died, he now hastened to send an unknown recipient with access to the prince instructions about how best to proceed in the new political environment. "Tell his Lordship there are three points to consider," he began. The first was that Condé must be set free and his innocence recognized so that neither he nor any of the other prisoners who likewise needed to be "relieved" would be subject to ongoing reproach or future trial for their recent actions. The second was that Navarre himself should act "manfully (*virilement*)" to ensure that he and not "a woman, indeed a foreign woman" dominate the regency council that had to be set up. The makeup of that council, furthermore, should be determined by the Estates-General—and not the assembly currently meeting at Orléans, since it had not been convoked specifically to deal with the question of the regency council, but a new gathering to be preceded by new elections

---

[21] *CO*, XVIII, col. 268, Calvin to Sulzer, undated but after the death of Francis II.

in which the Reformed would be able to participate more freely than they had in the elections for the Estates-General of Orléans. "The third point concerns religion. Here all that is to be sought is that the liberty given by the [edict of March 17] be preserved, the liberty to present requests." Two explicitly minimalist ("cold and meager") requests should initially be conveyed. One should demand an end to the persecution of all peaceable dissenters. The other should ask that those who could not in good conscience worship within the Roman Church be allowed to gather separately for worship if they agreed to sign up with the local royal officials and designate one of their number to report to the authorities anybody in their ranks who violated the terms granting them the right to assemble.[22] The call for a convocation of a new Estates-General and the emphasis on preserving and using the right of petition point to a major shift in the political tactics used by the Reformed in the changed environment of Charles IX's reign. Where the reign of Francis II had been a season of conspiracy, the period from the onset of Charles IX's rule to early 1562 would be what Daussy has called "*Le temps des requêtes*," a period in which coordinated action to win freedom of worship and advance the cause on the national level would rely above all on petitioning and electioneering.[23] This first year of the new king's reign would also be a period of even more dramatic growth in the number of Reformed churches and of even greater improvement in their legal situation than the spring and summer of 1560.

Disaster had been miraculously averted, and for the next year or more coordinated Protestant political action would chiefly employ new tactics that did not rely on the threat of armed action. But mobilization and sworn associations did not disappear from the toolbox of political practices employed by the Huguenot movement. Recourse to such tactics returned shortly before and during the First Civil War. When it did, many of the veterans of 1560 also returned to significant leadership roles within the movement, both nationally and locally.

---

[22] *CO*, XVIII, cols. 281–85, Calvin to unknown, undated.
[23] On the centrality of these tactics to Reformed political action in 1561 and early 1562, see Benedict and Fornerod, eds., *Organisation et action*, lxxxiv–cx; Daussy, *Parti huguenot*, 217–38.

It seems appropriate to end this study with some words about what became of those involved in the conspiracies of 1560. Some, of course, perished in the incidents or in the repression that followed, although just how many escapes calculation. In addition to the approximately eighty men indicated by contemporary sources to have been decapitated, hanged or drowned in the aftermath of Amboise, at least six executions followed the Maligny affair in Lyon and three the day of the kerchiefs in Angers. However, providing even an approximate order of magnitude for the number of those who died in skirmishes around Amboise, perished at the oar after being condemned to row in the galleys, or were captured and executed by the military authorities and judicial commissioners sent to Bas-Languedoc, Aquitaine, and Normandy in the fall is impossible. One thing nonetheless seems clear: Despite a not inconsiderable death toll, most participants survived the events, escaped punishment, and then returned home following the amnesty issued by the regency government of Charles IX. This is demonstrated most clearly by the fate of the group that might have been thought at greatest risk in the troubles, the captains named to lead the Amboise enterprise. Soon after that event, Chantonnay reported that the conspirators were believed to have appointed fifty captains. Of these, eighteen had been captured.[24] The Protestant historians La Planche, La Popelinière, and d'Aubigné identified fifteen captains by name. Of these, only two, Castelnau-Tursan and Mazères, are known to have been executed. Twelve unquestionably survived the event and its aftermath.[25]

---

[24] *ADE*, I, 216, Chantonnay to Philip II, Amboise, March 19, 1560.
[25] This analysis is based on the list of regional captains in d'Aubigné, *Histoire universelle*, I, 270–71, which amplifies a prior list provided by La Planche and repeated by Beza and La Popelinière. It thus excludes the overall commander La Renaudie, who also perished. The fate of one captain in this list is unknown for want of a secure fuller identification. This is the individual whom La Planche names "De Vailly Brezay," said to be captain for Poitou and Saintonge, and whom d'Aubigné names "Maillé Braisé," captain for the Angoumois, Loudunais, and Touraine. Daussy, *Parti huguenot*, 143, identifies him as Arthus de Maillé, seigneur de Brézé, but this seems questionable as Arthus was a prominent courtier and lieutenant of the duke of Aumale rewarded for his role in guarding the king at Amboise in March 1560. An alternative identification of him with Arthus's brother, Philippe de Maillé-Brézé, seems equally unlikely, for as a captain of the royal guard Philippe took Condé into custody after he arrived in Orléans. Ambroise Ledru, L. J. Denis, and E. Vallée, *La maison de Maillé. Histoire généalogique* (Paris: A. Lemerre, 1905), 144–45, 149–53; De Thou, *Histoire Universelle* (London, 1734), III, 568.

Ten of these twelve reappear in the annals of the civil wars as significant figures in Condé's Association or later Protestant military efforts. Whether the Maligny identified by d'Aubigné as the captain for Champagne and the Ile-de-France was the elder or the younger brother, he and his sibling both survived not only the Amboise adventure but also the September troubles despite a vigorous national manhunt for them that lasted into the next year. By the end of October, the crown had realized that their capture was improbable and condemned the younger brother to death *in absentia*, a sentence that was revoked not long after Francis II's death, like all the other sentences against fugitive participants.[26] Edme drowned soon thereafter swimming in Lake Geneva, but the elder Jean was able to inherit the title of Vidame de Chartres from his cousin François de Vendôme upon the latter's death, just before the end of the year 1560. Under his new name, he would carry out important diplomatic missions for Condé in late 1561 and 1562 and bring sixty gentlemen in his train when he joined the prince's Association at the beginning of the First Civil War. He would remain active in Protestant warfare and diplomacy until his death in 1586.[27]

Another of the Amboise captains to escape not once but twice was the man reported in the anonymous Avertissement as a central figure in the second phase of conspiratorial activity in Guyenne and Périgord, Denis d'Aix, seigneur de Mesmy. When, slightly over a year later, the churches of Haute-Guyenne and the Limousin established a structured militia at the December 1561 provincial synod of Sainte-Foy, Mesmy was appointed "protector" of the churches of the portion

---

[26] *CSP Ven*, VII, 264, Michiel and Suriano to doge and Senate, Orléans, Nov 1, 1560; BnF, Ms 500 Colbert 27, fo. 139 bis, unknown to unknown, c. Nov 1, 1560, fo. 218, Tende to Francis II, Aix, Nov 30, 1560; *ADE*, I, 460, Chantonnay to Philip II, Paris, Nov 4, 1560; Bastard d'Estang, *Jean de Ferrières*, 229–36; MS Français 4632, fo. 10, Charles IX to Tavanes, Orléans, Jan 6, 1561; *Lettres de Catherine de Médicis*, I, 164, Catherine to Tavanes, Orléans, Jan 17, 1561; Pingaud ed. *Correspondance des Saulx-Tavanes*, 60, Tavanes to Catherine, Dijon, Jan 18, 1561; Desjardins, ed., *Négociations diplomatiques avec la Toscane*, III, 447, Tornabuoni to Cosimo I, Orléans, Jan 10, 1561. Although the Triou deposition identifies Jean as the leader of the Lyon enterprise, Edme's dramatic flight from court at the moment of the Amboise conspiracy appears to have made him the brother most clearly identified by the royal administration as a plotter.

[27] *Corr Bèze*, IV, 98; David Potter, "The French Protestant Nobility in 1562: The 'Associacion de Monseigneur le Prince de Condé'," *French History* 15 (2001): 314n12 and the references therein; Bastard d'Estang, *Jean de Ferrières*, 58–158.

of the synodal province located within the jurisdiction of the Parlement of Bordeaux. In that capacity he went to Agen that same month to back the city's Huguenots, who had seized its seventeen churches. The show of strength was sufficient to dissuade that old warhorse then serving as royal lieutenant in the region, Blaise de Monluc, from going there with a small force to undo the action. Mesmy then led the Huguenot troops of the region at the outset of the First Civil War. Unfortunately for him, he soon proved to be less effective as a commander than as an organizer, "not that he was not an excellent man (*fort homme de bien*) and well affected [to the churches], but because he had never previously wielded arms because of his bodily indisposition." In the course of the conflict he was captured and executed.[28]

Two individuals whom we have already met because of their active involvement in the second phase of the plotting had particularly storied military careers during the early civil wars. The first was Charles Dupuy-Montbrun of Dauphiné. During the First Civil War, Dupuy-Montbrun was a key lieutenant of the man who took control of much of the modern Rhône-Alpes region in the name of the king and the prince of Condé, the redoubtable baron Des Adrets. As such, he was responsible for one of the most proudly advertised brutalities of the conflict, meant to strike fear in the enemy. In revenge for a prior Catholic massacre of the Protestants of Orange, no quarter was given the surrendering defenders of Mornas when that fortress in the Comtat Venaissin was taken. The corpses of those killed were thrown from the promontory overlooking the Rhône on which the citadel was located. They were then loaded into a boat that was released to float down the river, adorned with a sign reading, "O you of Avignon, let these bearers pass without paying; they already paid the toll at

---

[28] The documentation about Mesmy in this period is not always clear or precisely dated, but see *HE*, I, 888, 893–94, II, 893, 943; Blaise de Monluc, *Commentaires*, ed. Paul Courteault (Paris: Gallimard, 1964), 478; *Commentaires et lettres de Blaise de Monluc*, ed. Antoine de Ruble (5 vols., Paris: Renouard, 1864–72), IV, 130, Monluc and Burie to Charles IX, Cahors, March 18, 1562; Philippe Tamizey de Larroque, ed., "Antoine de Noailles à Bordeaux d'après des documents inédits," *Actes de l'Académie nationale des sciences, belles-lettres et arts de Bordeaux* 1876, 522–23n. The note on p. 1182 of Courteault's edition of the *Commentaires* placing Mesmy's death in 1560 seems erroneous. A letter of Noailles's dated October 28, 1562, provides details of his execution in that month and year.

Mornas." When Des Adrets subsequently lost the confidence of Condé and the more militant elements in the Southeast by discussing peace terms with the duke of Nemours, Montbrun helped effectuate his arrest. He fought no less fiercely and well in the subsequent civil wars. His exploit in crossing the Rhône in 1570 in the face of a far larger royal force as he led his men back into Dauphiné was immortalized in one of the prints of Tortorel and Perrissin. In the months of shock and dispiritedness after the Saint Bartholomew's massacre, he did more than any other person in Dauphiné to organize military resistance and inspire the Reformed churches to dare to meet again. He was captured and executed in 1575, but his legend lived on in a canticle set to the tune of psalm 43 published the following year, which hailed him as a "good servant of God and of the king of France" and "the first to take up arms in Christ's defense and to raise troops against the great Antichrist."[29]

Dupuy-Montbrun's Provençal neighbor and ally in the August 1560 capture of Malaucène, Paulon de Richieu, seigneur de Mauvans, actually had a better claim to have been the first to take up arms against the great Antichrist, since he began to raid Catholic churches in 1559 in reprisal for the disruption of a worship service in the family's house in Castellane. After abandoning Malaucène and being driven from the Rhône valley in September 1560, he may have gone to the Val Pragelato to fight alongside the Waldensians resisting the efforts of the restored duke of Savoy to put an end to Reformed

---

[29] Loys de Perussiis, *Discours des guerres de la Comté de Venayscin et de la Provence: ensemble quelques incidents* (Avignon: Pierre Roux, 1563), 56; Gabriel Brisard, *Histoire du Baron des Adrets* (Valence: J. Céas et fils, 1890), 73; Benedict, *Graphic History*, 380–82; La Popelinière, *Histoire de France*, II, 108, 176, 193–94; Stéphane Gal, Mark Greengrass and Thierry Rentet, eds., *Bertrand de Gordes, Lieutenant général du roi en Dauphiné. Correspondance reçu (1572)* (Grenoble: Presses Universitaires de Grenoble, 2017), passim; *Discours en forme de Cantique sur la vie et mort de Charles du Puy, seigneur de Montbrun et de Ferrassierres, Gentilhomme Daulphinois, bon serviteur de Dieu et de la Couronne de France* (n.p. 1576; my thanks to Mark Greengrass for furnishing me with a transcription of this work). Montbrun was also hailed for his deeds in the 1563 *Cantique des fidelles des eglises de France* and was the subject of a biography by the seventeenth-century Catholic historian Guy Allard, *Les vies de Francois de Beaumont, Baron des Adrets. De Charles Dupuy, Seigneur de Montbrun et de Soffrey de Calignon, Chancelier de Navarre* (Grenoble: Jean Nicolas, 1671), part 2. I quickly trace Montbrun's career as a Protestant champion in "The Lesser Nobility and the French Reformation," in *Ritterschaft und Reformation* eds. Andermann and Breul, 348–53. On his background, see Pierre-Henri Chaix, "Promotion sociale et Réforme. Charles Du Puy de Montbrun," *BSHPF* 121 (1975): 455–83. Additional details in Daussy, *Parti huguenot*, 379–82, 585, 598, 614–15, 620, 622, 697.

worship in the Alpine valleys of Piedmont.[30] He certainly was among the Protestant military men who placed themselves and their troops at the disposal of Antoine de Crussol after that favorite of Catherine de Medici was given a royal commission at the turn of the year 1561–62 to end both Catholic and Protestant disturbances in Provence, Bas-Languedoc, and Dauphiné. The *procès-verbal* of Crussol's mission indicates that Mauvans was present with a company of horsemen when Crussol took Barjols in February 1562 from the Catholic irregulars mobilized by Durand de Pontevès, seigneur de Flassans, who had been terrorizing the Protestants of the surrounding region. During the First Civil War Mauvans was one of the leaders of the Huguenot forces in Provence. Greatly outnumbered by their Catholic enemies and rapidly pushed into a few strongholds, they made Sisteron their last redoubt. Here, Mauvans distinguished himself in the long defense of this stronghold before slipping away via an unguarded ledge in the jagged rocks around the city, just before the city fell. He then went to Lyon to continue the fight and, two months later, assisted Montbrun in arresting Des Adrets. He again led forces from Provence in the Third Civil War, organizing his own successful crossing of the Rhône against improbable odds at the beginning of that conflict that would also be praised in song. The troops he led were able to join up with a larger Protestant army in Guyenne. Not long thereafter, in October 1568, he died in battle near Périgueux.[31]

Six more of the Amboise captains can also be determined with confidence to have raised men or fought in the subsequent religious conflicts. Even though Pierre Desprez, seigneur de La Cour de Chiré, captain for the region of Châtellerault, became a Reformed pastor, this did not prevent him from saddling up in several of the civil wars. He was wounded at Dreux in 1562, named governor of Fontenay by

---

[30] This is suggested by the eighteenth-century prior of Castellane and *érudit*, who provides considerable information about the Richieu family in his local history of the town: Joseph Laurensi, *Histoire de Castellane* (Castellane: A. Gauthier, 1898), 267.

[31] BnF, MS Français 15873, fo. 22, bishop of Riez to cardinal of Lorraine, Riez, Sept 17, 1560; AD Bouches-du-Rhône, B 3328, fo. 780; "Mémoires de Claude de Cormis," 541–42; Pierre Louvet, *Histoire des troubles de Provence* (Sisteron: Jean-Pierre Louvet, 1680), 157; Laurensi, *Histoire de Castellane*, 252–72; Guiraud, *Réforme à Montpellier*, II, *Preuves*, 140; Brantôme, *Oeuvres complètes*, V, 424–26, which mentions the song, a "vaudeville soldatesque"; Daussy, *Parti huguenot*, 381, 585, 614–15, 693, 707.

Condé in 1568, and killed when the Catholics took the priory of Mouzeuil in 1570.³² Another Poitevin, Tanneguy Du Bouchet, seigneur de Puy-Greffier and Saint-Cyr, rallied to Condé's side at Orléans and would be one of the captains put in charge of that Protestant citadel in the late stages of the First Civil War after Condé and Coligny rode out to do battle. He also served as a prominent commander of the Huguenot troops in the subsequent two civil wars and fell at Moncontour.³³ François d'Acigné, seigneur de Montejean, captain for Brittany, led a unit of 150 gentlemen to Orléans and then fought alongside Montgomery in the First Civil War. He also raised troops in Brittany at the beginning of the Second and Third Civil Wars. He was killed at Jarnac.³⁴ Although hailing from nearby Normandy, François de Cocqueville, captain for Picardy, mobilized men from both provinces in the summer of 1568 and led them on an expedition into Artois meant to be coordinated with other incursions in support of William of Orange. The plan failed. Cocqueville and his men withdrew to France and seized Saint-Valery-sur-Somme. They were soon forced to surrender to a royal army under Timoléon de Cossé-Brissac. Cocqueville was tried and decapitated for treason, after which his head was brought to Paris and exposed in the Place de Grève.³⁵ More long-lived was the captain for Normandy, Nicolas Aux Epaules, seigneur de Sainte-Marie-du-Mont, who rallied to Con-

---

[32] *CO*, XIX, 309–12, Desprez to Calvin, Chiré, March 1, 1562; "Lettres adressées à Jean et Guy de Daillon, comte du Lude," 136, Charles IX to Lude, Paris, May 21, 1563; Auguste Lièvre, *Histoire des protestants et des Églises réformées du Poitou* (Paris: N. Bernard, 1856–60), III, 311. Chiré was not the only minister to bear arms in the civil wars. A fraction of Reformed pastors did not consider warfare incompatible with their vocation. Philip Benedict, "Prophets in Arms? Ministers in War, Ministers on War: France, 1562–1574," in *Ritual and Violence: Natalie Davis and Early Modern France* Past & Present Supplement no. 7 (2012), 169–76., eds. Graeme Murdock, Penny Roberts, and Andrew Spicer.

[33] As a commander in Orléans and "homme de bien et grand ennemy de vice," Saint-Cyr would oversee the execution in March 1563 of a prominent adulterous couple, an action recorded and lauded by Beza and that merited him a notice in Pierre Bayle's *Historical and Critical Dictionary*. *HE*, II, 328; Pierre Bayle, *Dictionnaire historique et critique* (5th ed., Amsterdam, 1740), IV, 121–22, s.v. "Saint-Cyre"; *FP²*, V, 552–54; Daussy, *Parti huguenot*, 585.

[34] *Mémoires de Charles Gouyon*, 27, 51; Joxe, *Protestants du comté de Nantes*, 60, 162–63; Daussy, *Parti huguenot*, 586, 613, 617.

[35] La Fosse, "*Mémoires*," 78; La Popelinière, *Histoire de France*, I, part 2, 55, who identifies Cocqueville as a "gentilhomme normand"; De Thou, *Histoire universelle* (Basel: Brandmuller, 1742), IV, 77–78; *FP²*, IV, 486–87; James Westfall Thompson, *The Wars of Religion in France: The Huguenots, Catherine de Medici and Philip II* (Chicago: University of Chicago Press, 1909) 360; Kristen Neuschel, *Word of Honor: Interpreting Noble Culture in Sixteenth-Century France* (Ithaca, NY: Cornell University Press, 1989), 52–53.

dé's Association with two of his close relatives in 1562 and fought actively in Normandy. He was still alive and loyal to the Protestant cause in 1580.³⁶ On the other hand, the Saintonge captain, François de Pons, baron de Mirambeau, broke with the Huguenot party in the later 1570s because of a serious affront to his honor after participating in and surviving five civil wars. Although he was trusted enough to undertake negotiations for the cause at court in 1575 and was elected by the heavily Protestant nobility of Saintonge to the 1576 Estates-General of Blois, he aroused the suspicion of the young Henry, Prince of Condé (Louis's son), by entering into discussions at these meetings about a possible exchange of lands with the crown. The Huguenot army leader feared that he planned to surrender control of the strategic port of Brouage and relieved him of its command. Stung, Mirambeau ended his long engagement in the Protestant military cause.³⁷

Many of the more obscure figures met in these pages similarly survived the conspiracies and occupied significant roles in the First Civil War and subsequent conflicts. The core group of conspirators in Lyon all managed to evade arrest after the discovery of the arms they had stockpiled in the houses of Constantin and Terrasson. Most returned in 1561 or 1562 to the city whose military seizure they had tried to organize in 1560. After the Huguenots successfully took control of the city at the outset of the First Civil War, Pierre Nadal and Jean Darut were appointed to the political council set up by the Reformed to share in government. Antoine Vincent received a commission to recruit Swiss troops to aid in the city's defense, a task he carried out with the assistance of Claude Le Maître, one of the

---

³⁶ Potter, "French Protestant Nobility in 1562," 326–27; *HE*, II, 729; David Potter, ed., *Foreign Intelligence and Information in Elizabethan England. Two English Treatises on the State of France, 1580–1584*, Camden Fifth Series, Vol. 25 (Cambridge: Cambridge University Press, 2004), 144.

³⁷ *FP¹*, VIII, 287–89. It is harder to speak with confidence about one other captain of the conspiracy who may have fought in the civil wars. The leader for Anjou identified by the early Protestant historians simply as "La Chesnaie" could have been the "sieur [Guy?] de la Chesnaye Lalier" who seized Craon with a small band of men he raised in the vicinity in 1562, then joined Condé at Orléans, but was soon induced to turn his coat (*HE*, III, 668–70). André Joubert, "René de la Rouvraye, Sieur de Bressault," *Revue Historique et Archéologique du Maine* 10 (1881): 133–35, seems to accept this identification, but the same author's *Histoire de la baronnie de Craon de 1382 à 1626* (Angers: Germain et G. Grassin, 1888), 140–42, 145–46 insists that the conspirator was a second individual, Joachim de La Chesnaie, seigneur de Congnier, about whom he provides no further information but who could be the "Cognée" who was one of the Protestant captains who raised men in the Third Civil War, according to La Popelinière, *Histoire de France*, I, part 2, 63.

two men who had come to Triou to tell him to go to Lyon. A decade later, Darut would be among the victims of the *Vêpres lyonnaises*, the local Saint Bartholomew's massacre.[38]

Those in Montpellier and Nîmes identified by the Toulouse judicial commissioners as most centrally involved in organizing the "voyage of Lyon" likewise all survived and would subsequently reappear in a variety of local leadership positions in the First Civil War and after. Guillaume Sandre, seigneur de Saint-Georges, and Louis Toyras, seigneur de Saint-Jean, the two commanders of the Montpellier contingent that left for Lyon, were pursued deep into the Cévennes by Villars and his men in the autumn crackdown but managed to escape. When the clouds of civil war gathered around Montpellier eighteen months later, Saint-Georges was one of four men elected to take charge of the city's defenses. When the city came under siege in August 1562, "Toyras"—perhaps Saint-Jean, perhaps his father—led one of the companies that assured its successful defense. Pierre Combes, seigneur de Combas, one of those who provided the money for the contingent, led a unit from Montpellier that came to the defense of Béziers when it was threatened by Joyeuse's troops in June 1562. By early 1563 he was the city's first consul.[39] Meanwhile, Claude Formy and Francois Maupeau, "deacons of the voyage of Lyon," both became ministers, with Formy serving Montpellier's church until his death in 1581.[40] Guillaume de Sauzet, "leader of the schemes and raids" in Nîmes, also began to prepare himself for the pastoral ministry, but he died fighting in the region in the First Civil War before he judged himself ready to receive the laying on of hands.[41]

Other noblemen of the Midi encountered here likewise fought in 1562. Ardoin de Maillane, after dutifully obeying the order of the Geneva Council that he remain in the city for a year after his December 1560 interrogation, returned to his native region early in 1562 and

---

[38] Information kindly provided by Natalie Zemon Davis.
[39] *HE*, III, 166, 169, 201; Guiraud, *Réforme à Montpellier*, I, 401, II, *Preuves*, 225, 262–64, 266, 274. Combes would still occupy an important place in the church in 1570.
[40] Maupeau briefly served as pastor to the nearby churches of Lunel and Mauguio before disappearing from the historical record after 1565. "A Montpellier au XVIe siècle d'après les registres d'état civil huguenot," *BSHPF* 48 (1899): 78, 80, 83–85; Guiraud, *Réforme à Montpellier*, I, 461, 478, II, *Preuves*, 255–57; *HE*, III, 166, 169; Loirette, "Catholiques et protestants," 515.
[41] Benedict and Fornerod, "Deputies," 314, 330.

soon thereafter was placed at the head of a company of troops created to guard Beaucaire after it was taken by the Protestants from Nîmes. He was also named to the political council established in November 1562 by the Estates of the Protestant-controlled portion of Languedoc as part of the set of new institutions created to oversee the war effort and government of the province. One of his younger brothers—the source does not indicate which one but indicates that he was a "good commander (*bon officier*)"—died fighting in this conflict just outside the walls of Montpellier.[42]

Similarly, Raymond de Valette, seigneur de Cardet, who accompanied the younger Maligny when the latter visited Toulouse (and whose chateau would be destroyed by Villars's men in November 1560 in retribution for his behavior during the summer) led the group that took over the cathedral of Nîmes by force and destroyed its images in December 1561. Two months later, he directed the recruitment and reviewing of the troops that the congregation placed at the disposal of Antoine de Crussol when that trusted courtier sent to pacify the Southeast neared the region. Cardet subsequently led one of the companies from Languedoc that went to Orléans after Condé raised the standard of revolt there.[43] Jean de Fay-Virieu-Malleval, who brought the urgent message to Maligny to cancel the Lyon enterprise and subsequently helped organize the successful extraction of the conspirators from the city, became governor of Tournon for the Protestant forces during the First Civil War. His elder brother, Antoine de Fay-Peyraud, also involved in the Maligny affair according to Saconay, filled the same post in Montpellier. A decade later, Malleval would find himself in Paris at the time of the Saint Bartholomew's massacre, renounce his faith after his life was spared, and subsequently serve under the moderate Montmorency-Damville as commander of artillery in Languedoc, service that enabled him to earn membership in the order of Saint Michael.[44] Even François Bordon, the second-generation Genevan arrested in Bourg-en-Bresse on suspicion of involvement in the Lyon enterprise, set off again to fight in France,

---

[42] Naef, 235; *HE*, III, 176–77, 208–09; Vic and Vaissette, *Histoire générale de Languedoc*, V, 232, 239, 243; Daussy, *Parti huguenot*, 368, 544.
[43] Ménard, *Nismes*, IV, 253, 317–18, 336; *HE*, III, 156.
[44] Nicod, "Maison de Fay-Peyraud," 325–27; Guiraud, *Réforme à Montpellier*, II, *Preuves*, 93.

requesting and receiving permission from the Small Council on July 23, 1562, "to go to the aid of the church of Lyon." He survived the conflict, returned to Geneva, but disappears from the city's records after 1564.[45]

The engagement of so many of those deeply involved in the conspiracies of 1560 in the Huguenot war efforts of 1562 and beyond should not be taken to imply that most of those who led the latter efforts were veterans of the earlier plotting. No firm evidence connects the great majority of Condé's chief lieutenants in the First Civil War to the events of 1560. During the intervening sixteen months, the Reformed churches grew dramatically in size, number, and capacity for institutional coordination. Many of the Protestant commanders of 1562 may have been drawn to the faith in this period. Among the military leaders of the Protestant cause in 1562 was even to be found the man entrusted at the end of August 1560 with delivering the letter to Antoine of Navarre summoning him to court, Antoine de Crussol, who seems to have been convinced by his experience in attempting to pacify the Southeast in early 1562 that militant Catholicism posed an even greater threat to respect for royal authority than the Reformed churches, which by then had won the legal right to assemble. Nevertheless, the extent of the continuity between the militants of 1560 and the captains and commanders of late 1561–62 suggests that the view that the conspiracy of Amboise was the first act of the Wars of Religion contains a good measure of truth. The conspiratorial activity of 1560 had shown the French Reformed churches and their aristocratic champions how military units could be organized on their behalf and identified individuals who could take charge of organizing them. It was a fateful legacy.

Gilles Triou meanwhile remained imprisoned for twenty months, considerably longer than others arrested in connection with the troubles of 1560. In the course of his detention, he was transferred from Lyon to Orléans for interrogation during the November 1560 trial of Condé, then subsequently moved to the Conciergerie in Paris, most likely for re-examination after the second round of proceedings began the next year to clear the prince's name. The records of the

---

[45] Naef, 209n.

Parlement of Paris reveal that he was released from the Conciergerie on April 30, 1562, "by the good pleasure of the king and queen [mother]." Jacques de La Sague, the messenger arrested a week before him with the incriminating evidence from the vidame de Chartres, went free at the same time. Their liberation shows the accuracy of the early histories that asserted that both had been promised that their lives would be spared if they cooperated with their interrogators. The crown kept its word, if belatedly. But with the clouds of civil war gathering as they were released—the Protestants had seized Orléans four weeks previously—the tranquility of the realm demanded that they not be allowed to go wherever they wanted. Both were banished forever from France on pain of immediate hanging if found again within its borders.[46] Did Triou nonetheless set out for Orléans for the second time in his life to serve the prince of Condé and the Huguenot cause? Did he return to Lyon, which the Protestants seized on the very day he was liberated and controlled throughout the First Civil War? Or did he obey the order and live out his remaining days in exile in Geneva or elsewhere under one of his multiple names or aliases? No clues to his subsequent whereabouts have yet been found, but they may still be, just as I hope more will yet be learned about other of the obscure individuals encountered in these pages.

---

[46] AN X2a 923, April 22, 1562; AN X2b 33, April 23, 1562; AN X2a 129, fo. 648; La Planche, 699–700; Sylvie Daubresse, *Conjurer la dissension religieuse : la justice du roi face à la Réforme (1555–1563)* (Seyssel: Champ Vallon, 2020), 152. I owe a great debt of thanks to Dr. Daubresse, who recently discovered the documents in the Archives Nationales revealing the liberation of Triou and La Sague and was kind enough to share this information with me and furnish the relevant pages of her book prior to publication. Her work also reveals that two cousins of Malleval who had been arrested shortly after "le faict de Lyon" and fruitlessly interrogated about it, François and Imbert de Fay, seigneurs de Changy, were released from the Conciergerie eight months earlier, on August 2, 1561, just after the edict of July. On the Changys, see La Planche, 591–92; *HE*, I, 250, 389, 514, III, 263, 323–24, 347, 361, 363; Nicod, "La maison de Fay-Peyraud," 323–25.

Appendix

The Deposition of Gilles Triou

The deposition of Gilles Triou is preserved among the papers of the house of Foix-Albret-Navarre transferred from the chateau of Pau to the Archives Départementales des Pyrénées-Atlantique in the nineteenth century (call number ADPA, E 582 [13]). It is a clean copy.

This transcription follows the principles outlined in Bernard Barbiche and Monique Chatenet, *L'édition des textes anciens, XVIe–XVIIIe siècle* with one significant exception. In order not to obscure the ambiguity of certain passages and the problems of interpretation involved, I have inserted only a minimum of punctuation into a manuscript entirely devoid of it, and then only by inserting periods at the end of each paragraph and between phrases in cases where the division of a paragraph into several sentences seems obviously appropriate. Annotation has also been kept to a minimum because identifying information about most of the people mentioned in the document can be found in the text and footnotes. The Index may be used for locating this information.

ADPA, E 582 (13)

[fo. 1] du huictiesme de septembre cinq cens soixante par devant Me Fournel Pourret et Chastillon[1]

---

[1] Jehan du Fournel was the lieutenant civil of the sénéchaussée of Lyon. I have not been able to identify the other examining magistrates.

Pierre Menard ne vouloit faire aultre responce que celle qu'il feit hier par devant monsieur le gouverneur ledit Fournel et plusieurs aultres.

Se nomme come dessus est menuisier natifz du Surgieres pres La Rochelle d'aige de cinquante ans ou envyron.

Fut hier faict prisonnier estant au faubourg de Veze[2] logis de la croix blanche.

Ne scayt la cause s'il n'est l'esmute qu'avint en ceste ville mercredy dernier passé.
Fut tout ledict jour de mercredy en la maison de Jehan Constantin orphebvre en rue longe enseigne sainct martin.

Dit que sur l'heure de huict à neufz heures du soir ceulx de la ville vindrent audit logis de Constantin estoient ausdit lieux assemblez de quarante à cinquante homes. Ne scayt à quel effaict.

Respondant est en ceste ville dez digmenche derniere est venu en ceste ville de Genebve ou il se tient pour en faire amener quelques meubles qu'il avoyt bailli en garde audit Contastin.

Qui est la cognoissance qu'il a eu avec luy avec lequel il a veu quelquefoys Pierre Tarrasson.

Ne cognoist Jehan Badier que pour l'avoir veu une foys en passant ung sien amy. Luy dict que ledit Badier estoit homme de bien et faisoyt beaucoup de charité aux pauvres.

[fo. 1v] A ouy parler d'aultres foys que ung gentilhomme qui se nomme Belimes ou Belimour qui venoit en la maison dudit Constantin. Mais ne cognoist la lettre dudit Belimes que luy a esté exinee en datte du dix-septieme aoust.

Luy ont esté exinees trois autres lettres cottés B C D.

Plus ung petit memoyre escript en lettre ytalliene et aultres comensant Sire Constantin.

---

[2] Vaise, a suburb of Lyon just up the Saône from the walls of the sixteenth-century city.

Ne le recognoist.

Idem une feuille de papier portant rolle d'armes et forme de bataillon.

Confesse y avoir escript ces motz arquebuz pistolletz morrions manches peicques chifre et aultres motz y escriptz.

Et fut escript sur ledit Constantin icelle dictant sellon les rolles que ledit Constantin avoit en sa main.

Luy ont exinees rolles comensant l'un d'iceulx Me Pierre de Prouvence — ix a c qu'il a recogneu estre l'un d'iceulx que tenoit lors ledit Constantin.

Aussi le rolle comensant Memoire de Guilleaume Guay ix^a finissant par ces motz Claude Richard r/r/bien.

Ledit rolle en doce de neufs lignes portant le nombre comensant l'enseigne des veloutiers bien armés finissant Pierre Anthoine Rurcaille le tout recogneu par le respondant et signé et que lesdits rolles se faisoient pour scavoir le nombre d'armes et hommes que l'on auroyt.

L'on disoit à Genefve que le roy de Navarre se vouloit saisir de la ville de Lyon et s'en parloyt en diverses sortes. Luy dict Constantin que ledit Roy se vouloyt saisir de ladite ville pour y faire tenir les estatz et donner ordre à la religion.

[fo. 2] Oultre les armes pourtez par ledict rolle /O/ en furent apportés aultres en la maison dudit Constantin ledit jour de mercredy environ quatre vingtz corcelletz et furent les gaigne denier payés par ledit Constantin le respondant present.

Ne scest le jour qu'il debvoit executer leur entreprinse parce qu'ilz attandoient l'arivée des compaignons de jour à aultre et remettoient le tout soubz l'advis du Sr de Sainct Cyre cappitaine principal qui estoit logé chez Tarrasson.

Bien a ouy dire audit Constantin que ladite ville saisie ilz auroient nouvelles du Roy de Navarre. Ilz fairoient cryer en ladite ville de par les Roys de France et de Navarre aux citoyens et habitans de ladite ville ne molester l'un à l'aultre et que nul ne bodgeast de ladite ville sur peine de la hard. A ceste fin envoyeroyt le prince de Condé son frere avec ces lettres patentes pendent que l'on donneroyt ordre que lesdits estatz y feussent tenuz pour la police et ordre du gouvernement de ce royaulme et affaires de la religion.

Que ledit jour de mecredy n'estoit le jour de l'execution entreprinse mais en advint le tumulte parce que Claude Mandur de la ville arriva en la maison dudit Constantin qui vit plusieurs balles d'armes et demanda ledit Constantin qui n'estoit lors à la maison et depuis advertit ledit Constantin le fit scavoir audit cappitaine qui estoyt logé chez ledit Tarrason lequel cappitaine comanda faire armer ses gens dixaine à dixaine.

Peu apres sur la nuyt comme lesdits homes s'armoient survindrent les gens de ladite ville qui voulurent entrer en ladite maison de Constantin. Ce que le respondant oyant se cascha dans la cave dudit logis comme fit aussi ung arquebuzier de ladite ville jusques à ce que le bruict fut passé.

[fo. 2v] Entendit que ceulx qui sortoient de ladite maison Constantin avoir leur mot de guet Crist l'apel et y eust grande meslee de personnes.

Le respondant sortit de ladite cave envyron les unze heures de nuict s'en alla à la maison de Claude Nouyer menuisier pres Confort ou il couscha et ne scait que devindrent les homes de ladite meslee.

Avoyt veu le mardy precedent au matin Bussillon qui parla audit Constantin estant encores en son lict et a signé sa responce Pierre Menard Fournel.

Par devant M. Torneon

Ledit jour nous estant à la chambre de la question ledit Meynard confronté à Bussellon ledit Bussillon dit qu'il a ouy appeller ledit Meynard Maitre Gilles le Gaultier. Ce que ledit Meynard a recogneu et dit s'appelle Gilles Triou et avoyr changé son nom de peur d'estre cogneu. Requerant au surplus qu'on eust pitié de luy et qu'il avoit dict verité comme il avoyt deliberé dire cy apres.

Confronté audit Bussillon qui a soustenu.

Le neufiesme dudit moys lesdits Fournel et Pourret continuans

Dict qu'il a changé son nom à cause cy dessus et que son vray nom est Gilles Triou comme peult tesmoigner Monsieur le procureur du Roy à Molins où le respondant s'est marié y a sept ou huict ans.

[fo. 3] Est sa femme à Genefve depuis la sainct Jehan dernier passé ou ledit respondant avoyt demouré quatre ans auparavant.

Nota que ladite responce pour son regard est inparfaicte et finist en la derniere ligne dicelle a changé son dict.

Ledit jour

Dict qu'il a changé sondit nom parce qu'il avoit esté distributeur des aulmosnes que l'on faisoit en ceste ville aux pauvres fidelles et aultres necessiteulx ce qu'il avoit faict soubz le nom de maitre Gilles.

Luy avoit esté donné charge de ladite distribution par Anthoyne Vincent duquel il avoit eu cognoissance par le moien de sa belle mere qui est de Mollins lors estant le respondant logé prez d'elle audit lieu de Molins et depuis elle estant en ceste ville cinq ans y a passez elle luy bailla cognoissance dudit Vincent.

Luy a dict ledit Vincent puis deux ans en ca que s'il scavoyt quelques pouvres gens esquelz il eust pitié il luy bailleroit argent pour leur distribuer et conferoient ensemble de la religion.

Ce faisant s'assembloient quelque foys Pierre Nadard, Jehan Darud, Julien Calendrin et Pierre Davailles imprimeur qui se tient de present à Genefve.

[fo. 3v] Ledit Darud luy bailla la premiere foys quarante testons estant le respondant logé en la maison de Gazeau libraire en rue Merciere. Aussi ledit Vincent et Nadard luy en ont baillé par plusieurs foys. Ne scauroit dire les somes parce que si tost qu'il les avoyt distribuez leur en rendoyt compte lui en bailloient d'aultres.

Estoit de ce temps logé en la maison Mannilliane à present femme de Francoys de Gabiane rue Merciere ung predicant nomé maitre Michel Millet de Normandye qui est de present à la Rochelle.

Dict que le comencement de ceste conspiration ne fut faict en ceste ville. Et est vray que par le moys de Janvyer dernier ilz vinrent le Sr de la Riviere de Chateau Neufz qui a du taphetas noyr au bout du nez qu'il a couppé estoient logés à la pomme firent assembler en la maison dudit Tarrasson en la chambre la plus haulte lesdits Vincent Constantin Nadard Claude Gousset et y fut appellé ledit Jehan Darud qui dict qu'il ne s'y vouloyt trouver disant que estoyt chose de grand consequance n'en vouloyt ouyr parler. Aussi s'y trouva ung ministre du nom duquel n'est recors logé chez ledit Tarrasson.

Là ledit de la Riviere propose que les eglises de france s'assembloient pour tenir journee et deliberer de grandz affaires. Requerat que les susdits declairassent s'ilz vouloient estre de ladite assemblee et deliberation et s'i trouver. Ce que les seigneurs assistans accordarent pourveu que ce ne fut contre l'honneur de dieu ny du Roy et qu'ilz n'en entendroient aultre chose jusques à ce que la journee se tiendroit en laquelle s'ilz y vouloient venir y seroient receuz.

[fo. 4] Depuis ledit Chateau Neufz retourné en ceste ville par le moys de fevrier ensuyant peu avant karesme parla esdits Vincent et Nadard à chacun d'eux particullierement. Ne scaict s'il parla à d'aultres.

Peu apres s'assemblerent en la chambre de Jehan Darud dez membres de la maison du Sr George Aubret scavoir lesdits Vincent Nadard Constantin Gousset ledit Darud et le respondant. N'est recors s'il y en avoyt d'autres.

Fut à ladite assemblee et par l'un d'iceulx n'est recors par qui rapporté ce que ledit chateau neufz leur avoit dict assavoir que journee avoit esté tenue à Nantes où s'estoient trouvez plusieurs gentilzhommes et conclud lever gens qui se trouveroient en armes là par où la court seroyt dans le dixieme ou douziesme de mars ensuyvant que ledit S^r prince de Condé conduyroit l'entreprinse pour eulx saisir dez personnes dez messieurs de Guise, leur faire rendre compte des grands tortz et griefz qu'ilz avoient faict au Roy et à ce Royaulme et apres faire tenir les estats pour faire mectre order à la police des estatz et religion.

Les susdits assemblés prinrent resolution d'envoyer vingt cinq homes et que l'on fourniroit quelques armes.

Si en furent envoyés dix que le respondant ne vid parce que lesdits Constantin et Gousset prindrent charge de les choisir et de les faire rendre à Orleans.

[fo. 4v] Furent envoyés audit Orleans par la conduicte d'un serviteur de Pierre Nadard vingt cinq pistolletz vingt cinq paires de manches de maille et dix huict jacques de maille desquelles le respondant en vid une partie et ne les compta parce que ledit Constantin avoyt eu charge d'acheter lesdits mailles et ledit Gousset les pistolletz.

Les susdits dix homes partirent de ceste ville pour aller audit Orleans sur le comencement dudit moys de mars. A ouy dire audit Gousset que ledit Nadard luy bailla cinquante escuz pistolletz pour paier lesdits pistolletz.

Le respondant depuis le partement desdits homes demoura en ceste ville jusques sur la fin dudit moys de mars que arrivarent ledit Sr de la Riviere un aultre nomé le Garet logés au griffon. Mandarent querir lesdits Constantin Gousset et le Respondant. Leur dirent s'ilz avoyent le coeur failli et s'ilz ne vouloient mectre en debvoir d'assembler homes et armez en ceste ville. Que ledit prince de Condé estoit jà mis en danger et y failloit donner ordre.

Feirent responce qu'ilz n'avoient le moien et ne le vouloient entreprendre. Resoulurent que lesdits Gousset et respondant yroient par devers ledit prince pour entendre sa deliberation.

N'y estoient lesdits Vincent Darud Nadard et Tarrasson.

Ledit Gousset et le respondant partirent de ceste ville ensemble. Ledit Gousset fournissoit ses despens. Ledit Constantin bailla dix huict escuz et pistolletz audit respondant. Allarent de canpaignie jusques à Orleans. Ledit Gousset demoura cependant le respondant s'en alla à Paris où il entendit que ledit prince estoyt à Condé où le respondant fut. N'y trouva ledit prince.

[fo. 5] Fut de compaignie audit Condé avec ung gentilhome de Champaigne duquel il ne scayt le nom et ne le recognoist que pour l'avoir veu depuis à Genefve.

Arrivez audit Condé vint à eux de la part de madame de Condé leur demander d'où ilz estoient et ce qu'ilz demandoyent.

Feist responce ledit gentilhomme qu'il estoyt venu pour avoir responce d'un pacquet que ung gentilhomme de Mectz avoyt escript audit prince enquerant où il estoit. Leur fut dict que ledit prince estoyt allé à Frontevaux veoir sa tante et le trouveroient à Tours à l'entree du roy par son retour passeroyt par Orleans.

Lors ledit gentilhomme et le respondant s'acheminarent audit Orleans y trouverent encores ledit Gausset et sejournarent quelques jours attendant ledit prince qui passa en poste sans qu'ilz feussent adverty.

A l'occasion de quoy ledit gentilhomme et respondant prindrent la poste devers Estampes ou trouvarent ledit prince logé à l'escu de France et ne peurent parler pour se soir jusques au matin ensuyvant se dressarent à ung secretaire sien que luy a fit le rapport.

Entrarent en la chambre dudit S^r qui estoyt encores au lict. Dirent qu'ilz estoient envoyés de la part de l'eglise de Lyon pour entendre sa volunté sur ce que lesdits de La Riviere et Lagaret leurs avoyent dict d'avoir force dans Lyon et s'ilz auroit le coeur failli que ledit prince estoyt exposé en danger estoyent prestz d'obeyr à sa volunté.

[fo. 5v] Ledit prince leur feist response que desjà les troupes estoient rompues. Ne scauroyt quel ordre y donner. Protestoyt devant dieu ne vouloir rien entreprendre contre son roy qu'il en communicqueroyt à son conseil pour y donner ordre que chacun ce pendant se tint en paix. Estoyt marry d'avoir sceu que quelque peu auparavant on avoyt pendu en effigie le cardinal de Lorraine qui ne servoyt que de scandalle et d'irriter le roy qui s'en estoyt dressé audit Sr de Condé.

Ladite response faicte, ledit gentilhomme et le respondant se retirarent, ledit gentilhomme à Paris et le respondant à Orleans où il trouva encores ledit Gousset. Communicqua avec luy avec le Sr de la Bergerie et de la Fontayne ministres de l'eglise d'Orleans qui prindrent pour lors resolution de tenir les affaires en paix.

Ledit Gousset revint à Lyon ou trouva lesdits de La Riviere La Garet et Constantin. Communicquent ce que dessus et resoluent de vivre en paix qui fut sur la fin du moys d'avril ensuyvant.

Par ledit moys de mars et au temps de l'assignation donnée à Amboyse arriva en ceste ville le cappitaine qu'on appelle Goulayne à la prince rouge qui se disoyt envoyé de la part dudit prince et chargé si les affaires y succedoient d'attendre lettres du Roy pour garder qu'on ne pillast et saccageast et parce que lesdits affaires d'Amboyse ne succedarent s'en retourna et lors que le respondant parla à luy estoyent present lesdits Vincent Nadard Constantin et Gousset.

A despuis veu ledit gentilhomme qui se disoyt aller en Bourgogne en la maison du Sr de Maligny.

[fo. 6] Le respondant avoit faict rapport de son voiaige à Orleans aux susnomez se retira à Genefve où il a demeuré jusques au xxviii aoust sans avoyr entendu aultre chose desdits entreprinses s'il n'est par comun bruict qu'il couroyt à Genefve que l'on se vouloyt saisir de ceste vile mais que les affaires se menoyent secretement entre les principaulx à ce qu'ilz ne feussent descouvers comme ilz avoient esté à la precedente assemblee.

Bien ouyst dire que par d'advis des Srs Calvin de Beze Passy et Pastereau auroyt esté envoyé en Allemaigne deux gentilzhommes l'un desquelz s'appelle Maligny le jeune qui se surnomme le Boys et ung autre nommé Vezine qu'il ne cognoist pour lever gens qu'ils auroyent trouvé. Mays le roy de Navarre ne ceulx de Genefve n'accordoient qu'on leur fit descendre en France de peur qu'il fut mal aysé les en retirer. Et ainsi l'a ouy dire audit S^r de La Riviere par ung nommé Florent que aultresfoys a demeuré chez ledit Sr Aubret et de present demeure à Genefve.

Dict oultre que ledit jour xxviii aoust le Sr de Vareynes qu'on appelle aultrement Guillaume Trye et Claude Maitre vinrent chercher le respondant en sa maison à Genefve. Luy dirent qu'il falloyt aller à Lyon pour s'ayder à l'entreprinse de se saisir de ladite ville et qu'il y pourroyt beaucoup servir. Luy en parlarent touz deulx ensemblement et separement.

Le prierent de se haster et admener et parce que Jehan Frellon alloyt à la foyre de Flanquefort qui avoyt ung cheval de retour à Lyon le respondant alla souper avec ledit Frellon et vinrent en la maison de la fille dudit Vincent autresfoys marié audit Genefve et de present vefve.

[fo. 6v] Dit là le respondant audit Vincent que lesdits Trye et Maistre l'avoyent chargé de venir à Lyon pour les affaires qu'il scavoyt.

Lors dit ledit Vincent qu'il n'en scavoit qu'en dire et avoit peur que cestre entreprinse reusist et print aussi mal que la premiere. Et à son advis ledit Frellon ne scavoyt rien desdits propoz car pendant le soupper ledit Vincent enqueroyt dudit Frellon quel bruit et nouveau y avoit à Lyon.

Le jour suivant qui fut le penultime d'aoust le respondant partist de Genefve pour venir en ceste ville. Logea et arriva le dymanche au soir en la maison dudit Constantin.

Ledit Vincent donna charge au respondant de parler à son fils et luy dire qu'il gardast tout le vin qui estoyt en la cave et en vendit le moins qu'il pourroit ce que le respondant n'a faict et n'a parlé audit filz.

Le respondant mena le cheval chez ung chassemarre où il demeura jusques au lendemain et fut rendu en la maison dudit Frellon par ung jeune garcon que le respondant ne cognoist.

Dit que des Srs de Genefve aucun ne bailla charge au respondant que les sur nomez et tenoient lesdits S^rs les affaires secretz audit repondant.

Ledit respondant arrivé en ceste ville en fit entendre l'occasion audit Constantin qui luy dit que ledit Sr de Saint Cyre aultrement nommé le Sr de Maligny l'aisné estoyt en ceste ville logé ches ledit Constantin qu'il estoyt chefz de ladite entreprinse et toute la sepmaine debvoient arriver gens de toutes partz.

[fo. 7] Ledit respondant souppa ledit soir seul avec ledit Constantin.

Le matin ensuyvant ledit Sr de Saint Cyre, adverty par ledit Constantin de l'arivee dudit respondant, ledit Constantin vint querir ledit respondant pour aller parler audit Saint Cyre, ce qu'il fit et le trouva seul en la maison dudit Tarrasson au plus haute hetage.

Et ledit S^r luy demanda s'il avoit rien de nouveau audit Genefve et s'il estoit allé par ceste ville sans y estre cogneu.

Fit responce qu'il n'y avoit rien de nouveau audit Genefve et que de luy n'ozeraoit aller par ceste ville tant il y estoit cogneu.

Ledit Sr de Saint Cyre lors serra les espaules en disant retirez vous en votre logis. Il ne faut pas faire du fol.

Le respondant demeura ledit jour à disner au logis dudit Tarrasson avec lesdits Srs de Saint Cyre de Bellimes La Riviere Chateau Neufz Constantin et Terrasson et demeura ledit jour audit logis jusques apres souppé sans en auser sortir de poeur d'estre cogneu.

Apres ledit souppe arriva ung gentilhomme de grande stature barbe noyre qu'il a ouy appeller le Sr de Maleval logé à la couppe que l'on dit luy appartenir.

Lesdits Srs de Saint Cyre et de Maleval se retirarent ensemble à part ne scayt quelz propos ilz eurent.

[fo. 7v] Vid cependant entrer un souldat logé au mesme lougis avec aultre qu'il a entendu y estoient mais ne les vid.

Couscha en la maison dudit constin y demeura jusques sur le disner le lendemain à lire ce pendant ledit Constantin alla par la ville et ung sien serviteur ledit jour entrarent quelques souldatz audit logis qu'il ne pourroit recognoistre sans les veoir.

L'apres disnee dudit jour luy et ledit Constantin commancerent à faire les rolles et memoires qu'il a recogneuz cy dessus.

Plus aultre rolle depuis treuvé comencant "vers les cordelliers" et finissant "il y quarante cinq sans arnoy et ausquelz fault quinze corselletz deux arquebuzes le reste hallebardes."

Aultre rolle comencant "comme à son fort" finissant "ceux qui ne sont poinct armés huitante cinq homes tous halebardies piquiers et harquebuziers."

Qui sont rolles sur lesquelz a esté dressé le calcul et bataillon susdit et en signe de cela le respondant les a signé par devant nous.

Ne scayt le nombre d'homes qui se devoient trouver à ladite entreprinse et d'où ils debvoient venir. Bien a entendu que ledit Sr de Vezines en debvoit venir et faire venir dudit Genefve secretement troys cens homes par ce que lesdits Srs de Genefve ne se vouloient desaisir d'homes de la peur qu'ilz ont du duc de Savoye.

[fo. 8 (erroneously numbered 6 in the manuscript)] Ledit Constantin dit au respondant qu'on ne scavoyt le jour de l'execution de l'entreprinse et le tout deppendoyt dudit Sr de Saint Cyre qui attandoyt de jour à aultre nouvelles du roy de Navarre et prince de Condé. Et lui tardoit fort qu'il n'en avoit nouvelles et que ledit gentilhomme luy debvoyt bien quatre vingtz livres de despence.

Ne scavoyt qui fournisoyt argent. Bien a entendu dire audit S^r de La Riviere que ledit roy de Navarre debvoit emprumpter soixante mil livres et que luy en avoit parlé audit George Aubret ce qu'il avoyt refuzé.

Se faisoit ladite entreprinse par gentilzhomes qui se donnoient parolle de l'un à l'aultre.

Disoit ledit Constantin que les Srs de Montbrun et de Moutvans de Prouvence debvoient venir au secours avec leurs gens qu'ilz avoient ja levez et que ledit Roy de Navarre faisoit aussi gens pres de luy de maniere que l'assemblee seroyt bien forte.

Ledit jour de mercredy ledit Constantin ne fit que aller et revenir par la ville. Le respondant demeuroit seul au logis de peur d'estre descouvert.

Sur le soir ledit jour arrivarent armez à la maison dudit Constantin à la conduicte d'un homme Rousseau ung peu blessé au visaige. Le respondant a ouy dire estre arsnetier (?).

A recogneu les nommez en un rolle qu'il a signé que ledit Constantin luy a dit avoir faict promesse pour servir à ladite entreprinse.

[fo. 8v] Ledit Constantin avoir adverty ledit Sr de Saint Cyre de ce qu'ilz estoient descouvertz lesdits Saint Cyre et de Bellimes firent armer ceulx qui estoient à leur suicte desdits armes portez chez ledit Constantin. Ledit de Bellimes distribua à chacun d'eulx son harnoys les apportant de dixaine en dixaine et n'en distribua au respondant parce qu'il n'avoyt arquebuze ny hallebarde et n'estoyt de sa charge.

Se armarent les susdits pour la poeur qu'ilz eurent d'avoir esté descouvers et non pour l'execution de leur susdite entreprinse qu'ilz ne pouvoient encores executer.

Et comme ilz comensoient à s'armer le respondant qui se purmenoyt en la court a perceu venir quelques gens entre lesquelz on disoyt estre le cappitaine de ladite ville. Entrarent en ladite court de Constantin et parce qu'ilz vouloient faire effort à la porte de ladite maison le respondant se jecta dans une cave où il se tint casché. Bien entendu que ceulx qui sortirent de ladite maison Constantin repoulsarent les gens de la ville qui estoient là venuz de force que l'un dez harquebuziers de ladite ville se cascha en ladite cave.

Et peu apres ledit harquebuzier et respondant sortirent comme il a dit cy dessus.

Survint quelcun que le respondant ne cogneust qui appella les soldatz estans en ladite maison Constantin disant qu'ilz sortissent et que le guet estoit rompu, ce qu'ilz firent jusques à la porte de ladite maison mais n'arrestarent pas beaucoup de rantrer.

[fo. 9] Et audit rentrer estoient lesdits Srs de Saint Cyre, de Bellimes et ledit Sr de Maleval. Ne se print garde s'ilz estoient armez ou non.

Bien ouyst qu'ilz parlamentoient ensemble et disoient qu'il failloyt porter les armez en la maison dudit Tarrasson ce qu'ilz fisrent.

Disoient aussi qu'ilz en avoient blessé quelques ungs et s'ilz eussent voulu eussent tous tué et que deux dez leurs avoyent esté blessez l'un à la teste d'un coup de pistollet l'aultre au cousté d'un coup d'arquebuze lesquelz il ne vid.

Vid bien lesdits Srs de Saint Cyre de Maleval de Bellimes qui n'estoient blessez.

Tous s'en allarent mesmes la femme dudit Constantin chargée son enfant sur son col et se voulant retirer à la maison de son pere fut refuzee.

Revint ledit Constantin soubdain de la maison dudit Terrasson disant tout est perdu que lesdits Srs de Saint Cyre et Maneval se voloient sauver luy avoient baillé charge d'aller vitement chercher ung batteau et faisoient conduire ses artres (?) au logis de la couppe.

Ne scait le respondant ce qu'en fut faict.

Le jour suyvant le respondant alla prez la poste chez ung menuysier nommé Claude pour chercher logis ou il couscha.

[fo. 9v] Le jour ensuyvant fut le respondant prins comme il alloit à la croix blanche prez chappeau roge prez les faulxbourgs de Veze.

A oublyé nous dire que ez premieres assemblees s'est trouvé et a esté convocqué Jehan Bertrand papetier. Et a signé le contenu esdits rolles de ses responses dudit jour ainsi signé Fournel Tryou Pourret.

Du xiiie dudit moys par devant lesdits M Fournel et Faye

Repeté en ses responces perciste adjouste qu'il a demeuré quelque temps avec ung religieux en Normandie ou il aprins à chanter en musique, a suyvy beaucoup de pays tant aux allemaignes que ailleur et a aprins ledit mestier de menuisier à Bordeaulx, se retira à Mollins y a viii ans à la toussainctz dernier ou il s'est marié avec Jehanne Pellisson vefve d'un nommé Jacques d'Aloy à laquelle il print acointance parce qu'ilz estoient instruitz en mesme religion.

Ont aussy demeuré troys ans audict Mollins, et de là venuz en ceste ville parce que les voisins murmuroient contre eulx parce qu'ilz n'alloient à la messe. Dez lors apporta lettres de recommandation audit Vincent qui luy furent baillez par le prieur des Carmes nommé Du Cret.

Plus que ledit Terrasson n'estoit present en l'assemblee qui fut faicte en sa chambre par le moys de janvier dernier.

Que on n'avoyt garde de tracter de telz affaires en presence de Jehan Du Poing parce qu'il estoyt legier de sens et parloit aussi tost pour luy que contre.

N'a sceu que personne de ceste ville ayt esté en ladite assemblé de Nantes.

Adjouste que ez propoz tenuz en l'assemblee faicte en la pomme rouge par le Sr de Goulayne disoit ledit S^r que que (sic) debvoient venir gens de Piedmont Dauphiné et Prouvence pour donner order qu'on ne saccageaste et pillast ceste ville que nul bogeast.

[fo. 10] Demeura ledit cappitaine environ troys sepmaines en ceste ville et ayant entendu que l'entreprinse d'Amboyse ne sortoyt effet se retira et le treuva le respondant à Rouhaine[3] ainsi qu'il alloyt au susdit voyaige d'Orleans et furent de compaignie par eaue jusques prez de Size[4] ou ledit gentilhome print terre disant qu'il s'en alloyt vers le Sr de Maligny.

---

[3] Roanne (Loire), a river port on the Loire.
[4] Decize (Nièvre), a river port on the Loire 120 km downstream from Roanne.

Bien luy dit le respondant qu'il s'en alloyt vers ledit S^r prince de Condé fit ledit Goulayne responce que s'il scavoyt ou il seroit qu'il luy escriroyt.

Est vray que le respondant estoit auparavant venu en ceste ville pour amener sa femme à Genefve.

Ne scavoit rien le respondant de l'entreprinse de ceste ville que ce qu'il en avoyt entendu par ledit S^r de La Riviere et ledit Florand.

Luy a esté exibé ung rolle escript en grosse lectre ytalliene commensant Anthoyne Utor dit qu'il ne scest que c'est.

Lecture facite d'icelle dit qu'il cognoist ung nommé Pierre de Villeneufve Philibert Courtoys Maitre Quentin le Petit Martin Pierre Bussillon Jehan Bertrand Pierre Martin Jehan du Poing au logis duquel du Poing il vid quatre hommes lors qu'il revint de Genefve qui fut par le moys de mars dernier et disoient estre venuz en ceste ville parce qu'en leur pays y avoit garnison pour [?] de la religion.

A oublié de nous dire que ledit Constantin luy avoyt dit faisant les rolles qu'il a cy dessus recogneu que ledit Saint Cyre luy avoyt defendu de ne riens dire de l'entreprinse à ceulx qui estoient desnomez esdits rolles et que ladite entreprinse estoyt pour bon affaire auquel il ne fauldroyt frapper ny ruer.

Bien estoit ladite entreprinse du Sr de Saint Cyre dresser bataillon aux portes et se saisir des clefz de la ville sans rien piller mais n'en disoyt rien à ceulx qu'il enroullouent si n'est à aucuns que c'estoyt pour faire prescher l'evangille. Ainsi signé Fournel Triou.

[fo. 10v] Fault à noter qu'il y a eu autres responces premieres par lesquelles ledit Gilles dict que en mars ou au cemencement d'avril l'aisné Maligny bailla à son frere 1500 écus pour aller en Allemagne lever gens.

Index

A

Abry, Claude (Geneva conspirator), 150–54
Agen (Lot-et-Garonne), 12, 113, 116, 188
Agen, synod of, 113
Agenais, 117n
Aigues-Mortes (Gard), 144
Airebaudouze, Pierre d' (minister), 153, 156
Aix-en-Provence, 66–67, 86, 90, 92, 159
Albiac, Charles d', alias Duplessis (minister and conspirator), 107–08, 118, 138
Albret, Jeanne d', 46, 48, 70, 72, 174
Aloy, Jacques d', 211
Alvarotti, Giulio (Ferrarese ambassador), 11, 15, 28, 110–11, 117–18, 132, 136, 172–73
Amboise, conspiracy of
  Beza and, 20, 22, 25–26, 45, 65–66, 68
  Calvin and, 3, 5, 20–27, 45, 48, 65–66, 68, 156–61, 165–66, 168–69, 181
  captains of, 30, 34–35, 186–92
  Condé and, 6, 27–29, 34, 49, 91, 93–94, 168–69
  details of the event, 10–14, 18–19, 38, 64
  England and, 15, 55–63, 77, 80, 172, 174
  financing of, 49, 55, 62, 75, 77, 91, 93, 171–74
  foreign involvement in, 11, 15, 53, 75, 77, 172
  Genevans and, 23, 25, 64–68, 147–66
  nature and goals of, 5, 10–37, 39–43, 49, 52–53, 60, 67, 90–91, 159, 174–78, 202–03
  Navarre and, 6, 27–29, 49–50, 52
  organization of, 29–30, 38, 76–77, 84–93, 168
  pastors and, 25–26, 52–53, 60–61, 168–69
  Reformed churches and, 19–20, 53–53, 66–70, 73–74, 92–95, 147–48, 168–70, 178–79
  repression following, 15, 179–81, 186
  royal letter of about March 31, 16–17
  scale of, 171n–72n
  Scotland and, 15, 55–62, 80
  sociology and beliefs of participants, 5, 53, 73, 148–65, 169–71
Andelot, François de Coligny, seigneur d', 38
Anduze (Gard), 115, 120, 123, 151, 153
Angers, 137–38, 144, 186
Angoumois, 65n, 186n
Anjou, 126, 128–29, 138, 192n
Annonay (Ardèche), 120, 124
Antoine of Navarre, *see* Navarre
Aquitaine, 12, 42, 62, 110–18, 137, 139, 169, 172, 175, 186
Arles (Bouches-du-Rhône), 64n–65n
arms purchases, 91, 173, 203
Arran, James Hamilton, Earl of, 57, 59, 61, 108–09, 169
Artois, 191
Aubigné, Theodore Agrippa d', 35, 38–39
Aubonne, meeting at, 38, 159, 169
Aubret, George, *see* Obrecht
Augsburg, 14
Aunis, 135, 169
Auvergne, 98, 133
"Avertissement," 113–17, 133
Avignon, 119, 151, 188

B

Badieu, Jean (Lyon conspirator), 84, 87–88, 198
Baillet, Jacques (Geneva conspirator), 150–52
Banc, Arnaud (minister), 66–67, 123, 170, 179
Barjols (Var), 190
Barran, Pierre Henri (minister), 113, 133
Barsonnay, Jean (Geneva conspirator), 150–52
Basel, 87
Bastard d'Estang, Jean-Denis Léon de, 35
Bataille, Pierre (Geneva conspirator), 150–52, 154
Bazadois, 117n
Béarn, 115, 117
Beaucaire (Gard), 65n, 194
Beauce, 95
Belime, Claude de Veyny, seigneur de, 98
Belime, Joseph de Veyny, seigneur de, 98
Belleforest, François de, 42, 105
Bellimes (var. Belimour), seigneur de, conspirator, 9n, 98, 100, 198, 207, 209–10
  possible identification, 98
Bertrand, Jean (Lyon conspirator), 87, 101, 210, 212
Berwick-upon-Tweed, 59
Beza, Theodore, 3–6, 8, 20, 22, 25–26, 29, 36, 37, 39, 45–47, 49, 54, 64–66, 68–73, 75–77, 80, 95–96, 99, 104, 125, 128–31, 133–36, 139–40, 142–43, 148, 152, 158, 175, 181–83, 191n, 205
  gives psalm to La Renaudie, 22, 26, 66
  in Nérac, 45–46, 70–71, 99, 135–36, 139, 142
Biron, Armand de Gontaut, Baron of, 141
Blaurer, Ambrose, 25
Blois, 10, 30, 34, 91, 137, 173, 192
Boisnormand, François de, alias Dugué, La Pierre (minister and conspirator), 28, 69, 114–16, 126, 133, 138, 169
Bonnet, Pierre, see Provence, Pierre Bonnet dit de
Bordeaux, 63, 84, 116n, 129–30, 211
Bordon, François de, seigneur de Compeys, 158, 163–64, 194–95
Bouchard d'Aubeterre, François (conspirator), 76, 161, 163
Bouchard, Amaury, 134, 166
Bouchavannes, Antoine de Bayancourt, seigneur de, 33
Bouillon, Henri-Robert de La Marck, Duke of, 137
Boulanger, Florent, 9n
Bourbon, Antoine de, see Navarre
Bourg-en-Bresse (Ain), 93, 163, 194
Bourges, 95, 135, 137, 151
Brie, 35
Briquemault, Adrien de, see Villemongis
Brittany, 33, 60, 63, 92, 93, 110, 126, 129, 139, 160, 174, 191
Brouage (Charente-Maritime), 192
Brown, Elizabeth A. R., 73–74
Bruslart, Pierre, 10
Bullinger, Heinrich, 22, 24, 48, 71, 136, 139, 142
Burgundy, 108, 110, 205
Bussillon (var. Boussillon), Pierre (Lyon conspirator), 101–03, 200, 201, 212

C

Caiazzo, see Sanseverino
Calais, 55, 58
Calandrini (var. Calendrin), Giuliano, 9n, 105n, 201
Calvin, John, 2–6, 10, 17, 20–26, 29, 45–49, 52–55, 57, 64–66, 68, 70–

71, 73, 77, 79–81, 95–97, 99, 104, 106, 108, 111–13, 125–26, 128, 130–31, 136, 139–43, 146, 148–54, 156–61, 163–69, 173–76, 182–84, 205
- change of heart in May–June, 182
- denies involvement in Amboise conspiracy, 3, 20–26, 65–66
- encourages Navarre to act, 47–48, 55, 111–12, 141–43
- friends and associates, 88, 97, 104, 158–61, 163
- letter to Coligny, 22–24, 77, 125
- letter to Sturm, March 1560, 21–22, 90, 181
- letters concerning Maligny affair, 45–46, 70–71, 99

Camialle, Yves, 95n
Cardet, Raymond de Valette, seigneur de (conspirator), 114–15, 121n, 123, 194
Casteljaloux (Lot-et-Garonne), 115
Castellane (Alpes-de-Haute-Provence), 89, 189
Castelnau-Tursan, Charles de (captain), 13, 15, 18, 19, 39–40, 42, 111, 131, 162, 171n, 186
Castres (Tarn), 144
Castres, Baron de, 119, 133
Catherine de Medici, 9, 11, 15, 30, 87, 107, 112, 124, 136, 145, 178
Cecil, William, 56–59, 61, 63, 80, 109
Cenesme, Jean de (Geneva conspirator), 150, 152–54
Cévennes, 140, 144, 193
Châlons-en-Champagne, 12, 173
Champagne, 35, 93, 204
Chandieu, *see* La Roche Chandieu
Changy, François de Fay, seigneur de, 196n
Changy, Imbert de Fay, seigneur de, 196n
Chantonnay, Thomas Perrenot, seigneur de (Spanish ambassador), 11, 14, 15, 28n, 52, 55n, 91n, 132n, 136–37, 141, 172, 174, 180n, 186–87
Chastillon, examining magistrate, 197
Châteauneuf, conspirator, 85, 89–91, 94, 169, 175, 202, 207
- possible identifications, 85–86
Châteauneuf, Charles de, seigneur de Mollèges, 85–86
Châteauneuf, Jean de, 86
Châtellerault (Vienne), 56, 61, 137, 169
Chaumet, Etienne (Annonay conspirator), 124
Chauvet, Raymond (minister), 163
Chiré, Pierre Desprez, seigneur de La Cour de (captain), 61, 169, 190-91
Clairac, synod of, 138
Claude, cabinetmaker in Lyon, 210
Cocqueville, François de (captain), 191
Coderc, Jean (Nîmes conspirator), 9n, 123, 170
Coligny, Gaspard de, 20, 23, 125, 159, 161, 178, 180, 191
Colladon, Germain, 97, 163
Combes de Montaigu, Pierre, seigneur de Combas (Montpellier conspirator), 120–21, 193
Comtat Venaissin, 100, 118, 188
Conames, *see* Cenesme
Condé (Aisne), 93, 204
Condé, Eléonore de Roye, Princess of, 205
Condé, Henri de Bourbon, Prince of, 192
Condé, Louis de Bourbon, Prince of, 2, 6, 9, 15, 27–29, 32, 34–36, 39, 43, 47, 49, 53, 54, 91, 93, 94, 99, 103, 105, 109–10, 113, 125, 127, 130–33, 139–40, 143, 145, 168–69, 183, 184, 187–89, 191, 195, 200, 203–05, 208
Condomois, colloque of, 113
Constantin, first name unknown, wife of Jean, 100, 210

Constantin, Jean (Lyon conspirator), 1, 87, 89, 91, 93–94, 97–103, 118, 133, 173, 192, 198–200, 202–10, 212
Cop, Lucas, 154
Cop, Michel, 154
Corbier (Pézenas conspirator), 123, 170
Cossé-Brissac, Timoléon de, 191
Courtois, Philibert (Lyon conspirator), 101, 212
Cousturier, Noel (Annonay conspirator), 124n
Crespin, Jean, 37, 41, 162
Crest, Jacques de Savoie, seigneur de, 164–65n
Crouzet, Denis, 175
Crussol, Antoine de, 132–33, 190, 194–95
Cussonel, Guillaume (Annonay conspirator), 124

D

Damville, Henri de Montmorency, Count of, 32, 194
Dareste, Rodolphe, 45
Darut (var. Darud), Jean (Lyon conspirator), 87, 89, 91, 103, 105n, 192–93, 201–02, 204
Dauphiné, 47, 55, 92, 98, 100, 101n, 118, 125, 128, 129, 133, 141, 188–90, 211
Daussy, Hugues, 35, 75–77, 85, 168, 185
Davailles, Pierre, 201
David, Pierre (minister), 28
"day of the kerchiefs," 138, 186
Decize (Nièvre), 93, 211
Des Adrets, François de Beaumont, Baron, 188–90
Dieppe, 144
Digne, Antoine, dit seigneur de Bargement, 159–60, 166
Doumergue, Emile, 23, 47–49,
Doupoin, Jean (Lyon conspirator), 9n, 101–02, 211, 212
Dreux, battle of, 190

Droz, Eugénie, 88
Du Bois, alias of conspirator, 114, 116
Du Bouchet, Tanneguy, *see* Saint-Cyr
Du Bourg, Anne, 96
Du Cret, heterodox Carmelite of Moulins, 211
Du Poing, *see* Doupoin
Du Tillet, Jean, 21, 73–74
Dufour, Alain, 3, 8, 35, 70–73, 76, 81, 97, 148
Dumas, Antoine, 102–03
Dupleix, Scipion, 42
Dupuy, *see* Montbrun
Dureng, J., 55, 58

E

Ecole des Chartes, 50, 53
Elizabeth, Queen of England, 56–59, 61–63, 75, 77, 80, 109, 127, 132
Emmanuel-Philibert, Duke of Savoy, 182, 189
Estates, Estates-General
 of Blois (1576), 192
 crown decides to convoke, 131, 137
 of Languedoc, 194
 preliminary electoral assemblies for Orléans (1560), 137–38
 preliminary electoral assemblies for Pontoise (1561), 177
 in thought and plans of conspirators, 2, 14, 18–22, 30, 34, 36, 54, 58, 71–72, 74, 90–91, 107, 128–29, 134–35, 137–39, 175–77, 184–85
Etampes (Essonne), 93, 131, 204
Etampes, Jean de Brosse, Duke of, 33, 126–28

F

Farel, Guillaume, 31
Faure, Antoine (Annonay conspirator), 124
Fay, Antoine de, seigneur de Peyraud, 98, 194
Fay, Jean de, seigneur de Virieu and Malleval (conspirator), 98, 99, 194
Faye (examining magistrate), 211

Ferrara, ambassador of, *see* Alvarotti
Fétigny (Jura), 87
First Civil War, role of conspirators in, 187–95
Flanders, 114, 117
Flanquefort, *see* Frankfurt
Flassans, Durand de Pontevès, seigneur de, 190
Florent (var. Florant), 206, 212
Florentine ambassador, *see* Tornabuoni
Fontaine, Jacques, minister, *see* La Fontaine
Fontainebleau, Assembly of Notables at, 32, 72, 129, 131, 180
Fontenay-le-Comte (Vendée), 190
Fontevraud, 204
Forez, 98, 133
Formy, Claude (Montpellier conspirator), 120–21, 170
Fournel, Jehan du, 197–98, 200–01, 210–12
Franche-Comté, 87
Francis II, King of France, 55–56, 116
  goes to Orléans, 136–37
  illness and death, 141, 145, 184
  new forcefulness, 137
François, François de, dit seigneur de Gardanne, 159–60, 166
Frankfurt, 206
Frellon, Jean, 206
Frontevaux, *see* Fontevraud

G
Gabiane, François de, 202
Garraut, Pierre (Geneva conspirator), 150–52
Gascony, 15, 107, 109, 111, 114, 134, 172
Gazeau, libraire, 202
Geneva, 1–4, 11, 15, 20–26, 37–39, 42–43, 46–47, 52, 55–57, 63–72, 76–77, 79, 88, 93–97, 99–101, 104–06, 115, 117–18, 122–23, 125, 128–30, 139–40, 147–66, 168–72, 176, 182, 193–95, 198, 199, 204–08, 212

Germany, 34, 56–57, 59, 75, 95–96, 205, 212
Gévaudan, 118
Gex, bailiff of, *see* Mülinen
Gilbert, Pierre, alias La Bergerie (minister and conspirator), 95, 205
Gontaud (Lot-et-Garonne), 116
Goulaine, conspirator, 91–93, 108, 110, 205, 211–12
  possible identification, 92
Goulaine, François de, 92
Goulaine, Jacques de, 92
Goulaine, René de, 92
Gousset, Claude (Lyon conspirator), 87, 89, 91, 93–94, 202–05
Grammont, Antoine de, 132
Groslot, Jerome (suspected Orléans conspirator), 141
Guagnon, Jean (minister), 163
Guay, Guillaume (Lyon conspirator), 102, 199
Guéraud, Jean, 102–03
Guibray (Calvados), 180
Guise family, 2, 11, 14, 15, 17–20, 30–34, 36–37, 43, 45, 49, 53, 58, 61, 73, 90–92, 110, 112, 124, 128–30, 134–36, 140, 143, 175–77, 181–82, 203
Guise, François, Duke of, 11–12, 27–28, 127
Guise, Mary of, 11, 56, 63
Guizot, François, 44
Guyenne, 111, 115, 118, 132, 138, 187, 190

H
Hainaut, 118, 132
Hauser, Henri, 51, 52
Heu, Gaspard de, 31–32
Hotman, François, 18, 22, 32, 45, 49, 57, 59, 61, 67, 76, 86, 96, 152, 158, 160, 172n, 173, 177

I
Ile-de-France, 35

J

Jarnac, battle of, 191
Jarnac, Guy de Chabot, Count of, 135, 179
Jeanne d'Albret, *see* Albret
Jouanna, Arlette, 8, 69, 74–76, 85
Joyeuse, Guillaume de, 115, 118, 133, 193

K

Kingdon, Robert M., 8, 69–70
Knox, John, 56

L

La Bergerie, alias of Pierre Gilbert, 94, 205
La Bigne, Jacques de, 9n
La Borde, Jean de, 9n
La Chesnaie, captain, 192n
La Fontaine, alias of Robert Le Maçon (Orléans minister), 94, 116, 205
La Fontaine, conspirator, 114, 116
  possible identifications, 116
La Fontaine (var. Fontaine), Jacques, minister, 116
La Fredonnière, château of, 30
La Garaye, Charles Ferré, seigneur de (conspirator), 93–94, 109–10, 159–60, 163, 203–05
La Garde, Antoine Escalin des Eymars, Baron de, 119, 133
La Gaucherie (preceptor of Henry of Navarre), 133
La Haye, Robert de, 9n
La Motte Gondrin, Blaise de Pardaillan, seigneur de, 118–19, 133
La Place, Pierre de, 29–33, 35, 37, 161–62
La Planche, Louis Régnier, seigneur de, nephew, historian, 8, 30, 33–39, 43–44, 67, 71–74, 79–80, 85, 89–91, 94, 97, 99–100, 107–10, 115, 117, 124, 134–37, 168, 173, 176, 186
La Planche, Louis Régnier, seigneur de, uncle, 30, 33
La Popelinière, Lancelot Voisin, seigneur de, 37, 186
La Quadra, Alvaro de (Spanish ambassador to England), 62
La Renaudie, Jean Du Barry, seigneur de (chief conspirator), 14, 18–19, 21–23, 26, 29–32, 34, 38, 40, 42–43, 53, 65–66, 73–74, 76, 89, 159, 161–62, 168–69, 175, 181
La Ripaudière, Guillaume Morice, seigneur de (minister and possible conspirator), 163, 166
La Rivette, Pierre de (Lyon conspirator), 103
"La Riviere de Château Neufz," conspirator[s?], 84–85, 98, 202, 207; *see also* La Rivière, Châteauneuf
La Rivière, alias of Jean Le Maçon (Paris minister), 86
La Rivière, conspirator, 85, 93, 109–10, 202–08, 212
  possible identification, 86–87
La Roche Chandieu, Antoine de (minister and conspirator), 21, 26, 52, 62, 68–69, 76, 87, 168–69, 181
La Roche Chandieu, Bertrand de (conspirator), 21
La Rochefoucauld, François de, 53
La Sague, Jacques de (probable conspirator), 131, 143, 183, 195
Landier, Jean, 9n
Languedoc, 64, 66, 77, 85, 118–19, 123, 126, 129, 134, 137, 140, 143–44, 164n, 172–73, 177, 186, 190, 194
Larmurier, Leonard (Annonay conspirator), 124n
Lausanne, 14, 22, 65n, 86, 107

Lautrec, Antoine de, seigneur de Saint-Germier (possible conspirator), 157–59
Lauzun, Robert de, abbot of Valmagne (conspirator), 164n–65n
Le Bois, alias for Edme de Maligny, 205
Le Camus, court furrier, 107–08, 124, 128
Le Fleur, Matthieu (suspected conspirator), 117n
Le Frère de Laval, Jean, 2, 8, 42
Le Gantier (var. Le Gaultier), Gilles, alias of Gilles Triou, 1–2, 105, 200; see also Triou
Le Garet, see La Garaye
Le Maçon, Jean, alias La Riviere (Paris minister and probable conspirator), 86–87
Le Maçon, Robert, alias La Fontaine (Orléans minister and conspirator), 95, 116, 205
Le Maître, Claude (Geneva conspirator), 95n, 97, 99, 104, 105, 173, 192, 206
Lebrun, Pierre (Annonay conspirator), 124n
Lenzi, Lorenzo (papal nuncio), 11, 180n
Limoges, 36, 72, 129–30, 134–35
Limousin, 117, 129, 187
Little Martin (Lyon conspirator), 212
London, French church of, 95
Lords of the Congregation, 56–60, 80
Lorraine, 151, 173
Lorraine, Charles, cardinal of, 11–15, 27–28, 32, 34, 55, 58, 63, 67, 94, 174, 176, 205
Loudunais, 186n
Lucca, 152
Lunel (Hérault), 193n
Lyon, 1–3, 12, 24, 35–36, 42–44, 46–52, 55, 68, 70–72, 75, 83–95, 97–106, 109–10, 113, 117–28, 132–33, 142–43, 153, 164, 186, 190, 192–93, 195, 206
Lyon, enterprise of, see Maligny affair

M

MacCaffrey, Wallace, 62
Maillane, Ardoin de Porcelet, seigneur de (conspirator), 64–67, 85, 91–92, 120, 122–23, 148, 156–57, 159–60, 166, 193–94
Maillane, Jean de (probable conspirator), 64n, 122, 156–57, 159
Maillane, Robert de (probable conspirator), 64n, 122
Maillé Braisé, captain, 186n
Maillé, Arthus de, seigneur de Brézé, 186n
Maillé, Philippe de, seigneur de Brézé, 186n
Maistre, see Le Maître
Maitland of Lethington, William, 59
Maitre Quentin (Lyon conspirator), 101, 212
Malaucène (Vaucluse), 100, 114, 119, 189
Maligny affair
  Beza and, 3, 5, 45–47, 70–73, 112–13, 125, 141–43, 182–84, 205–06
  Calvin and, 3, 5, 6, 45–48, 70–73, 112–13, 125, 141–43, 182–84, 205–06
  Condé and, 6, 93–94, 132, 200
  details of the event, 1–2, 70–72, 83, 100, 200, 209–10
  financing of, 95–96, 101, 132, 208
  foreign involvement in, 63, 95–97, 104, 205–06
  nature and goals of, 5, 47, 54–55, 98–99, 104, 128–29, 199
  Navarre and, 6, 49, 63, 111–17, 132, 199, 206, 208, 209

Maligny affair *(continued)*
  organization of, 95–104, 108–26, 199, 208–09
  overlooked by historians, 3, 7–8, 32, 79
  Reformed churches and, 104, 119–23
  reinforcements from outside Lyon, 100–01, 118–24, 208–09
  repression following, 102–03, 143–45, 183–84, 186
Maligny, Edme de Ferrières, seigneur de ("Maligny le jeune"), alias Le Bois, 27, 35–36, 45, 95–97, 104, 108–09, 112, 114, 118, 125–26, 130, 140, 187, 205
Maligny, Jean de Ferrières, seigneur de ("Maligny l'ainé") alias Saint Cyr, later Vidame de Chartres, 35–36, 53, 95, 97–99, 104, 108–10, 124–25, 130, 187, 199, 207–10, 212
Maligny, seigneur de, unspecified one of the two brothers, 15, 24, 35–36, 45–50, 68, 70–73, 205, 211
Malleval (Loire), 98
Malleval, seigneur de, conspirator, 98–100, 207, 210
  probable identification, 98
Mandur, Claude, 200
Maneval, *see* Malleval
Mannilliane, 202
Mantuan ambassador, *see* Strozzi
Marennes (Charente-Maritime), 134
Mariéjol, Jean-Hippolyte, 54, 76
Martin, Pierre (Lyon conspirator), 101, 212
Mary of Guise, regent in Scotland, 11, 56, 63
Mary Stuart, Queen of Scotland and France, 55–56, 58
Mauget, Guillaume (minister), 67, 121–22

Mauguio (Hérault), 193n
Maupeau, François (Montpellier conspirator), 120–21, 170, 193
Mauvans, Antoine de Richieu, seigneur de, 89
Mauvans, Paulon de Richieu, seigneur de (conspirator), 23–24, 55, 89–90, 100, 114, 119, 125, 129, 189–90, 209
Mazères, François de La Salle, seigneur de (captain), 15, 115, 171n, 186
Melun (Seine-et-Marne), 152
Melwin, Walter, laird of Rethes, 60
Mémoires de Condé, 44–45, 58
Menard, Pierre (var. Meynard), alias of Gilles Triou, 1, 198, 200; *see also* Triou
Mérindol (Vaucluse), 66–67, 89, 170
Mesmy, Denis d'Aix, seigneur de (conspirator), 114, 116–18, 126, 187–88
Metz, 31–32, 59, 88, 158, 168, 204
Mézeray, François Eudes de, 44
Michiel, Giovanni, Venetian ambassador, 11, 12, 15, 27n, 45, 53, 111, 132n, 141n, 172–173, 187n
Millet, Michel (minister), 202
Minard, Antoine, 96
Mirambeau, François de Pons, seigneur de (captain), 192
Moncontour, battle of, 191
Monluc, Blaise de, 188
Monod, Gabriel, 53
Montagnac (Hérault), 120, 123n, 165n
Montargis (Loiret), 65n
Montbrun, Charles Dupuy, seigneur de (captain), 55, 100–01, 114–15, 119, 125–26, 129–30, 132, 140, 188–90, 209
Montejean, François d'Acigné, seigneur de (captain), 92, 191

Montgomery, Gabriel de Lorges, Count of, 191
Montpellier, 118, 120–21, 126, 144, 170, 172, 178, 184, 193–94
Morel, François de, seigneur de Collonges (minister and conspirator), 65, 69, 76, 152, 163, 169
Morély, Jean (possible conspirator), 25–26, 158–59
Mornas (Vaucluse), 188–89
Moulins (Allier), 84, 201, 211
Mouvans, *see* Mauvans
Mouzeuil (Vendée), 191
Mülinen, Ludwig von (bailiff of Gex), 64, 68, 91, 172
Mundt, Christopher, 61, 96, 109

N
Nadal (var. Nadard), Pierre (Lyon conspirator), 87, 89–91, 105n, 192, 201–05
Naef, Henri, 4, 21, 25, 63–69, 74, 81, 86, 149–50, 173
Nantes, assembly at, 29–30, 34, 38, 60, 66–67, 69, 77, 85, 89–93, 170, 174–75, 203, 211
Navarre, Antoine de Bourbon, King of, 2, 9, 21, 48, 73, 94, 96–97, 106, 125, 128, 141, 168, 183–84, 199, 206, 208, 209
  and Amboise conspiracy, 27–28, 49
  Calvin feels betrayed by, 142–43
  Calvin seeks to advise again, 184–85
  informed about Amboise conspiracy, 28
  and international Protestant diplomacy, 31, 57, 61, 76, 168
  invites Beza to Nérac, 112
  journey to court, 135, 139–40
  and Maligny affair, 6, 28, 36, 46, 49, 71–72, 99, 101, 109, 183–84
  pressured by Protestants to act, 34, 36, 45, 47, 49, 54–55, 71, 80, 94, 109, 111, 113, 128–30, 134, 143
  and Protestantism, 28–29, 65, 108, 111, 115–16, 168
  role claimed for him under Francis II, 21
  role in government under Charles IX, 9, 145
  summoned to court, 132–33
Nemours, Jacques de Savoie, Duke of, 19, 39–41, 164–65n, 189
Nérac (Lot-et-Garonne), 27–28, 36, 45, 46, 54, 70–71, 75, 94, 99, 109, 112–14, 116, 125, 132–35, 138
Nesle, Louis de Saint-Maur, Marquis of, 60n
Nesle, Renée de Rieux, Marchioness of, 60
Nijenhuis, Willem, 182
Nîmes, 66–67, 69, 94, 114, 115, 118, 120–23, 144, 157, 170, 172, 184, 193–94
Noizay, chateau of, 19, 40–41
Normandie, Laurent de, 161
Normandy, 61, 63, 84, 111, 114, 118, 126, 132, 134, 137, 191–92, 211
Nouyer, Claude, 200

O
Obrecht, Georges, 101, 202, 206, 208
Olhagaray, Pierre, 113
Orange (Vaucluse), 188
Orléans, 33, 34, 64, 70, 75, 88, 91, 93–95, 116, 135–36, 140–41, 144, 168–71, 173, 184–85, 191, 194, 203–05, 211

P
Paris, 21, 22, 26, 31, 33, 34, 44, 53, 62, 65, 67–69, 71, 75, 76, 86, 88, 93–96, 113, 137, 144, 147, 151–53,

Paris *(continued)*
    158, 168, 173, 182, 191, 194, 204–05
Parlements, 176
  of Aix, 85
  of Bordeaux, 117, 175
  of Paris, 16, 18, 96, 195
  of Toulouse, 119–23, 157
Passy, *see* Spifame
Pastoureau, Jacques, 95–96, 205
Pau, 9, 52, 113, 115, 197
Pellisson, Jeanne, wife of Gilles Triou, 211
Périgord, 117
Périgueux, 116, 137
Perrissin, Jean, 37, 166
Peyraud (Ardèche), 98
Pézenas (Herault), 120, 123
Picardy, 33, 191
Piedmont, 92, 189–90, 211
Pinchenat, Joseph, 159–60, 166
Pithou, Nicolas, seigneur de Chamgobert, 144
Poissy, colloquy of, 87
Poitiers, 32–33, 75, 109, 113–14, 133, 136, 140
Poitou, 15, 33, 61, 109, 126–27, 129–30, 134, 172, 186n, 190–91
Potter, David, 99
Poujol, Jacques, 59–61, 73, 174
Pourret, examining magistrate, 197, 201, 210
Prouvence, Pierre de, *see* Provence, Pierre Bonnet dit de
Provence, 21, 23–24, 33, 36, 47, 55, 66, 71, 75, 77, 85–86, 89–90, 92, 100, 109–10, 113–14, 116–19, 124, 125, 128–30, 134, 156, 159, 169, 170, 173, 179, 190, 211
Provence, Pierre Bonnet, dit de (Lyon conspirator), 102, 199
Puy-Greffier, *see* Saint-Cyr

Q
Quercy, 144

R
Régnier de La Planche, *see* La Planche
Renée de France, Duchess of Ferrara, 65n
Rennes, 127
Richard, Claude (Lyon conspirator), 102, 199
Roanne (Loire), 211
Robinson, Marilynne, 3
Roget, Amédée, 46–48, 55, 70
Romier, Lucien, 5, 35, 50–55, 59, 62, 63, 68–70, 74–76, 88–89, 129–30, 172
Romorantin (Loir-et-Cher), 110
Romorantin, edict of, 180
Rousseau, 209
Ruble, Alphonse de, 2–3, 5, 35, 48–52, 62–63, 71, 84–85, 88–89, 129–30, 148, 164n
Rurcaille, Pierre Antoine (Lyon conspirator), 102, 199

S
Saconay, Gabriel de, 2, 42–44, 72, 84–85, 98, 103, 194
Saint Cyre, alias for Jean de Maligny, 97, 199, 207–10, 212
Saint-Amand, *see* Vellut
Saint-André, Jacques d'Albon, maréchal de, 163
Saint-Cyr, Tanneguy Du Bouchet, seigneur de Puy-Greffier and (captain), 191
Saint-Jean [de Gardonnenque], Louis Toyras, seigneur de (Montpellier conspirator), 120–21, 193
Saint-Valery-sur-Somme (Somme), 191
Sainte-Foy, synod of, 187–88
Sainte-Marie-aux-Mines (Haut-Rhin), 65n
Sainte-Marie-du-Mont, Nicolas Aux Epaules, seigneur de (captain), 191–92
Saintonge, 76, 129, 135, 169, 186n, 192

Sandre, Guillaume, seigneur de Saint Georges (Montpellier conspirator), 120–21
Sanseverino, Gian Galeazzo, Count of Caiazzo, 164–65
Sauzet, Guillaume de (Nîmes conspirator), 121–22, 170, 193
Savoy, 53, 75, 101, 158, 182, 189–90
Savoy, Emmanuel-Philibert, Duke of, 208
Scotland, 11, 55–63, 127
Sénarpont, Jean de Monchy, seigneur de, 33
Servetus, Michael, 97
Sipierre, Philibert de Marcilly, seigneur de, 137
Sisteron (Alpes-de-Haute-Provence), 190
Souchet, Guillaume (Geneva conspirator), 150–52, 155
Spifame, Jacques, seigneur de Passy, 38, 88, 95–97, 160, 173, 205
Strasbourg, 14, 21–22, 26, 48, 52, 57, 61, 67, 76, 86–87, 109, 111, 141, 168
Strozzi, Herculo (Mantuan ambassador), 11, 14–15, 19n, 91n, 132n, 172n, 180
Stuart, Robert, seigneur de Vézines (conspirator), 95–96, 100, 104, 206, 208
Sturm, Jean, 21, 26, 45, 90, 96, 111–12, 135, 147, 158, 166, 181
Sulzer, Simon, 142
Surgères (Charente-Maritime), 1, 198
Sutherland, Nicola M., 59, 61, 63, 68
synods of Reformed churches, 65n, 113, 138, 187–88
Swiss cantons, Switzerland, 11, 75, 136

T
Tende, Claude de Savoie, Count of, 33, 129–30
Terrasson (var. Tarrasson), Pierre (Lyon conspirator), 84, 87, 97–98, 100, 102–03, 198–200, 202–03, 207, 210–11
Thermes, Paul de La Barthe, maréchal de, 117, 137
Thézé, Louis, 95n
Thou, Jacques-Auguste de, 8, 43–44, 58, 80
Throckmorton, Nicholas (English ambassador), 19n, 56–57, 59–63, 80, 109–10, 127
Tornabuoni, Alfonso (Florentine ambassador), 15, 109, 111, 141n, 187n
Torneon, examining magistrate, 200
Tortorel, Jacques, 37, 40
Toulouse, 113–15, 118, 123, 194
Touraine, 15, 172, 177, 186n
Tournon (Ardèche), 194
Tours, 32, 108, 110, 168, 169, 171n, 204
Tremayne, English agent, 60
Trie, Guillaume, seigneur de Varennes (Geneva conspirator), 97, 99, 125, 104, 206
Triou, Gilles, aliases Gilles Le Gantier, maître Gilles, Pierre Menard
 deposition of, 2–4, 9, 49, 51–52, 83–105, 197–211
 life and actions of, 1–2, 83–85, 91, 93–102, 195–98, 200–01, 210, 212
Troyes, 87, 144
Tuininga, Matthew J., 3

U
Utor, Antoine (Lyon conspirator), 212

V
Vaise, faubourg of Lyon, 198
Val Pragelato (Piedmont), 189–90
Valence (Drôme), 70
Valmagne, abbot of, see Lauzun
Valvignières (Ardèche), 118
Varennes, see Trie
Vaud, Pays de, 108, 115
Velay, 118

Vellut, Adrien de Saint-Amand, seigneur de, 158–59
Vendôme, François de, Vidame de Chartres, 9n, 35, 53, 131, 187
Venetian ambassador, *see* Michiel
Vermigli, Peter Martyr, 24, 27
Veyrac, Claude d'Anduze, seigneur de (Geneva conspirator), 150–53, 159
Vézelise (Meurthe-et-Moselle), 151
Vézines, *see* Stuart
Vidame de Chartres, *see* Vendôme
Vigner (vars. Vignier, Vinay), Pierre (Geneva conspirator), 150–52, 154–55
Villars, Honorat de Savoie, Count of, 119, 133, 137, 140, 144, 193–94
Villefuesne, Annonay conspirator, 124n
Villemongis, Adrien de Beauvais de Briquemault, seigneur de, 20, 23, 57, 161–62, 166
Villeneuve-sur-Lot (Lot-et-Garonne), 117
Villeneuve, Pierre de, 101–02, 212
Vincent, Antoine (Lyon conspirator), 84, 87–91, 97, 104, 166, 192, 201–03, 205–06, 211
Vincent, Emerance, daughter of Antoine, 206
Vincent, first name unknown, son of Antoine, 206
Viret, Pierre, 163
Vivarais, 118–19, 126, 133, 140

W

Watt, Jeffrey, 149
Winterthur (Switzerland), 25

Z

Zurich, 24, 141